Three-Cornered Heart

Also by Anne Fremantle

Three-Cornered Heart

ANNE FREMANTLE

The Viking Press

NEW YORK

First published in 1970 by The Viking Press, Inc.
625 Madison Avenue, New York, N.Y. 10022

Published simultaneously in Canada by
The Macmillan Company of Canada Limited

SBN 670-70696-5

Library of Congress catalog card number: 73-124321

Printed in U.S.A. by Vail-Ballou Press, Inc.

Second printing March 1971

The sections on Lady Gregory (pages 261–68) and on Evelyn Waugh (pages 286–92) were first published in *Vogue* in slightly different form. "Balm in Gilead" originally appeared in *The New Yorker* in slightly different form.

ACKNOWLEDGMENT: To Methuen & Co. Ltd.: From *A Victorian Childhood* by Annabel Huth Jackson. Reprinted by permission.

The author wishes to thank Anthony Root for photographing Sargent's portrait of Tiny, and Horace Gilchrist for photographing Arthur Hughes' portrait of Lady Grant Duff and Adrian.

FOR A.J.

who will never read this book

Christmas Day, 1970, is the centenary of your birth. You have been dead twenty-seven years. But since, in the words of your favorite poem, "Still are thy pleasant voices, thy nightingales awake," I have tried to listen and to repeat something of what they say.

The whole round world is not enough to fill
The heart's three corners, but it craveth still;
Only the Trinity, that made it, can
Suffice the vast triangulated heart of man.

—from *Schola Cordis* (1622)
by Christopher Harvey

Contents

Illustrations

A Victorian Child

I

Tiny

Tiny's first memory was of sitting on a green lawn. She was so small the daisies came up all around her. Suddenly she was aware how beautiful her mother was, sitting near her on the grass, how beautiful the sunlight. But was aware almost simultaneously that her mother was objecting to the daisies: she was saying the lawn badly needed mowing. Later she learned her mother insisted the lawns be kept smooth as velvet; her father loved the pink fat daisies.

Her daughter Anne's first memory too is of grass, of a long green slope, and of rolling her younger sister, Clare, down it, over and over. A green smear appeared on Clare's white batiste frock, and Anne was scolded. Anne's son Richard's first memory is of that same green slope, of being rolled down it by an elder brother. His strongest sensation was fear of the rough gravel at the slope's end, which he knew would hurt; it did. Thus for three generations, an initial perception of the world's greenness was contemporaneous with the perception of dissension, shame, or fear.

Tiny, born in London on December 25, 1870, was named Clara Annabel Caroline, but from the first, as she weighed only three pounds at birth, was called Tiny. Her christening was recorded in her father's diary on March 11, 1871. Benjamin Jowett, Master

of Balliol—to which college Tiny's father, her grandfather, two
of her brothers, her husband, her only son, a son-in-law, and a
grandson went—"comes to stay with us to christen our little girl.
The godmother, Lady Henley, and the godfather, John Warren,
had arrived, when the most comical difficulty arose from Jowett's
being unable to read the print of any prayer-book in the house.
It was evening and we had to send in all directions for one in
which the service was in larger print. We wholly failed, but at
last he contrived to get through the ceremony with infinite
trouble."

A few days later Tiny's father rented Hampden, on top of the
Chiltern Hills. Murray's handbook describes the house: "Shrouded
in ancient woods and approached through a long beech avenue.
The original house remains, much disfigured by modern white-
wash and stucco. John Hampden was brought up here and hence
he led his four thousand men on June 18, 1643, to Chalgrove,
where he was killed." Here Tiny was first aware of the cowslip in
perfection, the wild hyacinth making blue lakes in the woods,
the hawthorn and laburnum in glory, the lilac in flower, the ash,
chestnut, and tulip trees coming into full leaf. Behind the daisied
lawn of her first awareness were great cedars, and through the
long summer when she was two she heard the call of the pea-
cocks as they went to roost in the branches. Each morning she
would watch them fly, ungainly, down out of the trees, and she
would follow them around, watching until a male spread out the
whole glory of his tail. A day without this revelation was a lost
day.

Under the cedars grew toadstools, and she told her nurse that
toads sat on them. Nurse said, "Don't talk nonsense." Tiny caught
a toad and sat it on a big brown boletus, where it remained, too
scared to move, while she fetched Nurse, who, not deceived,
slapped her hand. In the orchard, in a hollow apple tree, lived a
tame toad, and Tiny, trotting after her big brothers, was adept at
collecting slugs with which to feed it daily. Accused of eating a
slug, she did not deny it, "but I only tasted the worm."

There were three older brothers, Arthur, Evelyn, and Adrian, and they seldom left her in peace. They had invented a game called Doggyland, with complicated laws, a history and geography she had to learn, and lots of fighting with long lances, short daggers, and swords, all cut by the carpenter from lengths of spare wood, with sharpened points. Why they did not put out each other's eyes she never knew. She hated it all, especially when she was taken prisoner and tortured. Her own favorite game of Little Houses, which consisted of quietly keeping house and going out to look for food, was considered a crime, and she was punished when she was caught playing it.

Adrian, nearest Tiny in age, was nice to her when the older boys were not around. The worst was Evie. "God bless my brothers," she would dutifully say each evening, adding, "not Evie." Once, when she was five and he had been teasing her unmercifully, she seized a carving knife from the dining-room sideboard and lunged at him, with deliberate intent to kill, but was restrained by the butler, who impeded her from behind.

The boys' holidays were pure nightmare. However, when she was six she one day heard her nurse and nursemaid discussing a local suicide. " 'E just couldn't take it any more," Nurse said. "The funker," scoffed the nursemaid. The man had thrown himself off a roof. Instantly Tiny slipped away, rushed upstairs to the attic, and opened a trapdoor to the roof. Pursued by the nursemaid, who had noticed her disappearance, she announced, "I am going to commit suicide." She was dragged down to her mother, who expatiated on the heinousness of Tiny's crime and had her tied to a table leg every day for a week. Even when taken out for her walks, she was led on a long string. Still she felt triumphant: she had learned there was always a way out.

Tiny had been four when her strict Baptist Nurse Maunder, cruel, clean, honest, and self-righteous, took her down to her mother one day because she had come to table with dirty face and hands. Her mother thrashed her with a small gold-topped rhinoceros-hide whip she used when riding, and for days afterward Tiny slunk about in shame, thinking all the gardeners knew and despised her. Tiny herself had begun riding when she was three, in a long habit, on a Shetland pony that would eat no hay, only seaweed. Soon after she was four, a groom put her on her pony and then lunged it. She was so terribly frightened that when it was over she picked up the tail of her long habit, went to her father in the library, and said, "I have had a tewwible nervous sock and will never ride again." He father forbade her being put thereafter on a horse, nor was she until she was eight, when she asked to ride because a friend had a pony.

She could read by the time she was four, and later could remember on her fourth birthday reading aloud to her maternal grandfather a parody about Gladstone and Huxley:

> Who filled his soul with carnal pride?
> Who made him say that Moses lied
> About the little hare's inside?
>   The Devil.

Gladstone, then Prime Minister and leader of the Liberal party, was Tiny's father's chief. Mountstuart Elphinstone Grant Duff, Tiny's father, eldest son of James Cunningham Grant Duff, was born in Scotland on February 21, 1829, at Eden, which had been in the family since 1712. It stands above the River Deveron and marches with the properties of James's cousins, the Duke of Fife, whose family name is Duff, and the Earl of Seafield, whose family name is Grant, and who then owned over three hundred square miles of land. Another cousin living nearby in James Grant Duff's day was George Gordon, Lord Byron, with whom James Grant Duff went to school at Banff Academy. James remembered the first time the ten-year-old Byron was addressed by his title on his succession; he burst into tears.

In 1804 James set off by sea to India to seek his fortune but was wrecked off the Cape of Good Hope, losing all his family papers and valuables (Anne remembers an old picture of the good ship *Corriemulzie*, in which he had sailed). James was picked up by a boat sailing for South America, which landed him at Buenos Aires, where James saw the Holy Inquisition, in the year after Trafalgar, still sitting. Thence he sailed again to India, and fought in the third Mahratta War, under the Duke of Wellington, who was then Arthur Wellesley. James's French opponent was General de Boigne. When the two men met at war's end, de Boigne said, "Financial difficulty—you British can never have a financial difficulty in India; you always have one certain resource open to you." "What?" inquired James. "*Plonder* China," was the reply.

James remained in India after the war for some time as resident at Sattara, where he wrote the classic *History of the Mahratta War*. But the climate affected his health, and he returned to Eden and married the daughter of Sir Whitelaw Ainslie, long resident in Madras, author of the *Materia Medica of India*. The Ainslies owned Delgaty Castle, one of the

> Six great castles of the north,
> Fyvie, Findlater, and Philorth,
> And if ye wad ken the other three,
> Pitsligo, Drum, and Delgaty.

At Eden, James devoted himself to agriculture and introduced shorthorn cattle to the north of Scotland. His herd was famous. He continued writing, "enlivening the world with an essay on livestock," as he put it. This "masterpiece on the rearing of swine," as he wrote to his cousin Huntly Gordon, Sir Walter Scott's secretary, in 1828, "is not a bit more inviting than the progress of the Mahrattas, of which I was as sick as I should be of the Pork." He also composed light verse, including a poem entitled "To a Young Lady Found by Accident in a Chaffinch's Nest." James was devoted to his mother-in-law and two daughters (one of whom died young), but never cared much for his wife and two sons.

Mountstuart grew up a solitary child, exploring the bleak country around his home and becoming a passionate botanist. He kept this interest all his life, and later, when he was Governor of

Madras, had the local flowers hand-painted by an Indian artist; the two bound volumes are magnificent and accurate to the last petal. Mountstuart would botanize wherever he was, and had several friends with like tastes; one of his greatest friends was Sir John Lubbock, later Lord Avebury, whose daughter Ursula married Mountstuart's son Adrian. The two men took a house together near Algiers, which they kept for many years, where they studied plants to their hearts' content, while Mountstuart's wife painted. She also embroidered beautifully, and some of her very accurate flower embroideries remain.

Mountstuart went to school at the Edinburgh Academy and on to Balliol. At the age of eighteen he began to keep a diary, and wrote in it every day of his life. Its fourteen volumes (1851–1901) were published by John Murray, and it is an admirable source book of Victoriana, although, since he "carefully eliminated from it almost all reference to the working part of my life," it is ineffably trivial. At Oxford, Mountstuart made lifelong friends of Benjamin Jowett—who was his tutor—Mark Pattison, Matthew Arnold, and many others. He fenced well, was influenced by the Oxford Movement, and also began lasting friendships with John Henry (later Cardinal) Newman and William George Ward.

On leaving Oxford, Mountstuart read for the bar, and he took a doctorate of laws at London University. On November 19, 1857, he was returned as Member of Parliament for the Elgin Burghs (a seat he held until 1881), and on February 4, 1858, made his maiden speech on Lord Palmerston's India Bill. He was a tiny man, only five feet four, a poor speaker with a weak voice, and painfully shy. But he wrote well and clearly and published his ephemeral speeches, which are better read than heard. He fell in love first with a beautiful friend of his sister Alise's, Emily Lodwick, who died of consumption. Then in 1858 he saw Julia Webster at a party given by her aunt, the widow of one of the Annesleys, and proposed after seeing her six times. They were married on April 13, 1859, and immediately went north to Eden to fight an election campaign. Mountstuart won again.

Julia's father and uncle were so handsome that when they walked into church people would stand up to stare. Tiny remembered being taken to see her grandfather Webster when he was dying and being lifted up to kiss him: he was still handsome *in extremis*. Tiny's mother's father's people were a wild lot: in a single night one of them played away first his money, then his wife's jewelry, and finally his estate; he walked out of the house next morning roofless and penniless. Julia's mother, his wife, who came from Smithills Hall, Bolton-le-Moors (a house that later played a great part in Tiny's life), had been born an Ainsworth. One of her forebears, a niece of Dr. Samuel Johnson's great friend Dr. Taylor, ran away with a handsome gypsy boy, by whom she had a large family. Her own parents refused ever to have anything to do with her again, but Dr. Taylor, hearing that one of her sons was promising, sent for him and made him a footman in his establishment. After Dr. Taylor's death, when his will was to be read and all the relations were assembled to hear it, this boy came into the room carrying coals to make up the fire. "Go upstairs and take off your livery, William," said the old family lawyer. "You will never need to wear it again." Dr. Taylor had left him his whole fortune. The boy went up to Oxford, later married, and became Tiny's great-grandfather.

James Grant Duff's second son, Ainslie, inherited Delgaty Castle and became a diplomat. While *en poste* in Russia, he married Frances Morgan, the beautiful daughter of an English merchant in St. Petersburg. Anne remembers her at eighty, still a lovely woman. She was supposed to be grandly illegitimate and certainly had whims and manners more like those of a Russian aristocrat than of the wife of a Scots laird.

Alise, the only sister of Mountstuart and Ainslie, fell in love with Lord Arthur Russell, who did not reciprocate; Alise went into a decline and was sent to Switzerland. There, as ill luck would have it, her doctor looked like Lord Arthur. Alise transferred her affections and married Doctor Obrist. Her family never spoke to her or saw her again, though Mountstuart kept her

portrait in his room. Tiny was grown up before she was allowed
to write to her aunt; to marry a Swiss doctor was as unthinkable
in Victorian days as earlier it had been to run away with a gypsy.
Actually, Dr. Obrist's family were good Swiss *bourgeois* and
lived in an old house at Zollikon, near Zurich. But Alise could not
long take a society in which nobody dressed for dinner and where
she was expected to take an active part in household management. After a few years (and four children, two of whom died of
neglect) she left her husband and retired with her two remaining
sons, Aloys and Hermann, to Weimar. They met Richard Wagner, and Aloys actually lived with the Wagners for some years;
he was a child prodigy, and Cosima Wagner made him play the
piano in public at the age of four. Later he became the conductor
of the Dresden orchestra.

Mountstuart enjoyed his ancestors, who included Joan Beaufort,
daughter of John, Earl of Somerset. As a young girl in the early
fifteenth century, she was walking in the gardens of Windsor
Castle, and a young man imprisoned within, looking at her
through the bars, fell in love with her. He wrote her some of
the loveliest—and some of the earliest—Scots poems. In the *Kingis
Quhair* (Quest) he describes Joan

> walking neath my prison tower
> Full secretly, new coming here to prayer
> The fairest and the freshest young flower
> That ever I beheld before that hour.
> Entranced I gazed, and with the sudden start
> Rushed instant all my blood into my heart. . . .
> My heart became her thrall
> For ever of free will.

He was James, son of King Robert III of Scotland and Queen
Annabella. He had been captured by King Henry IV of England
while on a ship being sent to France. Henry IV and later his son,
Henry V, the victor of Agincourt, kept James prisoner for eighteen years. Only in 1424 did James marry his Joan and go back to

Scotland as King. There he reigned wisely and well, but briefly, for in 1437 he was murdered at Perth by a group of rebel nobles, including James's own uncle, the Earl of Atholl. Within forty days all the murderers were caught except two, who fled to France. Those caught were tortured, then beheaded, torn limb from limb, and quartered. After each was dead, Joan breathed into her dead husband's decomposing ear, "He suffered more than you did." Then she married Sir James Stewart of Lorne, whose son married as his second wife Margaret Douglas, daughter of the fifth Earl of Douglas, Duke of Touraine. Their daughter Catherine Stewart married John, sixth Lord Forbes, and their daughter Elizabeth, who married Grant of Grant, was the ancestress of Helen Grant of Ballintomb, mother of Alexander Duff of Braco, Mountstuart's great-great-grandfather. Through the Gordons of Lesmoir, too, Mountstuart went back to the same Joan Beaufort.

John Duff, another ancestor of Mountstuart's, was out with Montrose in the Civil War in 1645 and again in 1650, and was saved in a dramatic way. John (born in 1624 and son of Adam Duff of Clunybeg) was made prisoner by Colonel Strahan's soldiers after Montrose's defeat at Carbisdale and was being taken through the Cabrach, en route to be hanged in Edinburgh. He was well known at the inn where they lodged, and hinted to the landlord that the guard should be filled up with whisky while he himself took care of the officers. When they were all drunkenly snoring, John crept down to the stable and found one soldier asleep across the door—whose throat he cut with a penknife— took a horse, and set off. When he had been riding a short while he heard the thunder of hoofs behind him and knew he was being pursued. He rode all night, and when dawn broke he turned and saw he was being followed by a troop of riderless horses that had followed the one he rode out of the stable. He proceeded to Buchan, sold the horses, married, and lived happily ever after.

The Duffs, though Scots, were mostly on the English side during the 1715 and 1745 uprisings, but the Grants were loyal to their lawful lords—first to James Stuart and then to his son

Charles (Bonnie Prince Charlie). The result was that many Grants were sent to the colonies, and Grants and Gordons abound on some Caribbean Islands and in the southern United States, descended from Scots sent out as indentured servants.

One who broke from his family's Whig traditions was James Duff of Hatton; he ran away from home to "follow Prince Charlie" in 1745. His son George, at the age of nine, also ran away and at thirteen started to serve under his great-uncle, Admiral Robert Duff. George's last letter was written as captain of the *Panther* about an hour before Trafalgar on Monday morning, October 21, 1805:

> My dearest Sophie,
>   I have just time to tell you we are just going into action. I hope and trust in God that we all behave as becomes us, and that I may yet have the happiness of taking my beloved wife and children in my arms. Norwich is quite well and happy. I have, however, ordered him off the Qr. deck.
>   Yours ever and most truly.

Norwich, Captain Duff's only son, did not obey his father's order to leave the quarter-deck, and witnessed his father's death. He gathered up from the scupper the actual piece of grapeshot, from a French canister, that had carried off his father's head, and brought the shot home to his mother. Mountstuart's granddaughter Anne as a child often held it in her hands—a ball of metal weighing two pounds, verified as French by the Woolwich arsenal. It had been fired from the *Fougueux*. Anne also remembers meeting Norwich Duff's daughter as an old lady.

Tiny and Adrian in their nursery were at the mercy of their keepers. Nurse Maunder punished continually and unjustly. Even when the head gardener gave the children apples, she insisted they had stolen them, and while Adrian screamed, Tiny got a worse hiding from Nurse Maunder for refusing to and being stubborn. Adrian explained to Tiny that it was idiotic not to yell when beaten, as grown-ups only hit harder if one did not. As well as

the Calvinist Nurse Maunder there was the German Catholic
Fräulein Reinking, bigoted and ill-tempered, who broke wooden
rulers over Adrian's back and shut Tiny up in a dark cupboard.
Tiny had no fear of the dark, but she detested beetles and imagined them all around her. Fräulein would also often send Tiny to
bed at five, supperless, and the long summer evenings would be
wasted, though Tiny grew adept at hiding books under the mat-
tress and almost ruined her eyes by twilight reading.

But it was for saying that she had seen things that were not
there that Fräulein punished her most often. Once she saw an
enormous white puffball, as big as a washstand basin, in the park,
and dragged Fräulein out to see it. But when they reached it, it
had shrunk to ordinary size, and Tiny had to go about for days
with a cardboard on which LIAR was printed tied to her back.
The worst thing about the incident was that Tiny was sure the
huge puffball really had been there, and that Providence had con-
spired with the powers that rule the nursery to trap her. She felt
sure of its malevolence on another occasion. The great scientist
Lord Avebury came to stay. He always brought presents for the
children; as none was immediately forthcoming, Tiny slipped
into his bedroom to search and, finding a large bottle of eau de
Cologne and having heard her mother say it was delicious, took
enormous gulps, then lay on the floor writhing in agony for some
time. She dared not tell but suffered her blistered mouth for days,
feeling very ill. It firmly convinced her of the truth of Nurse
Maunder's warning: "There are all-seeing eyes to punish sin."

After Tiny and Adrian had measles, all their toys were burned
or otherwise destroyed. They accepted as legitimate the fate of
Adrian's straw tiger but did not see the logic of the same treatment for Tiny's china cock. They sat up in bed, singing a dirge
for the sacrificed toys, the holocaust one more example of grown-
up injustice and God's partiality.

Prompted by her Calvinist nurse and her Catholic governess,
Tiny at the age of seven became very religious. Her father gave
her the *Imitation of Christ,* and she and Adrian read aloud from it

every day with Fräulein. They always chose the shortest passages, but some of the white-hot passion of the writer got across, and Tiny came to see Christ as a living figure, a knight in armor, ready to help protect her from God, whom she hated, because He was so cruel, waiting around every corner to catch her out and punish her. One day she walked round and round the nursery table in a rage, yelling, "I hate God, I hate God, and I hope I *will* go to hell," for which Nurse Maunder gave Tiny a large dose of castor oil, one of the nurse's favorite punishments.

Tiny's mother was a complete agnostic. One day when Tiny said something about Christ removing lions from the path (at a time when she was afraid of lions and bears under her bed at night), her mother said, "Oh, but you must not think of Christ as anything supernatural." Tiny's faith instantly fell into ruins and she took refuge with the Greek gods of her favorite book, Edward Baldwin's *Pantheon*. From then on she preferred Apollo to Christ and erected an altar on a tree stump in the garden, where she kept a gallipot of fresh water and bunches of flowers. She would steal bread, and wine left in the glasses after lunch, and offer them up. Beauty was the only truth, and she hated ugliness with a hatred that grew more intense with every year of her life. Ugliness and cruelty: these were the great twin evils, so often present simultaneously. Her love of the Greek gods persisted all her life, and she later, as a married woman, as a widow, had plaster casts of the Venus de Milo in her bedroom, of the Apollo Belvedere in her boudoir, of the Praxiteles head of Psyche in the drawing room. As she grew up she found in German romantic writers the same passion for the Greek gods, and loved to read Novalis's *Disciples at Sais* and Gustav Fechner's books.

Tiny's mother was a poor manager, uninterested in domestic details and, though an astonishingly beautiful woman, seemingly uninterested in her looks. In addition to her fine embroidery, she wrote pleasant verse and painted charmingly. She loved having children and doted on babies, but once the babies grew out of

being infants into people she was bored with them, though she
tried to be fair and gave them the best available education. She
had ten children, of whom eight survived. Arthur, the oldest,
went to Balliol, where he was a member of the group that included George Nathaniel Curzon; they all wrote verses about
each other, and the lines about Arthur were:

> Here's Grant Duff, he's happy should a
> Friend be found to talk of Buddha.

Arthur went into the Foreign Office and served first in China,
getting to look Chinese, even to the eyes. He learned Chinese
thoroughly, also Sanskrit, and was a scholar of comparative religion. He subsequently became British Minister in several Latin
American countries, ending his career as British Ambassador to
Sweden.

One of Arthur's first posts was Mexico, where he met and
married Kathleen Clayton, the lovely daughter of the then
United States Minister to Mexico, William Clayton, who was
born in Washington, D.C., and later became the first Governor
of Arkansas.

His daughter, Kathleen, seemed to her nieces incredibly romantic, for she had been engaged to one of the Iturbides—the family
of the short-lived Agustín, who was Mexican Emperor in 1822
and 1823. Kathleen, chaperoned by her sister, Charlotte, who was
married to the Belgian Minister, Baron Moncheur, had gone on
a long train journey, then a long coach trip, to reach the *estancia*
of her fiancé's people. There had been a big fiesta to celebrate her
forthcoming marriage. Her fiancé, jumping on a Mexican saddle
in the rodeo, jammed the pommel into his private parts and died
in agony before her eyes. Kathleen married Arthur on the re-
bound. It was an ideally happy marriage, though childless. Arthur
was a delightful person, gentle and humorous. He always smelled
deliciously of lavender water.

The next brother, Evelyn, followed Arthur to Balliol and

thence to the Foreign Office, but in spite of being the cleverest member of a clever family he ended his career only as Minister to Switzerland.

After Adrian went away to school, Tiny wrote, "he came back for the first holidays and I realized he had *really* learnt to despise girls and no longer wanted to play with me. I went through several days of anguish and then put him out of my mind. We were never the least intimate after that, though I always had great respect for him." Adrian was a first-rate soldier and colonel of the Black Watch. He was killed at the Battle of Aisne, September 14, 1914, the first colonel to be killed in action since Waterloo. Heroically leading his battalion, he was mortally wounded. Tiny commented that all his life it had been his dream to lead the Black Watch into action in some great war, and "I have always thought he was the most fortunate of us all. Surely to die fairly young in the moment of fulfillment is the supreme luck of life?" Adrian was the person most responsible for the *War Book*, which played a great part in making the English mobilization at the beginning of World War I a success. It was a compendium of instructions for every government department on actions to be taken, in every contingency, upon the outbreak of war. Lord Haldane told Tiny he thought Adrian contributed more to it than any other single person. Adrian completed the first edition in May 1912 from material supplied by nine government departments; in the second edition, which appeared in 1913, eleven departments were represented and the system was extended to the whole British Empire. For the *War Book* Adrian was given the C.B. in 1913. His only son also went into the Black Watch and was killed in 1940 during the Dunkirk withdrawal.

After Tiny came Dot (Victoria), named for her godmother, the Crown Princess Frederick of Germany, who was Kaiser Wilhelm II's mother. Dot was Tiny's favorite among her siblings; though possibly the prettiest of all, she never married. Hampden was next. He became a sailor, retired early as a captain, and lived alone in a small flat in South Kensington, taking daily walks of twenty miles or more (never less). He lived spartanly, but gave his nephews and nieces fivers for Christmas, which he certainly could not afford. After him came Lily and Iseult, much younger than the others, who were devoted to each other.

Tiny's mother had to do a great deal of entertaining, for Mountstuart loved grandeur. He would rent splendid establishments such as Hampden—the home of the Earl of Buckinghamshire, where Tiny had first become aware of the grassy lawn and where her brother Hampden was born—and Knebworth, Hertfordshire, the Earl of Lytton's place. Here, on her sixth birthday, Tiny read her father the "most interesting of the many inscriptions in these gardens," on a dog's tombstone, ending with: "O solitary Master! what now will sigh for thy departure, or rejoice at thy return?" This, she later wrote, was in a "pretty nook surrounded by yew hedges." In a winter gale the griffins and other monsters that dotted the house dropped tails and ears in all directions. "We never go near the walls in wind, in frost, or after rain," a gardener told Mountstuart.

Knebworth had, too, a perfect garden for children. Here Tiny found her first primrose, great trusses of lilac and laburnum, and scented tree peonies. There were a Chinese garden, a Greek garden with the Three Graces in the middle, a rosery, and a chain of little lakes in the park. On an island in one of them was a cottage where old Lord Lytton had written all his novels, with great bulrushes and kingfishers around it. Eighteen gardeners watched over this paradise, and most were Tiny's friends until Evie told her to tell the ugliest one he was an Adonis. She did not know what it meant but told him anyway, only to be punished by Nurse Maunder for being impertinent. And she had made of the gardener an enemy for life.

But these great houses had not only gardens but also ghosts, and Tiny as a small child was equally aware of both. At Hampden, Tiny's mother heard each night a girl's light footsteps run along a passage that passed the long series of sitting rooms and ended at her boudoir. If her boudoir door was unlocked, it would burst open; if she locked it, someone would fumble with the handle. Tiny's father was in London for the session of Parliament; her mother was physically a strong and courageous woman, but after hearing the footsteps for three months she changed her boudoir. On another occasion, late one winter's night, her Blenheim spaniel ran down the passage to the great hall. She called, but he did not return, so she followed him. To her astonishment the whole place was brilliantly lighted. Her first thought was, "The servants have left the candles and we shall all be burned in our beds," for the hall was lit from a big fixture in the middle of the ceiling; but then, looking up, she saw the candles were not alight. As the dog came shivering back to her, she went quickly back to her room and locked the door behind her.

Knebworth was haunted by a woman spinning. Tiny, sleeping in the haunted room with her mother, woke screaming and had to be put into warm water in her mother's bath to calm her. A woman friend, sleeping in the same room later, after the Grant Duffs had left and the Lyttons had returned, heard a man in chains crawling across the floor, sighing; the chains clanked terribly, and his sighs turned to groans. The woman called to her maid, sleeping in the next room, "Alice, do you hear it?" To which the maid replied, "Oh, Miss Mary, for God's sake come to me, I cannot move." The guest slipped out of her bed and got to the maid's room, and both escaped into the corridor by another door. Everything was pitch dark, but the maid remembered seeing the governess's room earlier while being shown the house. The two women managed to get there; the governess gave them blankets, and they slept on her floor. In the morning Lady Lytton begged them not to say anything, as her mother had had exactly the same experience the previous year and would be frightened.

Lord Arthur Russell once told Tiny that he had stayed at Knebworth as a small boy, and that at breakfast a strange-looking old man in a shabby dressing gown came in and walked slowly round the table, staring at each guest in turn. "Don't take any notice, he thinks he is invisible," said Lady Lytton. It was Lord Lytton, himself an expert ghost-story writer.

At Knebworth during the Grant Duffs' tenure there were 283 entries in the guest book, which was signed by every guest who passed one night or more. At Hampden in six years there were 432 entries. In their first four years at York House, 566 people stayed a night or longer.

In 1877 Mountstuart bought York House, Twickenham, a Jacobean mansion built by Lord Clarendon on the remains of an older house, in which Queen Anne and her sister Queen Mary had been born. Twickenham, now a part of metropolitan London, was then still a village. Tiny's father bought York House from the Comte de Paris. The Duc d'Orleans, the Comte's son, lived close by, and there was an underground passage uniting the properties, which had been bricked up, where Tiny and her brothers kept stag beetles. The gardens were wonderful, full of Italian statuary, cypresses, pools in which blue lotuses grew, fountains, and lozenge-shaped beds of hyacinths and tulips in spring, of wallflowers and petunias later, of pinks in summer and asters in fall. York House is now the local town hall and municipal offices.

It too was haunted, and Tiny's first psychic experience took place there, when she saw a little pink and white pig sniffing at her governess's skirts. Tiny, already in bed, sat up and said, "Oh, Fräulein, do you see the pig?" Of course Fräulein didn't.

Another time, lying awake in bed, with Fräulein snoring nearby, Tiny saw a little white kitten in the moonlight by the window. She got up and tried to catch it, but it vanished. Back in bed, she saw it again, and again pursued, but only succeeded in waking the indignant Fräulein.

To the splendid establishments where she grew up, Tiny preferred her widowed grandmother's modest house at Ealing. Mrs. Webster had only a couple of fields and an old horse and brougham, an old butler called Peprel, an old maid called Vine, and an old cook called Reffold. But there Tiny was allowed to play quietly in the drawing room while her grandmother sat by the fire in an armchair, wearing a frilled tulle cap and black dress with white collar and cuffs of tulle. Tiny did not take her toys to the drawing room but played there with a small bronze copy of the Venus de Milo and a bronze inkstand made to represent the Temple of Vesta (which Anne now has). Two Misses Perceval (sisters of Spencer Perceval, the Prime Minister who was assassinated in 1812) came occasionally to tea. Tiny read there Miss Mitford's *Our Village* and Bewick's *British Birds*.

A generation later, when Anne and Clare came down to the drawing room after tea, they too never brought their toys but were allowed to play decorously with drawing-room objects. Anne remembers a lovely ivory of the infant Krishna sucking his toe, on an ivory leaf; a number of scent bottles carved in jade or quartz; and a collection of eggs made of semiprecious stones: sardius, topaz, ruby, emerald, sapphire, diamond, jacinth, agate, amethyst, beryl, onyx, and jasper, and many more; the girls liked to single out the twelve stones Exodus mentions as being in Aaron's breastplate, and snobbishly preferred these to others.

Until she was eight, Tiny often had a hard time—though never quite as hard as had Anne's father-in-law. He took her to see his old nurse's grave when Anne was first married and told her, "She used to hold my fingers on the red-hot bars of the nursery fire as a punishment." When Tiny was eight her mother took her to Algiers. She then told her mother about nursery conditions, with the result that Nurse Maunder and Fräulein Reinking were both dismissed.

That visit to Algiers was one of the most important events in Tiny's life. It was her first experience of dependable sunlight, and she was drunk with joy the whole three weeks. The villa was an old Moorish house with a great courtyard; the garden was hedged with rosemary and lavender. The sea was always blue, little blue irises grew in the sand, and Tiny and the gardener's daughter stuffed themselves with loquats and dates and chattered day-long in French.

It was a turning point in her life, and thereafter, though nursery meals continued inedible and brothers bullied as before, Tiny had learned that things could improve. The new German governess taught well; the new nurse was kind. As a result Tiny stopped having nightmares and began to have pleasant dreams. She also began to care for music, prompted partly by the lovely voice of her father's secretary, who taught her to sing *Lieder*, but more by a handsome choirboy who had been promoted to play the organ in Twickenham church. Tiny fell in love with him and shivered all over in delicious excitement if she saw him in the street. He became Sir Walter Alcock, organist of Salisbury Cathedral. Tiny met him only once many years afterward, but thought it better not to mention her childish infatuation.

One fall she was left alone at York House, in charge of only a nursemaid. She drank her tea as she liked it, frightfully strong and buttered; she had read in the Abbé Huc's *Travels in Tibet* that was how it was drunk there. She explored York House and read prodigiously. "Such times," she wrote later, "are enormously fruitful in a child's life. We hear so much pity for the only child, but we never hear any pity for the child brought up in a herd who prefers to be alone."

II

A Father and His Friends

Friends and books—Tiny's childhood was filled with both, for her father believed children should read anything, "provided it was not coarse," and his only instruction to the succession of governesses, Fräuleins, and mademoiselles that came and went was that they should encourage the children to read. Anne still has a little red leatherbound book given Tiny by her father on her tenth birthday, Christmas Day, 1880, in which she recorded everything she had read up until then: Grimm, Andersen, Lewis Carroll, Christina Rossetti, all of Juliana Horatia Ewing (*The Brownies, Lob-lie by the Fire, Jackanapes,* and so on), all of Mrs. Molesworth (imaginative fairy tales, such as *The Cuckoo Clock, The Tapestry Room, Four Winds Farm, Carrots*), and all George Macdonald's children's stories.

And friends. Tiny's father had a genius for friends and had them in all camps and creeds; Gladstone of course, but also Disraeli, Matthew Arnold and Thackeray, Karl Marx and Cardinal Newman, Ernest Renan and Charles Darwin. Many of these frequented York House. Books and friends sometimes coincided, or amalgamated: Mrs. Molesworth's daughter married Mountstuart's nephew. George Macdonald would leave nursery tea, explaining to Tiny, "I must be about my Father's business" (Tiny was shocked), and his illustrator, Arthur Hughes, drew Tiny's mother as the North Wind in Macdonald's *At the Back of the North Wind* and as the ageless great-grandmother in *The Princess and Curdie*, and also painted her as herself, complete with Adrian and a peacock.

Tiny loved poetry and learned it in great chunks, and this was what first really brought her to her father's attention. Mountstuart was bored by children, his own included, and her early recollection of him was of a red-bearded man with very bright blue eyes who always said, "Vanish, vanish," whenever he saw one of his offspring, so that they fled like hares. But Tiny learned by heart Matthew Arnold's "The Forsaken Merman" and "Calais Sands," which her mother suggested she recite to her father. She was alarmed, for it meant braving either Guard, the collie who inhabited the library, or the gray cockatoo that ruled over the purple study. She chose the library, and Guard flew at Tiny, seized her arm, and shook it, but though she was scared (he was almost as big as she), she proceeded to where her father was sitting in his puce coat, his "cat regnant," a great gray Persian called Lavender, as usual sitting on his shoulder. Tiny had long wavy hair she could sit on, and very pronounced dark eyebrows over eyes that Swinburne called "the bluest of things gray and the grayest of things blue," and her father really saw her, aged nine, as though for the first time. From that moment they became good friends, and she was with him often, both Guard and the cockatoo admitting her and no one else.

Matthew Arnold frequently came to the house, and Tiny would sit on his knee and repeat his own poems to him; Lord Houghton, too, whose verse today is forgotten. Tiny loved some of his poems, particularly "Why should a man raise stone and wood between him and the sky?" But she was terrified of his enormous teeth. She recited hymns to Lord Napier of Magdala, who was very pious, and Heine's lyrics to the unhappy Crown Princess Victoria of Germany. As Mountstuart was Undersecretary for India from 1868 to 1874, Tiny also learned many of Sir Alfred

Lyall's Indian poems and later taught her children the one about the cynical Old Pindaree who said, "I sowed the seed he gave me, but first I boiled the seed." She learned chunks of Macaulay too, and loved especially the lines about the trees at Nemi that Sir James Frazer took as the basis for *The Golden Bough:*

> The trees in whose dim shadow
> The ghastly priest doth reign,
> The priest who slew the slayer
> And shall himself be slain.

Mountstuart was a great clubman. A member of the Athenaeum, secretary of "The Club," member of the Society of the Dilettanti (the oldest of the London dining clubs, founded in 1764) and also of the Roxburgh Club, he was President of the Royal Geographical Society and of the Royal Historical Society, and originator of the Breakfast Club in February 1866. This club met for breakfast at the houses of various members while Parliament was sitting. But his favorite club was Grillions, founded in 1812, though he also enjoyed the Literary Society. In Victorian days, when houses were cold and crawling with children and servants, a man's club was a true haven.

Mountstuart, besides being Member of Parliament for the Elgin Burghs, was Lord Rector of Aberdeen University from 1867 on, which meant many trips north. On these journeys his wife, who disliked Scotland, did not accompany him, and there is no record that Tiny went north until she was quite grown up.

Because Mountstuart had been one of Newman's circle at Oxford, James Grant Duff had been afraid his eldest son would become a Roman Catholic. Many of Mountstuart's friends did—notably William George Ward, Lord Denbigh, Lady Mary von Hügel, and Lady Blennerhasset—but he did not. Yet out of fear of Mountstuart's "Romanizing" tendencies, his father, who inherited Delgaty Castle from his mother, left it and all his money to his second son, Ainslie. Mountstuart got Eden without the wherewithal to keep it up.

The great love of Mountstuart's life was a Catholic convert whom he never met: Alexandrine de la Ferronays. He knew only her sister-in-law, Mrs. Augustus Craven. Craven was a British diplomat, unsuccessful and badly off, so Pauline, his wife, wrote potboiler novels. She also wrote *Récit d'une Sœur*, a book of pious reminiscences revolving around her beloved brother Albert and his Russian wife, Alexandrine. Once Mountstuart had read this book he read it daily for the rest of his life, for he had instantly and forever fallen in love with the dead Alexandrine. He made pilgrimages to all the places Albert and Alexandrine visited together before Albert died of tuberculosis shortly after their honeymoon, and picked a flower from each spot. He designed a gold ring with serpents twined around a crystal, through which the faded flowers were visible. Tiny gave Anne this ring, which she loyally wore. But one day, to Anne's horror, it suddenly sprang open; a worm had hatched, apparently after a hundred years, and had burst its way out. Mrs. Craven gave Mountstuart Alexandrine's missal, filled with holy cards and scribbles, which Tiny left to Anne. One night Mountstuart dreamed so vividly of Alexandrine that when he woke he got up and drew her face, then and there; Mrs. Craven declared it to be the best likeness ever made of Alexandrine. It later stood in a gold frame on Tiny's writing table.

Tiny, on her way back from Algiers, had been taken to Paris to meet Mrs. Craven and various members of her family and circle, among them her nephews, Count Albert de Mun, the Christian Socialist, and the Duc de Blacas. They stayed often with the Grant Duffs at York House.

Ernest Renan, the author of the famous *Life of Jesus*, was another friend of Mountstuart, who loved the ex-seminarian dearly. Mountstuart had been introduced to him in October 1859 by Duke Frederick of Schleswig-Holstein, and he wrote, "Renan dined with us, and we had the first of a long series of conversations which were for many years among my greatest pleasures in Paris." A few nights later he heard Renan say at dinner to Richard Cobden, "*You* mark the end of England's great politics." Mountstuart published a book about Renan in 1893.

Mountstuart frequented Madame Turgenev's salon in Paris and described her husband as "one of the first Russians to take up seriously the question of Emancipation of the Serfs." At the same time Mountstuart made friends with Guizot and Michelet and also met Thiers and Lamartine, whom he found "with a bad headache and much knocked up, so that he said very little."

Mountstuart met Browning for the first time in London in 1862, and their friendship continued until the poet's death. Tiny once quoted to the poet some lines from his "Pauline" and asked what he had meant by them, to which he replied with a smile that he had forgotten. Mountstuart's first impression of Dickens, whom he met at Richmond in June 1862 with the man destined to be Dickens' biographer, John Forster, was unfavorable; Mountstuart thought his look "singularly unprepossessing" but revised his opinion later. He seems to have liked the curmudgeon Carlyle and quotes many memorable remarks, one being that the American Civil War was between people who preferred to hire their domestics by the year and those who preferred to hire them for life. He knew the leaders of the Italian *Risorgimento*, Count Cavour and Mazzini, and met Garibaldi and his young brother staying with the Seeleys in the Isle of Wight in 1864. "I had a pretty long talk with Garibaldi," he wrote in his diary on April 5, 1864, "walking up and down a long orchard full of fruit trees in flower. But his conversation did not at all impress me; he spoke only of trivial subjects." During this visit Garibaldi wore sometimes a gray and sometimes a red poncho.

Mazzini told Mountstuart he had given more thought to the "religious question" than to any other, but that he did not read much at all! Mazzini added that he had once forgotten most of his Latin, but took to it again in 1835, when hiding in a small presbytery in Switzerland, where there were some Latin books. "He said that the next great religion would be the religion of progress, but what the religion of progress might mean, I did not gather."

Mazzini occurs again in the year of Tiny's birth, 1870, when Mountstuart, visiting Bologna "in my capacity of Rector of Aberdeen," found the rector "of this mother of universities," Count Ercolani, very concerned with Mazzini's idea that the Roman Church should "make a close alliance with advanced Democracy." In a footnote he points out that on this idea "Manning acted in the last years of his life." For it was Cardinal Manning who wrote the text of the first of the so-called "social encyclicals," *Rerum Novarum*. And he settled the great dock strike of 1889 when, as *Punch* wrote in August, "a dying man went down to rescue a dead city." On September 14 of that year all parties signed "the Cardinal's peace."

Mountstuart gave an interesting account of meeting Karl Marx. "Lunched at the Devonshire Club with Leonard Montefiore, to meet Karl Marx. His talk was that of a well-informed, nay, learned man, much interested in comparative grammar, which led him into the old Slavonic and other studies . . . it was all very *positif*, slightly cynical, without any appearance of enthusiasm, interesting, and, I thought, often showing very correct ideas when he was conversing of the past or the present, but vague and unsatisfactory when he turned to the future. He looks, not unreasonably, for a great and not distant crash in Russia, thinks it will begin by reforms from above, which the old bad edifice will not be able to bear, and which will lead to its tumbling down altogether." (January 31, 1879.)

Mountstuart traveled constantly: to Moscow and St. Petersburg; to Greece; to the Balkans and Turkey; and also every year to Italy, France, and the Low Countries. He went for two purposes—to meet people and to botanize—and remarked joyfully even on a visit to Venice that, though one didn't go there to botanize, yet he had found two plants he had never met with before.

Among Mountstuart's greatest friends were the Russells; in fact, Tiny, when six, divided the human race into three—"men, women, and Wussells." His adored friend was Lady William,

whom he first met at Lady Palmerston's in 1860. Byron had eulo-
gized her in *Beppo* as the only "one . . . whose bloom could, after
dancing, dare the dawn." She was over seventy when Mountstuart
met her, but she was still striking, and he admired her then as the
most fortunate woman in England because she had the three nicest
sons. In extreme old age she said to Disraeli, "Am I not fortunate,
to have lived to see one of my sons the head of his family, and
another head of his profession?" (One had become Duke of Bed-
ford; another, Lord John, was Prime Minister.) At her own house
in 1874 she was taken fatally ill and as she left the room said,
"Amuse yourselves as well as you can when I am gone." These
were the last words Mountstuart heard her speak, and he commented, "They closed a remarkable life and the only *salon* which
has existed in my lifetime in London." Mountstuart's favorite
among her sons was Lord Arthur, with whom his sister Alise had
vainly been in love. Lady Arthur had been a Miss Peyronnet,
whom Mountstuart had known before her marriage. Her sister
once sat next to a charming man at dinner, and, on asking his
name, was told, "Pity me, my name is Browne." He was Lord
Sligo, and she married him. She produced twin daughters who
were contemporaries and devoted friends of Tiny's. They were
very fat and lived out of town, so a friend wrote:

> I thought I saw a butter pat
> Upon a Surrey down.
> I looked again and saw it was
> The Lady Mary Browne.
> O, is she standing up, I asked,
> Or is she sitting down?

But it was Lord John Russell's widow and her grandchildren
whom Tiny knew best. They lived at Pembroke Lodge, in Richmond Park. Bertrand Russell, in the first volume of his memoirs,
describes how fond of Tiny he was when he was four and she six.
Unfortunately she preferred his elder brother, Frank, who, like
Tiny's brothers, was beastly to little girls and used to tie her up

in trees by her long hair. Bertie, sobbing in sympathy, would disentangle her, but she still preferred Frank. Though she loved going to tea with the Russells at Pembroke Lodge, even as a child she realized what an unsuitable place it was for the two extraordinarily gifted boys. Bertie, in a blue velvet suit, was always solemn, like his aunt, Lady Agatha, who wore a white shawl, looked downtrodden, and spoke in hushed tones. Rollo Russell never spoke at all. He gave a handshake that nearly broke all the bones of Tiny's fingers, but was quite friendly. They all drifted in and out of the rooms like ghosts, and no one ever seemed to be hungry.

Tiny's godmother, Lady Henley, was a lovely woman with red hair and dazzling skin. She had lost a beloved daughter young, and Tiny to some extent took her place. Tiny was named Clara for her, and Tiny's granddaughter, Elizabeth Hobhouse, Konradin's daughter, married Lady Henley's grandson Michael.

Tiny's godfather, Lord de Tabley, was a much appreciated poet in his day. When Tiny, at the age of twenty, had her first poem published in *The Spectator,* her godfather brought her his latest slim volume of verse with the comment, "My dear, as we are both in the same line, I thought you might like this"—his last book of verse.

Children are well aware who likes them, and for Tiny no man ever understood children as well as Sir Charles Dilke. But every time he came to stay at York House he brought with him his mistress, Mrs. Mark Pattison, whom he later married, and very naturally wanted to talk to her, which annoyed Tiny. It was curious he could bring her to York House, as Mountstuart was so respectable that no one even ever told an off-color story in his presence. Indeed, when someone asked if the Orleans Club was "fast," the answer was, "Oh no, Grant Duff is a member."

Tiny wrote her first poem when she was nine.

> Through the glades of life we pass
> Never stopping, never,

> Death though always comes at last
> And we all shall sever.
>
> And when we shall part at last
> And we all shall sever,
> We shall never meet again,
> Never, never, never.

She was very proud of this effusion and showed it to everyone in the house. A nurserymaid suggested the last lines be amended, so Tiny changed them to:

> We shall someday meet again
> In the heaven yonder.

But, she noted then, the original version was the true one.

Also when nine, she was driven off in solitary grandeur for her first overnight visit alone, other than those to her Webster grandmother. She was sent to stay at Park Lodge, Wimbledon, with W. R. Greg and his wife. Greg was supposed to have been the inspiration for Rochester in Charlotte Brontë's *Jane Eyre.* Tiny read the novel at ten and was terribly frightened by the madwoman's tearing of the wedding veil. When she cheerfully put her oar into a grown-up conversation to say so, her mother and the female friend with whom she was discussing the book almost fainted with horror at the idea that Tiny had read it. W. R. Greg's small son Walter, quiet, with gray eyes like saucers, was delighted by Tiny. Greg's brother-in-law, the economist Walter Bagehot, was a friend of Tiny's father, as was his niece Lady Colefax, who later for many years had one of the greatest *salons* in London. (She was immortalized by E. F. Benson in his *Lucia* books, and also by the wicked remark of a less successful rival that during the two minutes' silence observed throughout England on Armistice Day, the only sound that could be heard was Lady Colefax climbing. She was, too, the heroine of Evelyn Waugh's short story "To Meet Jesus Christ.") Greg's second wife—the one Tiny knew—was a sister of Emilie Barrington (Mrs. Russell Barrington), who entertained the Pre-Raphaelites at Herds Hill in Somerset and in Melbury Road, Kensington. Mrs. Barrington's crowded houses were chockablock with Watts and Leighton drawings, de Morgan tiles and pots, Rossetti and Burne-Jones pictures and studies, Morris wallpapers and curtains. She was a perfect example of all that was most vital in the Victorian era, and Tiny throve in her atmosphere.

Laurence Oliphant, a frequent visitor, died at York House. He had come to stay for a week in September 1888 and remained until his death two days before Christmas. He had angina pectoris, and Tiny's mother refused to let Laurence's second wife, *née* Rosamond Dale Owen, granddaughter of Robert Owen, take him away, as she naturally wished to do. Tiny's mother was a loyal friend and never thought anything too much trouble for those she loved. So everything possible was done for the Oliphants, Lady Grant Duff giving up her sitting room to the sick man. Laurence had just remarried. The story of his strange "experiments with truth" in Europe and the United States has been the subject of several books.

Tiny felt it an immense privilege to know Oliphant, "that seer and sage," as she called him. One day when she was sitting with him he asked her to make him a promise.

"What sort of a promise?"

"I want you to promise never to go to séances."

"Why not?" she asked.

"Because," he replied, "you are very sensitive, and people get under very strange influences from which there is no escaping. I should like to feel that you are not in danger that way."

She gave the required promise, and he told her that on the border between this world and the next there are half-human creatures trying to get back to the things they enjoyed in this world, and to do so they use human beings as a medium toward attaining their wishes. They often satisfy their desires through people who are foolish enough to get into their clutches.

Laurence Oliphant had a curious Armenian servant called Yani, and when fearful attacks of pain from cramp in the heart came on, the Armenian and Mrs. Oliphant would hold his hand, and they certainly soothed him. The hand-holding seemed to establish some kind of mesmeric quality that helped the pain. The servant wore his own beautiful native dress. On the day Laurence died, Tiny's mother took her in to see his dead body. It upset her terribly, and she rushed to her room and cried for an hour at the sight of the corpse.

Tiny's mother sent her to friends for Christmas to get over the shock. When she returned, Mrs. Oliphant was still in the house. One day Tiny, sitting with her and holding her hand, suddenly felt a frightful electric shock. Tiny jumped up, screaming. "I'm sorry, my dear," Mrs. Oliphant said, "but it's quite all right. It was only Laurence, who just put his hand on my shoulder."

Mrs. Oliphant finally went off to Haifa, taking with her a handsome young man who had been around her before Laurence died, whom she eventually married. This young man later committed suicide. Mrs. Oliphant wrote *My Perilous Life in Palestine*. She influenced Tiny a good deal. "She made the next world extraordinarily real to me," Tiny said. Tiny felt that there was surely a continuance after death, yet also felt that "immortality is not a gift, immortality is an achievement; and only those who strive mightily shall possess it," as the *Spoon River Anthology* put it.

Tiny's parents for several winters rented a town house in Queen's Gate, then so rural that Mountstuart, coming home from the House of Commons, would say to the cabby, "Drive along the Cromwell Road till you come to a hedge, and then turn right." All Tiny remembered of London then was the blue-gray of Hyde Park on November afternoons and the black tree trunks against the sunset. Also the muffin man, who came by at dusk, ringing his bell, and the crossing sweepers who cleared the mud and horse dung from the crossings, and the coal-black chimney sweeps. If these latter responded to one's greeting—touched a cap or pulled a forelock—that was good luck for a day, a week, maybe forever. Above all she remembered the furry seed balls that dangled from the plane trees in the park. She wanted one of these more than anything on earth, but never could reach one until she was too old to care.

The Grant Duffs provided very little entertainment specifically for their children but did take them to the seaside in the summer, where they collected winkles, later eaten with a pin in the housekeeper's room. In town the children occasionally went to parties, often with cousins, where they always managed to commit *faux pas*. At one cousin's, Adrian announced that his mother's drawing room was "much prettier," while Tiny sang a hymn loudly to the embarrassed audience and was stopped only by an ice. Asked by another cousin to watch the Lord Mayor's show, Tiny greeted her host with "We've come to have some kind of scratch lunch." Taken to a pantomime of Cinderella, she screamed with fright at the large rats. Her first dramatic entertainment was Lily Langtry's first appearance on the London stage—she was already the Prince of Wales's favorite mistress—and Tiny remembered her father and Herbert Gladstone, the Prime Minister's youngest son, both equally lost in admiration of the Jersey Lily's beauty. Many years later, when her daughter Anne was at Oxford, Tiny watched Lily Langtry's grandson, Angus Malcolm, playing tennis. "I'd recognize that back of the neck anywhere," she said before he turned to be introduced. He had heard and blushed.

In 1880 Mountstuart accepted from Gladstone a Privy Councillorship on becoming Undersecretary for the Colonies and was even busier and more social than before. As he never recorded an unkind word or a painful incident in his diaries, they are bland as junket and give the general impression that their author was nothing more than an intellectual and social snob. But he was more. He was a devoted public servant, a perceptive critic, and intensely kind; he never forgot a friend, and would take immense pains to go and see some dreary old woman in a remote suburb because she had been good to him as a child. Also, his most intimate friends were all men of absolutely first-class brains: Sir John Lubbock, later Lord Avebury, who was almost Darwin's equal as a scientist; Matthew Arnold; Ernest Renan; and above all Benjamin Jowett, the greatest master Balliol ever had:

> First come I. My name is Jowett.
> There is no knowledge but I know it.
> I am the Master of this college,
> What I don't know isn't knowledge.

Jowett was the great translator of Plato and a cynic who set as a Sunday essay: "It is wrong to do evil that good may come. We go to church on Sunday to edify the lower classes. Reconcile these two propositions." Tiny loved the whiskery old master and felt flattered when he came to her wedding; his portrait later hung in her husband's bedroom.

To have been a friend of men as diverse as Walter Pater and Kinglake, Cardinal Newman and Charles Darwin, Lord Tennyson and Robert Browning, Montalembert and Mazzini, to have breakfasted often with Gladstone and had Cobden and Bright often to his home suggests a flair, if not a genius, for friendship. To have traveled as much as Mountstuart did, and to have had such agreeable posts as Undersecretary for the Colonies and for India, and the Governorship of Madras, would seem indications of a lucky life when it is remembered that Mountstuart was only the son of a Scots laird. Tiny thought he was quite as brilliant as most of his contemporaries, but he suffered from three major disabilities all his life—bad health, appalling eyesight, and small means—so he did not reach the highest rungs of either the political or the literary ladder.

Tiny also thought the mistake of his life was in being a Liberal. His father was passionately conservative, and they did not get on; probably Mountstuart's liberalism was his form of rebellion. But Mountstuart always preferred Disraeli to Gladstone as a person and as a point of view, and Tiny wrote in 1932: "Father could have had the Foreign Office if he had been in the Conservative Government." Dean Boyle told her that he happened to be with

Gladstone and other Liberal leaders when they were planning a Cabinet and someone suggested, "Why not give Grant Duff the Undersecretaryship at the Foreign Office? He knows much more about foreign affairs then anybody else." "Ah yes," Gladstone said. "He knows too much." "The terror of the expert together with admiration for the man who pleases the mediocre, seem to the outsider, then as now, the note of the Liberal," wrote Tiny.

Mountstuart's second great mistake was to oppose Home Rule for Ireland. It lost him years of interesting work in the House of Commons when Mr. Gladstone was doing something constructive and wise, and Tiny thought it had cost him a peerage. Had he gone back into the House on his return from India and supported the government, he would have had a much more absorbing sunset to his life. But he knew nothing of Ireland and of the conditions there and accepted second-hand the opinions of his intimate friends, amongst whom Lord Arthur Russell, the closest friend of all, was the most vehemently opposed to Irish self-determination. "My father was therefore absolutely convinced of the iniquity of a free Ireland. It is difficult nowadays to realize that the Liberals of last century were honest. With the plain speaking and plain thinking which is the great advantage of modern life, they seem to us like the most appalling hypocrites. Disraeli, who was the least hypocritical of people, once said of Gladstone, 'I don't mind Gladstone wanting to kill and eat Mrs. Gladstone, but I do not care for him saying that the Holy Spirit put him up to it.' Or, as the French Ambassador M. Cambon put it, 'Whenever Mr. Gladstone pulls the ace of trumps from his sleeve he always says the Holy Spirit told him to.' When Disraeli did a wrong thing," Tiny concluded, "he knew perfectly well why he was doing it, and, if he pretended for public consumption that it was for the highest motives, he did not ever deceive himself. Gladstone, on the other hand, failed to look clearly at his own motives, and really believed his own slogans." Mountstuart Grant Duff, Liberal though he was, could not pretend to go along with policies he fundamentally mistrusted, and after he split with Gladstone on Home Rule he never had another prominent appointment.

Nor did he suffer fools gladly. The kindest and gentlest of men, he did not enjoy blood sports and was endlessly good to animals, rejoicing when Tiny wrote him that she had found her Shetland pony happy and well—though very old—at some friends' country house on the family's return from India; going to "cat-sit" with twenty cats of a friend while she went away for the weekend. But he refused to sit next to any woman who bored him in his own house, regardless of protocol, and Tiny would often have to remodel a dinner party at home at the last minute.

His favorite reading was from the East, from his friend Friedrich Max Müller's translations of the Sacred Books. His favorite quotation was, "This also shall pass away." He himself "passed away" after a short illness on January 12, 1906, clear-headed to the last. (Tiny died on the same day thirty-eight years later.) He had received the Holy Communion two days earlier, his family and some friends receiving with him. He was buried in the ruins of the old cathedral at Elgin, near his forebear MacDuff, and pipers played him to his grave with "Lochaber No More."

III

India

Tiny was ten when she noticed that her father and mother were very excited about something, and many telegrams and important-looking visitors arrived. After about a week of this, her mother sent for her and told her they were going to India. "Your father has been appointed Governor of Madras."

Tiny asked, "And are the boys coming too?"

Her mother replied, "No, I'm afraid not."

Tiny burst into tears, and her mother kissed her because she thought it showed such nice feelings. Tiny, however, was overwhelmingly relieved at the thought that there would be no holidays in which she would be bullied and tormented. From then on life was one delirious dream. Tiny and her sister Dot had always been very simply dressed, but now whole trousseaux were produced for the two of them, and everyone gave them parting presents. Her parents gave a big afternoon dance to say good-by to their friends, and Tiny for the first time heard, and danced to, Strauss waltzes. They sailed at the end of October on the *Rome* from Tilbury, taking little Hampden—his nurse with him—and seen off by Tiny's grandmother and her three older brothers. Lily, the baby, was left with cousins, in the care of a nurse.

On board were two aides-de-camp, Lieutenants Cecil Charles

Cavendish and William Evans-Gordon, and the Government House doctor, Surgeon-Major John Mackenzie. A few days out it became hot, and at night the phosphorescent water lashed against the boat. Every incident of the voyage was a delight— Malta with its palaces, where they spent a day; Suez and Port Said, with their donkey rides and queer mixed people. Tiny thought Aden beautiful, though everyone told her it was a horrid place. And at last they came to Bombay and the wonder of an Indian town. In those days India had scarcely been touched by Western civilization and, for a foreign visitor at least, there was romance all around.

At Bombay the sirdars of the Deccan gathered in some force to greet the son of the historian of the Mahrattas. Tiny's father was met by the Governor of Bombay and went straight to stay at Government House there, but the nursery party was sent off to Madras by the night train and spent two delightful days watching India pass the carriage windows, not in the least minding the heat, which reduced nurse and nurserymaid to a state of soporific indignation.

When the children arrived in Madras they were met by a third aide-de-camp, handsome Captain Arthur Bagot. He and Tiny made friends at once. First he was a big brother for many years, and then a devoted friend until he died. "Magnificently good-looking," Tiny later wrote in *A Victorian Childhood*, "a perfect horseman, a wonderful dancer and a first-rate shot, to me he was for all the world like someone out of a fairy-tale. He took us from the station to Government House, and we were ushered into an enormous room where about twenty-five people were breakfasting. I was most terribly shy, nearly frightened to death, and of course swaggered in consequence, as children do. I remember sitting between a man called Lord Dalhousie and another man called Lord Abercrombie, who fed me and asked me endless questions. I was very thankful when we were taken off to bed to sleep off the effects of our journey in a great cool room under mosquito curtains.

"After a long rest we went for a drive in one of the State carriages with splendid horses and scarlet liveries. We were very carefully dressed, and I remember my surprise at being dressed up in this way to go for a simple drive. We drove along the sea front, and saw numbers of Anglo-Indians taking the air much as people do in England in Hyde Park, meeting friends and gossiping. We were very bored, and the next day we were allowed to go for a walk in the park instead, and I shall never forget the enchantment of it. There was a round pool fringed with coconut palms, with kingfishers flying in and out everywhere, and great butterflies nearly as big as the kingfishers. There were herds of little black deer so small they were not much bigger than a fox-terrier, and beautiful brown women with great brass pots on their heads, going down to fetch water.

"Everywhere there were the loveliest flowers and great crimson bushes or flowering trees, but it was not until I got to Guindy that I realized the wonders of India. Guindy is a palace built as a sort of country residence for the Governor some way out of Madras, but near enough to the sea for us children to go down to it very often. The grounds were full of exquisite flowers and there were acres of divine gardens, and outside were the paddy fields and a small miniature racecourse where one could get a good gallop in the early morning. Two beautiful Arab ponies were bought for Hampden and me, called Omar and Ali. Ali, the most beautiful, was given to me."

There were a hundred horses in the stables, each with its syce (groom), grass-cutter, and woman to boil its *dal*, a kind of lentil. The stables were kept like a drawing room and the horses polished with the naked hand. Tiny never saw a syce in their stables rough with a horse, though a groom brought by the Grant Duffs from England was rough enough and gave the others a bad example. Since Tiny had recovered from her "tewwible nervous sock," she practically had the run of the riding stables and, as her hands were good, the staff let her ride their mounts.

The house had a hundred servants, efficient and attentive and capable, and of course there were the numberless boys belonging to the staff and the gardeners and so on, outside. The indoor servants or peons were picturesquely dressed in long flowing robes with gold-and-red or red turbans, according to rank. Some of the superior servants wore only gold and red.

Everything moved on oiled wheels, and Tiny was glad for the first time in her life to live in a properly run establishment and to be well fed.

On her eleventh birthday, her first Christmas in India, there was a Christmas tree covered with little yellow balls (*Muiraya exotica*, noted Mountstuart) sent to Government House from Guindy. Tiny remembered how happy she was that evening, and how she was suddenly aware what Captain Gordon, who, with the other aide-de-camp, lived in Government House, meant to her. On the boat she had only found him delightful and enjoyed being with him. Then, there, he had been just one of her father's staff. This was different.

"He was one of those men with whom all women fall in love, and no one particularly knows why. He was good-looking—but no better-looking than many men in that age of tall, finely made men—with dark hair, a slightly reddish moustache, aquiline nose, and clear skin. He had a delightful baritone voice and was really musical, and he danced and rode and shot and played polo well. But in my youth these accomplishments were expected of any soldier. He was not nearly as handsome as Captain Arthur Bagot, though a cleverer man. But there was no doubt about his charm for women; it was universally admitted.

"Few people know how many children fall in love and what agonies they suffer," Tiny wrote. The day she was eleven she became aware of her absorption in Captain Gordon, but for some time she did not really understand what had happened. She just adored him and wanted to be with him always, and then suddenly came the comprehension, "This is what people mean when they say they are in love." The inevitable happened, and he fell in love with her, and for six months more their idyl endured, carefully protected by the Indian servants with their genius for intrigue, a beautiful thing, however foolish it may have been on her part and wrong on his. "Looking back—it is nearly fifty years ago—" Tiny wrote, "I marvel at the passion a child could feel . . . passion undisturbed by the faintest lust. I had not the remotest idea what sex love meant and I cannot be grateful enough that this unique experience was given me.

"I see now that my lover must have suffered a good deal. Sometimes when he held me in his arms and kissed me blind, he would suddenly say, 'Run away, quick, quick,' and I used to tear off wondering and very much hurt, and noticing as I went that his face was working horribly and very white. When I was a woman I looked back and understood. The supreme instinct that comes to women from their cradles onward came to me, and I became so fine an actress that no one except Arthur Bagot and the native servants ever guessed. My mother was naturally unobservant, and my father lived his own life and rarely saw us together. My governess could not conceive the possibility of a grown-up man falling in love with a child, and my small brother and sister never thought about anything at all.

"To Captain Gordon I owe a great deal of my love of music. He sang me Schubert and Schumann and was always telling me that nothing in life mattered like music. In his last letter to me before he went away he said, 'Keep your music, whatever else you do or do not do, take trouble over it. You will find it a solace and consolation when everything else leaves you.' He used to read me Lewis Morris's *Epic of Hades,* and Byron and Keats and Heine in his beautiful grave voice. He taught me to see effects of cloud and shadow over the hills, and, as he was passionately fond of flowers, I was always trying to find new ones and arrange them in his room. I owe him a great deal, though he broke my heart.

"I have always been like a man—my love affairs have not touched the rest of my life. And this absorbing first passion of mine, though it coloured every moment when I was alone, did not prevent my rushing about with other children and amusing myself in various ways when I could not be with my lover. When Captain Gordon left the hills in November we had a heart-breaking parting and I cried myself sick. But I thought he would be back in three months. However, when he got to the plains Arthur Bagot went to him and said, 'If you do not arrange to change into another regiment and leave the staff I shall go to His Excellency.' I only knew this later in life. When I got the news that he was not coming back [he was put in charge of the small states of Partabgarh and Banswara] I nearly went out of my mind. I used to wander over the hills, hiding in the woods and sobbing my heart out. And then I would wash my eyes in a mountain stream and go back in high spirits. No one ever had any conception of what it meant, and when my mother spoke to me about it a year or two later, I merely said, 'Oh yes, I was very fond of him, but not really as fond as I am of Arthur Bagot.' And there the matter ended.

"I am always glad that I had the one overwhelming experience which falls to so few women, very young. It gave me a standard to measure other men by. Probably had I not fallen in love as a child I should have fallen in love later and married the wrong man. As it was my marriage was a supreme success, because I knew that 'love' alone was not sufficiently strong a foundation to build marriage on. Had I married Captain Gordon it would have been disastrous."

The whole family moved from Guindy to Ootacamund on March 1, 1882. Tiny's mother was near yet another confinement, and it was supposed to be better for the children to get out of the heat. They had never seen the mountains before, and the drive would have been a joy had they not been so terribly frightened in the tongas. The little ponies dashed up almost perpendicular roads and frequently slipped back, every now and then falling while their incompetent drivers yelled at them from behind. On arrival, the children were put to bed, exhausted, but waking up the next morning to the mountains was an experience Tiny was never to forget. There were eucalyptus woods carpeted with white violets, and tiny streams meandering on every side; there were *sholas* (arbors) of great aboriginal trees full of jasmine and every kind of flower, and there were thickets of wattle covered with mimosa. There were belladonna and arum lilies and little wild narcissus everywhere, and here and there the great rare Nilgiri lily.

The new baby—a girl, christened Iseult—was born on March 12, and Tiny and Dot were left alone to explore the country in utter bliss. The girls were sent for lessons to a French convent run by delightful nuns, one of whom, Mère Antoine, was beautiful, tall, and pale, with gold eyebrows and eyelashes. She was so beautiful that Tiny could not think of anything else but her face when she was in the room. She was rebuked by a plainer Sister for staring, and replied that she could not help it in the presence of such beauty. "External beauty is a wile of the devil," said the plain nun; Tiny did not contradict but was quite sure the plain nun was wrong.

Tiny and Dot used to ride to the convent daily, lunch there, and ride back at night. Tiny loved going to Benediction; for the first time she realized what worship could mean. The children ate in the convent parlor: omelets and salad and Gruyère cheese, followed by pears in French red wine; nothing, Tiny told Anne years later, ever tasted so good again.

The nuns were very poor, and to raise money one of the sisters wrote a play about the French Revolution, based on an incident in the life of one of her own forebears. The story was of a twin sister who was smuggled into prison and died impersonating her brother to save the family line. Tiny was the heroine. At the dress rehearsal everyone was so moved that it had to be stopped: actors, managers, and audience were all sobbing. The play was given every day for a week and made lots of money for the nuns, besides giving Tiny the immense pleasure of seeing the audience mopping their eyes night after night. She felt terribly important riding over to the convent every morning with powdered hair and being given *sirop de fleur d'oranger* to clear her throat.

One of the joys of Ootacamund was hunting jackals in the Nilgiri hills. The field was never large, twenty to thirty people at most, and they all knew each other and each other's ponies. An early start, and then about four hours' riding over glorious country, with real danger, for it is no light thing to gallop straight down a hillside that most people would be scared to walk down.

Tiny would read to her father from seven to nine each morning when she did not hunt, and again for an hour at six. It was too much at the age of eleven, and the doctor told her mother she could not possibly do lessons and read so much to her father. Her father said, "Then she had better give up lessons," so she practically became his secretary. He did not like the way any of his staff read aloud, and his weak eyesight made it necessary for him to have someone always at hand. Tiny also wrote from dictation and made copies in French, English, and German, and he insisted on her learning the first four rules of arithmetic, which he said were all any woman need ever know. (Tiny had her daughters taught no more, with the result that when Anne sat for the School Certificate exam she new neither geometry nor algebra; she had to take botany instead.)

Tiny described her own complex approach to numbers: "Up to eight or nine I got my sums into dreadful confusion because to me numbers always suggested individuals and had such definite personalities that I objected to the ones who did not suit being placed together. 3, for instance, was a bad little girl, 5 a boy of weak character, and I had a strong feeling that 3 would corrupt 5 if placed near him. 9 was a grown-up woman with nearly unlimited power but not very trustworthy, and 8 a stupid servant. 7 was a man and on the whole beneficient, and 4 was a really attractive and wholesome boy. This sounds very cracky, and I never mentioned it to anyone till I was well over forty, and then, discussing childish things with my younger sister Iseult, I told her of this aberration. 'How odd,' she said. 'I used to do the same thing.' I do not know if it is usual for children to visualize numbers like this and I never met any other instance of it except in the case of Iseult."

Tiny also wrote: "Like nearly all observant children, I saw faces in clouds, in the grain of wood, and in the marks on ceilings. I am inclined to think that a certain school of painting is founded on this. A man sees significant form in something, it suggests an idea to his mind, and he elaborates it. He then gives the result a title. It is purely a literary faculty and has nothing to do with art as practised by all the great graphic artists since the world began, men who have tried to paint what they saw and not what they thought."

In later life Tiny kept enormous green leatherbound books—one for each of her five houses—in which she entered all expenses. She spent hours "struggling with accounts" or "doing the weekly books" and had an awesome double-entry system that no one else could comprehend. She bought from her husband's estate every potato, strawberry, or pint of milk. She would stay up all night if she got even sixpence wrong, and she terribly disapproved of Anne's habit, after she married, of balancing figures to the nearest shilling, or, after she came to the United States, the nearest fifty cents.

When the children lunched at Ootacamund it was always in the dining room with the grown-ups, but the hundreds of adults who came and went were as the shadows of shades compared with Captains Gordon and Bagot. Arthur Bagot taught Tiny riding, driving, dancing, how to write a decent letter, how to shake hands, how to come into and out of a room; warded off unsatisfactory acquaintances; got her out of two or three dubious love affairs (including the one serious one with Captain Gordon); and gave her a rudimentary idea of what was meant by good form. When he was with children he would take their point of view, and would understand perfectly when she wanted to gallop over the hills, get off her horse, and pick flowers or even scramble in and out of a stream.

The second winter, Tiny and Hampden were left alone at Ootacamund with a governess, the groom, his wife, and a nurserymaid. One Sunday the syces went out and left the ponies tethered on the grass in front of the house, and Hampden and Tiny immediately scrambled onto them bareback. The governess came out and also tried to ride bareback. The whole episode lasted only about ten minutes, for Tiny's horse kicked and flung her over his head. The sickening pain made her lose consciousness for a moment; then she got up and tried to pretend everything was all right, but presently had to crawl back to the house in agony. The governess tried to assure Tiny that she was not hurt, and was reluctant to send for the doctor, who was fifty miles away on a case. She worried her all afternoon with officious remarks, until Tiny, desperate with pain and nerves, said very quietly, "Please, go straight out of the room and don't come back until the doctor comes. Now— go—at once." To Tiny's surprise the governess burst into tears and went. Tiny registered the incident.

The doctor did not arrive until midnight. When he came the governess asked, "It's only a sprain, isn't it?" and he replied, "Only four bones broken and I have no chloroform." He set the bones as best he could.

That day marked an epoch in her life. First, it gave her a taste of unbearable pain, and second, it taught her that if you say something forcefully enough, people obey.

The pain lasted three days and then she was able to get about, strapped up and wearing a dressing gown. By this time the governess had lost any authority she had had, so Tiny spent her time playing with the groom and his wife and an old Texan called Brown, who was head of the tonga depot. The Texan taught Tiny a great deal about life, and he also taught her to become a past master at whist. The groom approved of Tiny but warned her not to "grow up to be the sort of woman who looks as if they was smelling mince pies in 'eaven."

It was in India that Tiny first had a room of her own. The boredom of sleeping in a nursery and constantly being wakened by the baby screaming, the nurse snoring, or the dog whining was exchanged for the joy of the Indian nights, when the moon flooded everything and she stayed on the veranda until all hours, watching the sleeping palms. She crept out to see the Muharram festival, awakened by the tom-toms and fifes, and watched the procession carrying the great silver filigree replica of Omar's and Ali's tomb, which was borne from the mosque and thrown into the river. She got one rupee a week pocket money, and saved enough to buy a Satsuma bowl and a cloisonné bowl; she filled them both with rose petals, which she collected fresh every morning.

She and Hampden used to go out together at night. They would roam about the woods for hours, each with a dog on a leash. They would chase the pariah dogs and visit the Toda tribesmen in their huts. Anne still has some brass Toda ornaments that Tiny got then from the one wife of seven brothers. They went together also to native weddings and would play in the Tiger's Cave across the valley, where they sometimes saw a tiger slink by in the moonlight. Tiny was often in disgrace—as when, one evening, when her mother gave a great ball and she had not been allowed to stay up for the first few dances, she revenged herself by dribbling sugar, from a gallery that ran across the hall, onto the dancers as they left the ballroom. She was well hidden, and at first all went well: the guests grew stickier and stickier but could not imagine why. And then rather too much sugar fell on Captain Bagot's uniform; he left his partner with a yell of rage, dashed upstairs, seized Tiny, shook her, and carried her to her bedroom while she bit him furiously. Another day, she persuaded Dr. Mackenzie's daughters to establish themselves with her on a hill overhanging the principal road to Government House. They rolled rocks down so that they jumped over the road and only just missed the dogcart containing the staff.

It was now that she discovered the power of her eyes. She found she could scare the Indian servants by focusing her eyes on them and walking slowly toward them. They would drop dustpan or broom and fly in terror. Her brother Hampden was even more terrified, as she used to wait until it was dark and then, murmuring, "Eyes, eyes," follow him round the night nursery, staring, staring.

The children had quantities of pets: Hannibal, a bird that had boarded the *Rome* as they were crossing the Gulf of Tunis, and who lived, fat and well, in the nursery at Ootacamund; a baby elephant, rather scary and bad-tempered, that did not live long; a talking myna bird; a Malabar squirrel; a green parrot; a samba fawn. Tiny's father had saved the fawn's life. He had been sitting under a banyan tree by a small Hindu shrine in a wild island of the Chilka Lake while his staff was shooting deer in the woods around. The beaters caught and brought him the fawn, which he took care of until the dogs were tied up. It grew very tame and followed Tiny everywhere. She used to curl up in its shed in the hay with her head on its shoulder, and was miserable when it died of cold. There was several dogs, and when one, a Yorkshire terrier, was killed by pariah dogs, Tiny's father put up a stone in its memory. Immediately offerings of flowers appeared on the stone; many of the natives thought the dead dog was an incarnation of His Excellency's god and needed propitiating.

Tiny met high-caste Indians too. Daoud Shah, a prisoner of the British government, lived in forced residence at Ootacamund; six feet eight, and one of the handsomest men Tiny ever saw, he came hunting on a cart-horse. The Maharaja of Mysore also came out hunting. Tiny's mother took her once to a zenana (women's quarters) to visit the ladies; they had mechanical toy dogs that were wound up and pranced around the room, dolls that spoke, little toy trains, and many other gadgets. The younger ones were pretty, the older ones fat and plain. They all seemed good-tempered and sweet to each other, and only one girl, a Mohammedan from the north, seemed unhappy; she told Tiny she pined for her garden.

Though Tiny loved Indians, from rajas to pariahs, she took a dim view of many of her fellow countrymen, perhaps agreeing with Demosthenes that a democracy cannot be imperial and survive. She wrote later: "Half the trouble in India is caused by the third-rate men and women who go out there simply to have a good time and who talk about 'dirty natives' and who never attempt to understand the culture that they have come into. When one thinks of the average Anglo-Indian bungalow, as it was in my time, full of the vulgarest kind of European stuff and tenanted by women who cared for nothing but self-indulgence and amusing themselves, one can scarcely wonder at the cynical disbelief the native has in the reality of European civilization. On the other hand, there are wonderful men who have given their lives for the country of their adoption and who care more about India than the Indians themselves. But in India as in England the Englishman's lust of pleasure has been his undoing."

Mountstuart was in his element as Governor. "Held a levee: 348 people," he wrote four days after arriving in Madras; the same day, "My wife held a reception: 400 people." In the preface to his published diaries for the years 1881–1886 he wrote: "When a man has for nearly a quarter of a century led the life of a member of Parliament ever critical when out of office, ever on the defensive when in office, it is highly agreeable to be able to say practically the last word upon almost everything. . . . To look at public affairs from the point of view of the local British Providence for between thirty and forty millions of men, after having looked long at them from the point of view of a member of a huge popular Assembly, taught one a great deal about human history." And about his botanical passion he wrote, "Of the pleasure I derived from the vegetation of the country, I cannot easily convey an idea."

Tiny was now old enough to accompany her parents on many expeditions. She would ride with her father up Dudabetta, nearly nine thousand feet above sea level; she spent a week at Kartary by the great waterfall, and camped on Droog Mountain, with a marvelous view down to the plains thousands of feet below: "A perfect camp, perfect servants, scarlet rhododendrons flaming on every hill." With her parents she did a round of more than eight hundred miles—Coimbatore, Cochin, Camp George, Tinnevelly, and Madura. Large, gorgeous butterflies sailed about in all directions; along the road the Indians burned incense for the travelers at intervals—a mark of attention to an earthly potentate that Mountstuart had not seen before. At Camp George there was primeval forest all around, and a great black eagle sailed above. The Shiva temple in Tinnevelly and the illuminations at Madura were notable, but some of the Indians were extremely shy, and the neighboring population fled when they heard that the Governor was approaching. "He is coming with an army," they said, "to fight the Raja of Cochin about the boundary, and we are sure to be impressed to carry the baggage."

After a year in Madras, Mountstuart wrote that he had had 1089 persons to dinner, had traveled 4875 miles, and had got to know 250 new plants. Government House, a large building of dazzling whiteness, had a park full of antelopes, and the kites were fed from the veranda every day after luncheon. The parties were many: at one, all the guests were asked to wear dresses made of Indian materials; Tiny's mother appeared in silver as Starlight, with powdered hair and diamonds. At another, Tiny's mother went as Anne of Austria, Mountstuart as the Duke of Buckingham.

The winter Tiny was thirteen her mother decided to take her to the plains and leave her sister Dot at Ootacamund. She came down from the great hills and the wide free life. Her mother began to teach her dull subjects such as a Commentary on the Prayer Book, and history from heavy volumes. Tiny's amusements were solitary; roaming the gardens, picking flowers and fruits, going down to the seashore, accompanied by her guinea pig, to look for shells. She was sometimes allowed to go to grown-up parties, and Captain Bagot taught her to waltz. She was already a beautiful dancer and wanted to be a professional. Dancing was her only real talent. She had a great facility for writing verse and music, and a pretty voice, but her hands were too small for a piano and her throat had been weakened by reading aloud too much to her father.

The highlight of that winter was the installation of the Nizam of Hyderabad, which the Viceroy and his complete staff attended. The installation was splendid beyond words, with the great salute of the elephants. As the Governor of Madras and his party rode through the old town on elephants, they could look through windows no European had seen into before. One of Tiny's father's aides remembered the last installation and told Tiny how the Nizam, after seeing a face he fancied in one of the windows, had stopped the procession, got down off his elephant, and gone up into the lady's room, where he had remained for twenty-four hours, while everyone else waited in the street, in line in the procession, sending for food and sleeping as best they might. After the twenty-four hours the new Nizam came down and remounted his elephant, and the procession and junketings continued as though no interruption had occurred.

On this occasion Tiny saw white marble staircases, darkness, water, architecture outlined by lamps, temples, watergates, quays, and gardens, all illuminated, the summit of every building outlined in light. The fireworks were unique, and even the moonlight played a role; there was just enough of it to add charm, not enough to detract from the illuminations.

Tiny loved the elephant kraals, with the huge beasts lying about on straw, like ponies in England. But she was afraid of elephants and described riding one: "When you go up you feel you are going to the devil—but when you come down you feel that you are going to nothing at all."

The first course of the great banquet given by the Nizam to two hundred people was served on gold plate, with succeeding courses on marvelous china. It spoiled Tiny for future parties, for none she ever went to later matched it in splendor or good taste.

After these gaieties she went back to Ootacamund, where she had a blissful month before the others arrived. She had a Eurasian maid, who taught her what Tiny described as "a lot of unnecessary knowledge about what are known as the facts of life." When her mother arrived with Captain Bagot, they decided Tiny was in a "bad way," having become very undisciplined, and must be sent back to England to school. Tiny's mother broke the news one evening, explaining that she herself would accompany her. Tiny almost fainted from shock. She rushed to her own room, locked herself in, and sobbed for hours. In the morning she was so ill she was sent back to bed. "To have been a child in India," she noted more than fifty years later, "was a joy such as nothing in after life could ever be, and I would willingly forgo all the rest of my life could I have those three years back. Of the misery of those months before I left India it is useless to write. It was a time of such concentrated agony that nothing later in the way of mental pain ever touched my strength. I thought of killing myself, but was afraid. I thought of getting someone to marry me, but knew that, though I could have pulled it off had I been Miss Smith, as the Governor's daughter the act would have involved the man in too much scandal. I consulted with my maid whether I could be smuggled into some native prince's house. But she saw it was too difficult. So I gave in and in the apathy of despair began to prepare for the awful day, fixed for the 25th of April. Arthur Bagot understood and was endlessly kind, though it was he who had prompted my mother to send me to school. My mother could never comprehend why I should object to leaving India, and was herself wild with joy at getting home. Every detail of that last day is printed on my memory. Early that fated morning I went to my father and read as usual. By chance I began the poem:

> Say not the struggle naught availeth,
> The labour and the wounds are vain,

by Arthur Clough, ending with the line

> But westward, look, the land is bright.

'We will stop there,' said my father, his voice quivering a little. I could not cry. I was dumb with grief.

"The drive down, ordinarily terribly frightening, left me cold. I longed to be killed. When we got to Madras, Arthur Bagot held me tight in his arms. 'Poor little woman—dear little woman,' he whispered. 'It will not be as bad as it seems.' But it was worse, much worse." Worst of all was that Tiny was not allowed to write to anyone in India except her father.

The long agony of the journey home—how different from the

radiant voyage out—was mitigated by one small pleasure. Tiny grew fond of a lovely three-year-old girl, Kitty Keyes. She had never liked her little sisters; their nursery was too badly managed and the babies constantly screamed and smelled, were always leaking at one end or the other. But Kitty was "just at the most interesting age, and I adored her. For the first time I remember feeling what a pleasure it must be to have children." As an old woman she mused on the development of the maternal instinct in women. Some have it, she reflected, quite young. With many women, especially Englishwomen, it awakens only with the advent of a child; many more literally never have it until they have grandchildren. Boys and girls brought up in large families often have an instinctive horror of children, while only children have an exaggerated idea of the pleasures of companionship. Men always want to have children, Tiny said, but that is doubtless because they have none of the trouble of having them and "look upon them as amusing playthings to be seen on Sunday when there is nothing better to do."

There are, it would seem, in the whole of life only seven relationships, and everyone cared for is either a repetition or a replacement of one of the basic seven. These are: grandparents and grandchildren; father and son; father and daughter; mother and son; mother and daughter; siblings; lovers. If one of these relationships is a success, succeeding persons are an attempt to repeat remembered perfection; if it is a failure, then the effort is to provide an *Ersatz*. Tiny was soon to find in several of her cousins and teachers either reminders of her beloved grandmother or *Ersätzer* for her inadequate mother.

One cold afternoon in May, she and her mother arrived at Tilbury and went to lodgings in Oxford Terrace, Paddington, where her brothers had taken rooms. She could never pass through that district later without recalling her horror of England—dull dismal streets, hideous people, drab clothes, crass Cockney accents. "And I was so cold. My brothers seemed the same. They no longer persecuted me physically, but they showed me unmistakably that they thought me dreadful, which I undoubtedly was. Conceited, lazy, self-indulgent, with a tongue that could defend its proprietor, I was that unpleasant creature, a 'flapper' who longed to be treated like a grown-up person."

IV

School

Tiny has given her own account of her teens; the gray days in London were followed by visits.

"A month after our arrival from India," she wrote, "we went down to Northampton to stay with my mother's cousin, Richard Ainsworth, at his hunting box, Winwick Warren. Northamptonshire is a dull county with the worst faults of an English landscape, but it is made exquisite at the end of May by the great masses of hawthorn on every hedge. I was thankful to get out of London, and I felt for the first time pleasure in England when Dick's wife, Nono (born Lily Vaughan), held out her arms, saying, 'So this is Tiny.' She was one of those women whom it is very difficult to describe. Quite ugly, with a receding forehead, protruding eyes and a weak chin, and no claim to beauty except pearly teeth and a good complexion and very white hands. But I do not think I ever met anybody, man, woman, or child, who did not fall in love with her straight off and remain her devoted slave. She was not particularly clever except as a psychologist; though she had never read a book on the subject, she had by sheer sympathy discovered most of the data that it takes years of hard study for the average person to arrive at. Nono had immense humour of a kind so delicate that most people never suspected it, and an innate refinement. She instinctively shrank from everything ugly, vulgar, or unworthy. And yet nobody tackled pain and wretchedness, and even sin, more bravely than she did, when necessary. She was the most deeply religious woman I ever knew. I wish the form it took had not been that of old-fashioned Evangelicalism, which led her into strange paths and company. For it was only with regard to religious people that her marvellous judgment of character was ever at fault. It was very difficult for Nono to believe that anyone professing to be a sincere Christian could be a hypocrite, and many undeserving people took advantage of this and gained great ascendancy over her.

"But I was far too young to realize all this during my first stay at Winwick. I merely saw her as gay and tender and infinitely understanding, the first person who was the least sorry for my having to leave India and all my friends. She mothered and petted me and I gave her my full confidence, so that my one idea when we left was to get back to her. Her husband was a good solid Lancashire squire, Tory to the backbone, a good rider and good shot, a perfect example of the English gentleman of the old school. He considered that 'Poacher' and 'Radical' were almost identical terms, and that both meant blackguards of the worst kind.

"We went back to London after a fortnight, and then the dismal day arrived when my mother was to take me to Cheltenham Ladies' College and leave me there for five weeks. After the summer holidays I was to return for good.

"It was a hot June day, and Cheltenham was at its loveliest. Most of the Anglo-Indian colonels and the retired dowagers who go there for sport and cards do not realize how romantic the town is, with its spacious Regency houses and wealth of flowering trees and shrubs. But the beauty of the place did not strike the small rebellious child who was being taken from India to go to school under Miss Dorothea Beale, the then very modern head of the Ladies' College, and one of the few great educators in England.

"My culminating horror was that I was going to school. Like all rather clever children I had a horror of the herd, the herd mentality, herd games, herd morals and manners, and I had not yet realized that if you show the herd you are not afraid of it you will be left alone.

"My mother and I arrived at the Queen's Hotel one morning, and after the usual English lunch proceeded to interview my new house mistress, to whom I took an instant and violent dislike. We then went to the Ladies' College, a frightful building, perhaps the ugliest in England, which did not tend to mend matters in my mind. But when we entered the little house alongside the College, and the grave, rather beautiful woman rose to receive us, I realized that in Miss Beale there was something different, something not quite common, something apart. She was short, but her dignity was marvellous. The only woman of her generation whose dignity was greater was Queen Victoria. Miss Beale had large, penetrating eyes and great humour in the corners of her mouth. She walked with an extraordinarily smooth long step, probably because she wore no heels. It was a sight to see her come up the long hall and fall upon some luckless child who had caught her attention from the further end.

"She shook hands with my mother and myself and then settled down to the usual conversation between parents and the heads of institutions. But all the time she was talking to my mother, she was really watching me and taking in my immense indignation. When we left she shook hands in a friendly way, saying, 'You must come and see me the first day you are in College. I shall send for you.' And the interview was over."

Next morning Tiny's mother left her at Lansdowne Villa, of which Miss Eales was housemistress. Cheltenham's thousand girls live in houses of some fifty each and go daily to study in its College. Two of the elder girls were for some reason not at College that day, and they kindly came to help Tiny unpack. Tiny, used to giving orders, and knowing exactly what she wanted done, thanked them and proceeded to tell them where to stow her belongings, with the help of hammer and nails she had brought with her. Their astonishment knew no bounds, and they were so surprised that they meekly did as she commanded. When she said, "No, two inches lower," or "You've got it too much to the left," they obeyed. "But," Tiny later wrote, "they registered black marks against this appallingly conceited and cocksure child, and I never heard the last of that morning. 'The damnedest cheek we ever met,' was their verdict."

It was the day of the school *exeat*, and after lunch they went to Weston-super-Mare on the Bristol Channel, where the whole house of fifty was to stay over Sunday. These half-term "breaks" were very pleasant. A girl seized on Tiny that afternoon and told her Miss Eales wished them to be friends. Tiny was quite prepared to agree. For twenty-four hours they were inseparable and, Tiny recorded, the girl taught her "many strange things." But at the end of that time they quarreled violently, and they scarcely ever again spoke to each other. However, Tiny had already learned a lot.

After this everyone tried to bully her. Of physical bullying there was none, and that, Tiny always maintained, is the only thing that breaks a child. No one can stand up against physical pain. But everything in the nature of sneers, innuendoes, accusations of snobbery or conceit or want of manners that could be applied, was applied. She minded, but it never touched her on the raw, for none of those people seemed to her to matter. Coming as she did from a very cultivated home, she saw the girls were ignorant and was too green to realize that there were plenty of interesting and valuable girls among them. That was to come later. And she saw that she knew twice as much as the other girls of her own age. That meant that she took an excellent place in College, and she could do the work required of her with really little effort. She also had a sharp tongue and a ready wit, and, though she was hideously unpopular, that term she managed to hold her own. She earned the wrath of a science teacher by quoting from a poem by May Probyn:

How wonderful it seemed, how right
The Providential plan,

That he should be a trilobite
And I should be a man.

Among teachers were ladies named Miss Knott, Miss Mold, Miss Buckle, Miss Soulsby, and Miss Hare. Another teacher was Mary Everest Boole, widow of George Boole, the self-taught mathematician who wrote *The Laws of Thought* and *Theory of Analytical Transformations*; she was the daughter of Sir George Everest, whose name was given to the mountain that Edmund Hillary and Tensing Norkay climbed because it was there. After her mathematician husband, much older than she, had died in 1864, leaving her with five little girls, she became a teacher and wrote pseudo-philosophical books such as *Logic Taught by Love* and *The Forging of Passion into Power*. Her daughter, Ethel Lillian Voynich, complained to Tiny's daughter Anne, "Our house was always full of intellectuals talking, and they *would* call God the Great Pulsator."

When the holidays came, Tiny and one or another of her brothers went first to Smithills Hall, her cousin Richard Ainsworth's real home. Next to Guindy, it was the house that meant most to her of all in which she lived. It is a splendid old black-and-white timbered hall, standing in a great park close to the town of Bolton-le-Moors in Lancashire. The oldest part was built in the reign of King John, but it is said that a house of that name stood there as far back as 597. It was here that the Protestant martyr Richard Marsh was tortured in the reign of Queen Mary. As they led him from being racked, he put his bleeding foot down on the stone pavement and said, "As sure as my faith is the right one, this mark will remain." The mark is certainly still there, and it does not do to tamper with it. Some foolish young men had removed the stone and thrown it into the shrubbery fifty years before Tiny first went there, and the most disastrous manifestations followed; everyone was so terrified by noises and the feeling of being touched by invisible things that it was very soon put back— and everything became quiet.

One room at Smithills had always been kept, in the rather grisly way of our fathers, as the place in which any deceased member of the family was laid out. This room was called the "dead room" until Richard Ainsworth married Nono. She said it was barbarous and would not have it so named. In spite of this unpleasant title it had always been used as a spare bedroom, but no one very willingly slept there, and Tiny herself thought the whole wing of the house haunted. There was supposed to be the ghost of a cat in this wing, and one day, after a group of rowdy cousins had been chaffing about the animal, Tiny and two other guests came down to breakfast next morning with long scratches on their faces for which nobody could account.

The moors came down to the edge of the park and were as beautiful as Scottish ones in spite of the great manufacturing city so close. There were acres of lovely gardens, and the town was cleverly planted out with trees so that the place never felt the least suburban. The Ainsworths' old home, Moss Bank, which marched with Smithills, occupied all the near landscape, so it was a perfect place for children. "The countryside belonged to us and we were always treated as the children of the house, my cousins having none of their own," Tiny wrote.

"The bleaching works, too, which were owned by the family and in which every man, woman, and child had grown up serving Ainsworths, were a great joy to us, and we were always wandering around watching the processes, inhaling the pungent odours. The mill hands were almost like part of the family. Old men would say, 'Ah, you are the daughter of Julia who was the daughter of Hannah who was the daughter of old Mr. Ainsworth up t'Hall.' The servants of the estate and many of the mill hands came to Smithills Chapel twice on Sunday. When we arrived a new chaplain had just been installed, a Mr. Standen, who was to revolutionize the old house, which was run on the lines of every big country house in those days, very lavishly. Mr. Standen was a man of great force with an uncanny knack of getting at people's souls. This power he used to both spiritual and other advantages.

We all hated him, but admitted his power. He tried very hard to convert us all in groups and singly, without much success. At one time when I was fifteen, a most inflammable age, he got me as far as the penitents' bench, and I remember walking in a Salvationist procession with a trumpet, but the emotion did not last. He took an enormous hold on my cousin and his wife and for many years almost ruled Smithills. He got rid of the old servants and filled the house with missionaries, some good and some bad. But the whole character of the place was very much changed, and it was no longer a charming meeting-ground for numbers of people.

"This did not, mercifully, prevent an excellent cook being kept and a great standard of comfort being adhered to. Nono always said firmly that she did not believe Almighty God the least wished us to be uncomfortable; a very sound view of the situation. But she expected us to attend countless prayer meetings and endless talks on religious subjects. If she had not been so charming I suppose we should have jibbed, but we were all so fond of her that we accepted the drawbacks of the place without question, merely grumbling about Mr. Standen to each other and setting booby traps for him. He must have dreaded the holidays, poor man.

"It was at Smithills that I read an account in the *War Cry* of the White Slave Traffic. I shall never forget my horror and misery, and wrote an impassioned poem on the subject which I asked Mr. Standen to get published for me. He was rather impressed, but Nono was terribly shocked at my knowing about such things and promptly burnt it.

"At the end of the holidays we were at York House. My brothers were always trying to get my precious diary, in which I recorded not only facts but all my beliefs and feelings. One day before I went out, I left it in charge of my mother's maid, Bachelor, who promised not to read it or let it out of her hands. She gave it to Evelyn, and my brothers read the cherished volume and told my mother of its contents. My mother sent for me and spoke very seriously about the 'dreadful revelations' of character

shown by the diary. She did not, however, seem the least shocked
at the treachery of Bachelor or of my brothers. She said she had
not read it but would if I preferred her to. I said no, the whole
was soiled and desecrated and I would like it burnt. She was terribly hurt but burnt it before my eyes. That finished any hope
of affection between any of us. I no longer disliked my brothers,
I simply never thought of them at all. Before, I had a lurking
suspicion that they might be my superiors and were right in despising me, but by this act of slyness they became so much my
moral inferiors, they no longer needed to be considered."

In September, Tiny's mother took her back to Cheltenham and
left her at Lansdowne Villa: "This going back was not nearly so
dreadful, since it was not straight from India, and I felt I knew
the worst. The discipline was excellent, and I was happy in College. I was happy in my house too, but I do not think it was a
very wholesome happiness. The conversation of certain pupils
was like any barrack-room, and they naturally tried to recruit
new girls. However, there were plenty of nice-minded girls as
well, and one was very soon able to distinguish between them.

"I disliked my house mistress very much at first, then came
absolutely under her influence and adored her, then finally returned to my first impression. She was a clever woman, and I owe
her a deep debt of gratitude for making me hear Wagner before
most people in England knew anything about him. She was a
great friend of the famous *prima donna* Malten, described Bayreuth and its marvels, and would have taken me there had my
parents permitted.

"The intimacy of other young things was most useful in de-
veloping the mind and character, and there was none of that
attempt at creating a type which is such a tragic thing in all big
schools nowadays. We played tennis, but we were not *made* to
play tennis; we could go for walks over the lovely country if we
liked. We did a certain amount of what were called calisthenics,
but they were not very exhausting, unless a girl had need for spe-

cial exercises. There was plenty of dancing, and the intellectual interests of girls were much more acute than they are now. I suppose this was partly because a woman of genius was at the head of things and because she had the wisdom to choose very remarkable women as her assistants and to leave them a great deal of liberty. The class mistresses knew their girls well, had them to tea two or three times a term, and were interested in their pursuits and their points of view. It was not a question of size, for Cheltenham in my time reached nearly a thousand girls, but it was the difference in attitude to life of those in charge.

"Miss Beale did not particularly care whether people passed examinations, though she was glad, of course, when they did. What she wanted was to make fine women who could influence their generation. Her own deep religious feelings had an immense effect on the school, and I have never forgotten my fervent reaction to hearing her read the first chapter of St. John's Gospel. One felt that this woman was reading the statement she considered the greatest in the world, and that she was somehow putting over to a class of little geese that it was immensely important. Afterwards I often heard her expound it, and I wish she had left in writing some definite memoranda of her teaching on the subject.

"There were many faults in the Cheltenham of my day. There was a great deal of very undesirable conversation and too much discussion of lovers and love; we wore whatever clothes we liked and there was a lot of foolish emulation and endless discussion about frocks. The adoption of a simple uniform is a marked improvement, and the school gymnastics and exercises are good. A certain amount of compulsory games may also be an advantage but can be overdone. Constant scurrying is bad for growing children. They never have a moment to themselves, and the old delightful intimacies are not encouraged. And the artistic, literary, and political interests of the children seem to be less. I would rather a girl of mine left her school a wild red Home Ruler and Feminist than that she left it unable to take anything seriously except athletics and cinemas. The devil in the schoolgirl is thrown out, perhaps, by organized games, strict discipline, and such constant occupation that she finds no time to get into mischief; but to the swept and garnished vacuum what seven devils enter in when she has left her carefully guarded scholastic establishment?"

Tiny spent Christmas at Smithills.

"Certain houses have curiously defined scents which seem to bring back in a moment everything connected with them. When I smell brown Windsor soap, I see the long passages at Smithills, the roaring fires against the black panelling, the texts hung promiscuously about, the faint odour of evergreen—Christmas decorations stayed up there longer than anywhere else—an occasional whiff of potpourri, Nono seated in an armchair by the fire, a boy or girl on the ground leaning against her knees, Cousin Dick reading the *Times* and interjecting angry comments on the heinousness of the Radicals. Prayers were at nine, and the day never passed without some child being taken for 'a little word' with Nono or Cousin Dick about religious matters. Off some of us it rolled like water off a duck's back. But I remember trying desperately hard to be 'saved' and never quite understanding what it meant. 'Give your heart to Jesus,' said Nono, but at fifteen one is not certain what one's heart is, and a boy's, and much more, a girl's will is the wind's will, and the thoughts of youth are long long thoughts.

"At moments the religious bias was distressingly comic. Nono, for instance, who was a mystic in very truth, would entirely forget that she was at lunch, surrounded by a greedy group of youngsters and, lost in ecstasy, her eyes closed and her head thrown back, would murmur, 'Jesus—Jesus, my Redeemer. To think that I shall see Him and touch His Hands.' Then suddenly waking to the realities of life, she would exclaim, 'Dick, if you eat more of that pudding, you *know* you will have an attack of gout.' But it never entered our heads to laugh any more than it enters the heads of an Indian village to laugh at the vagaries of its holy man.

"Children know sanctity when they see it. Once whilst I was there a mill girl, just converted, insisted upon being baptized by immersion. There were no conveniences for such a rite, so after endless discussion a large bath was introduced into the chapel and the radiant catechumen, wrapped in mackintoshes, was forcibly pressed under the water by Mr. Standen, after which joyful hymns burst from the congregation. I begged to be allowed to assist, but Nono said, 'No, darling, I *know* you would laugh.'

"We treated the various divines and missionaries who came to stay very differently. I remember one morning when I was the only one at Smithills and a mission was going on. Five clergymen were at the breakfast table, and towards the close I, who had come in late, heard my neighbour say suddenly, to my intense horror, 'There is one amongst us who is not saved. Now is the appointed time. Our Lord says, "When two or three are gathered together . . ." Let us all pray that she also may find Salvation.' The five clergymen fell on their knees and prayed with the greatest fervour for me, while I sat eating marmalade to cover my confusion, and feeling unutterably foolish. At the end they rose and sat with their eyes closed, expecting a miracle. But no miracle happened. I said, 'Thank you very much,' and went on with my marmalade. But they were right. Anyone who really believes in this curious conception of the Creator has no choice but to behave as they did.

"On another occasion, I was there with a young Salvationist, a handsome, attractive boy who took immense pains to convert me. I asked him one day, 'Why are you bothering so much about me? There are five other women in the house and they've all got souls.' 'Ah, but think,' he said, 'with your face what you could do for the Lord.' The idea of using prettiness to convert people seemed to me horribly immoral.

"My brothers, influenced by Nono, treated me quite well. They took me out snap-shooting, and we spent generally comfortable holidays. I marvel, looking back, at the contentment of children with scarcely anything to amuse them in a quiet old country house in bitter weather. An occasional day's skating, an occasional ride, long walks, some rabbit-shooting and much revolver practice [Tiny could kill a running rat or rabbit at fifty feet with a revolver]; nothing to do in the evenings but play chess or backgammon."

In December 1886 Mountstuart returned from India, and in the following spring he and Tiny paid various visits, one to Canterbury, to stay there with the Dean, William Fremantle, whose brother, Lord Cottesloe, was the grandfather of Tiny's future son-in-law Christopher. William Fremantle preached in the Cathedral a sermon on the Empire, in honor of Queen Victoria's Jubilee, in the course of which he quoted from Mountstuart's 1886 India Office Minute which begins, "What then are our duties there?" and adds, "Those who rule in this spirit are surely ministers of God." Mountstuart took communion from William Fremantle, "as I had done in the same place from Arthur Stanley thirty years ago" and thanked him "for a great and historical compliment."

During the summer Tiny and her father visited Mrs. Russell Barrington at Herds Hill, in Somerset, and went to Westmoreland, to Fox Howe, to stay with Matthew Arnold's niece, Mrs. Humphry Ward, *née* Mary Arnold. She was writing *Robert Elsmere*, chapters of which she read aloud, and the structure and content of which she discussed with Mountstuart. This novel, the last of the great Victorian novels, contained, as Gladstone, who reviewed it, wrote, "much more than twice the matter of an ordinary novel . . . the wealth of diction is never separate from the thought." It was a *roman à clef*: Walter Pater is one of the protagonists, as are H.-F. Amiel, the Swiss writer, and T. H. Green, the philosophy professor at Oxford to whose memory the book is dedicated. The book's aim was "to expel the preternatural element from Christianity, to destroy its dogmatic element yet to keep intact the moral and spiritual results," and so it marked a real turning point in Victorian belief. It appeared in 1888 and became one of the best sellers of all time; called "a great book" by Henry James, it was written out of the author's bitter experience of di-

vided Christendom. For her father, a younger son of Thomas
Arnold of Rugby, became a Catholic and left his family to work
under John Henry Newman at the Catholic University in Dublin.
His wife was fiercely Protestant and took the children to live with
her parents at Fox Howe; here, as then was the custom, the girls
were reared in their mother's faith. Mary Arnold married Humphry Ward, who was at first a don at Oxford, later worked on
the *Times*. *Robert Elsmere* sold sixty thousand copies in its first
two years, and altogether over half a million in the United States.
The very human hero "finds greater difficulty being morally
strong than intellectually clear." Mrs. Ward's family rented
Hampden, and Tiny admired Mary Ward. "She was a fine woman,
dignified, kind, and extremely thoughtful," though, Tiny remarked, "she did not seem very sensitive. But one day years later
I happened to be sitting with her and we were talking about a
mutual friend who had just had a baby. I said, 'I am so sorry for
her because I remember that for a year after my first child was
born I was so terribly upset by the horrors I had gone through I
could never bear to see a woman in the street who was going to
have a baby; I used to go home and cry.' Mrs. Humphry Ward's
eyes filled with tears and she took hold of my hand and said,
'Oh, my dear, did you feel like that? I did too, and I thought it
was morbid and no one else would ever understand.' I was very
much touched." Mrs. Ward had three children; Tiny, four.

The winter Tiny was sixteen, her parents accepted the loan
of Laurence Oliphant's villa at Haifa for the winter. They took
the three smaller girls with them and rode up Mount Carmel and
among the Galilean hills; visited the ruins of the great Crusader
castles such as Athlit, whose banqueting hall was still usable; visited
Druze villages and the Holy Places. But what moved Mounstuart
most was a "High Place" above Nazareth, sacred before Judaism,
Christianity, or Islam, and dedicated to older gods. And, of course,
Mounstuart botanized, writing home with enthusiasm of the wild
cyclamen carpeting the slopes of Mount Hermon.

Tiny, meanwhile, went to Smithills again for Christmas, where she and her brothers were "absolutely happy, and only asked that the holidays might go on forever." After Christmas she went to stay with Lord and Lady Arthur Russell in London. That memorable visit had a far-reaching effect on her. She loved the whole family, Lord and Lady Arthur and their children, Harold, Flora, Claud, Diana, Gilbert, and Conrad. In 1952, Claud wrote to Bertrand, "Like you, I have a happy memory of Annabel (Clara we called her), and I was often at York House. . . . She came to us for her holidays (she was at school), and I was much in love with her—I being then about 15–16 years old." Tiny found them the happiest family she had ever known. None of them had been to school. Lord Arthur was very wise and so was his wife, and both had a charming spontaneity and an aloofness at the same time. They were absolutely natural people and always did and said what they liked, for under their courteous exteriors was an iron certainty of what they thought right and wrong, and no amount of fashion or pressure from without made them change their minds. They had a wide influence in London, and their house was a center to many people from varying circles.

It was at Lady Arthur Russell's that Tiny met Robert Browning again. He was on a sofa and she sat down beside him; no one but a very young girl would have dared to do it. And instead of waiting till he talked, Tiny immediately told him in ardent language how much she adored his work. He talked to her for an hour about his poems and then listened while she spoke enthusiastically about her favorites.

He told Tiny about the secretary of a Browning Society who had written asking him the meaning of the poem "Childe Roland to the Dark Tower Came," saying that the society had discussed it at length but none of them could understand it. He replied that he had been trying to get a mood and atmosphere and had not thought of a meaning at the time. Whereupon the infuriated lady responded that she did not think there was much point to Browning Societies if there was no meaning in the poems. He was a carefully dressed, not very tall man, who looked, Tiny remarked later, as though he could have been a successful stockbroker.

Tiny had never been in London except as a small child, and Lord Arthur took her to see something new every day. He introduced her to Limoges enamel and Chinese jade and the toadstools at the Natural History Museum and the Elgin Marbles. He explained the characteristics of the Milanese, Florentine, and other Italian schools of painting. He took her frequently to the National Gallery and to the London Library, and also to the winter exhibit at Burlington House. In fact those three weeks were packed with pleasures. He also renewed her acquaintance with the Piccadilly goat, which had been one of the excitements of her infancy. As it lived in Hamilton Place, quite close to Lord Arthur's house in South Audley Street, Tiny saw it frequently. "It is funny how some Londoners do not remember it and non-Londoners do not believe in its existence," she told Anne. It became a stock joke later between Tiny and her husband. Whenever she mentioned the animal he would touch his forehead significantly and say to whoever might be present, "Poor dear Tiny, you mustn't take any notice of her. She thinks she used to know a goat who lived in Piccadilly." The goat actually *did* live in Piccadilly; it belonged to one of the Rothschilds, who paid the bus drivers not to run over it. It survived into the Edwardian era.

Tiny went back to Cheltenham with mental indigestion but feeling that she had a new family almost, so kind and helpful had the Russells been. They invited her to stay again for the next holidays, so her cup of happiness was full. She was allowed to go to some people named Chamier for the last Sunday before term. Their son George was at home, as was their daughter Alice, whom Tiny had known in India. George fell violently in love with her, and, though she did not return his feeling, she was delighted to be made a fuss of again. A year after, he proposed to her, and she refused. She was distressed at the time, since she did not realize "how much sooner men get over their affairs than women. I should have said 'got,' for women take love affairs more lightly than they did, and the misery of *peine d'amour* is a thing of the past," she wrote in the 1930s. "Men and women now love little and often, and the relaxed morals of today make it all very easy."

During her last year at Cheltenham the popular actor Sir Frederick Benson and his troupe came to town. "Miss Beale disapproved of the local theatre, probably with reason," Tiny said, "for the plays generally were not good. Though she would not relax her rule and let us go to the theatre, the theatre came to us. Benson performed *Macbeth, Hamlet,* and *Julius Caesar* in the Great Hall. The quality of his company's acting was such that even the sight of three middle-aged gentlemen circling round a wastepaper basket, wearing, as I recall, evening clothes, as the *Macbeth* witches, did not move us to unseemly mirth."

But for the most part her final year at Cheltenham was uneventful and, since she was not going on to the University, rather a waste of time. She was in the Cambridge class under a Miss Sturge, who was a good creature, but they did not get on: she thought Tiny a rotter and Tiny thought her a philistine. So Tiny was pleased to be going, although she was sorry to say good-by to Miss Beale, and she sobbed at Leaving Prayers on the last morning: "O God, Our Help in Ages Past" yelled by a thousand girls is quite impressive, as Anne found when her turn came to participate in the same final ceremony.

Miss Beale came to Tiny's wedding six years later. As she kissed the slim, diminutive bride—tiny indeed beside her six-foot-one groom—Miss Beale murmured, "The lower life, my dear child; the lower life." Small wonder one of her pupils wrote about her and her co-foundress, Miss Buss:

> Miss Buss and Miss Beale
> Cupid's darts do not feel.
> How different from us
> Miss Beale and Miss Buss.

V

Coming Out

It was 1888 and school was behind her. Tiny was now considered grown up. The stern work of husband-hunting lay ahead, while three younger, plainer sisters waited impatiently in the wings. The most important quarter of life was over, Tiny opined, writing in a diary, which she left to Anne. "For if our appointed term is three score years and ten, then that is four times seventeen and a half. Everything we are is decided in those first seventeen years; we can develop or shrink later, but cannot change. And until education is directed not to cramming a child with knowledge but to teaching it to live in this difficult and complicated world, there is not much hope of pulling us out of the quagmire of blundering unhappiness in which three-fourths of us spend our days. We *could* be so happy. So much of the world is infinitely enjoyable and amusing and beautiful. If *only* human beings were taught to live!"

Tiny appraised her elders and betters with hindsight in later years: "The people of ninety years ago were, I think, wiser in their dealings with the young than the people of today. They were harder, less tolerant, less sentimental, but they were much more what the Germans call '*Realmenschen.*' They brought up their children with a view to a real world with real problems where people constantly had to do things they disliked and where it was not all soft and pleasant."

Tiny thus describes herself: "Seventeen and a half, quite nice-looking, healthy, and with an average amount of brains; that is to say, luckier than most people. Several of us were leaving school together, and apart from our distress at saying good-bye to many friends at Cheltenham we were strangely sobered for the first hour or so by the fact that we really were grown up. It was hot July weather and we were all dressed in the cloth garments we called travelling dresses; it was not considered suitable to take a train journey in light cotton clothes. We were hot and sticky when we emerged at Paddington Station, where my sister's old nurse met me and took me across to Waterloo and so to Twickenham."

This nurse, who was called Nana, was Mrs. Reffold, a great character and a most important factor in Tiny's life. She had taken Tiny's sister Lily to Smithills when the others went to India in 1880, as Lily was considered too delicate to face the Indian climate. Nana was the ideal old nurse out of a storybook, and Tiny always wished she had presided over her own youth. Very strict, just, infinitely kind, with strong common sense and an instinctive refinement, Nana allowed nothing unsuitable in the nursery. Tiny's sisters came back from India clamoring for pickles and chutney at every meal; they had no discipline and no knowledge of careful hygienic rules. When Tiny came home, she found that the nursery and schoolroom ran very smoothly.

Nana was always angelic to Tiny, adored her and slaved for her, and was the person she loved and trusted most. "I am good today, am I not, Nana?" Tiny would sometimes say. "When you're in bed and asleep, miss," Nana would answer firmly. It was she who invented that beautiful verb "to buffle." "I shall do it all right if you don't buffle me, miss," she would say, combining "ruffle" and "baffle." She had a tremendous and complete admiration for Tiny's father and mother, and though Mountstuart frightened her to death she would have gone through fire and water for him. One day, after Tiny's marriage, one of Tiny's family was seen unsuitably dressed, and a servant where she had been staying had criticized the individual. Nana, in tears, came to Tiny and protested, "I said as 'ow it wasn't true, ma'am. It couldn't 'ave 'appened in such an 'igh family, could it, for you *are* an 'igh family aren't you, ma'am?" "That was her line all through life," wrote Tiny. "If you belonged to decent people, you *couldn't* let them down. In her own class she considered the same rule held, and it was a very good and safe rule. *Tenue* will often save a human being from sin and folly when religion, affection, and fear of consequence do not deter."

Nana had many beautiful bits of china and furniture, and Tiny thought she might have been the last member of some old family. She kept her person, and later on her little home, utterly spick-and-span. Her clothes were, even in those days, very old-fashioned, and she never altered her attire. Frank Millet, many years later, did a beautiful portrait of her, and Nana's pleasure in being hung on the line at the Royal Academy was a thing to see. She lived to be a very old woman, ending her days in a beautiful convent in Chiswick, in the house in which Thackeray's Becky Sharp and Amelia are supposed to have received their education. The nuns let her have her own furniture, and she died surrounded by Grant Duff pictures, in great peace and happiness.

The governess, Fräulein Ihlefeld, also lived to a great age. Tiny made a pilgrimage to see her in the Feierabend Haus where she spent her last years, on a lovely lake at Waren in Mecklenburg. These excellent *Stiften*, or homes, for unmarried women of every economic standing are found throughout Germany. A governess, for instance, pays so much a year to an institution and, when no longer able to work, is received into it. Fräulein Ihlefeld had her charming bed-sitting-room with all her own furniture, the walls lined with pictures of Tiny and her sisters. She made her own coffee in the morning, so could get up when she chose. Her meals were provided, and common sitting rooms and dining rooms were shared with other old ladies. She seemed happy and comfortable. There were pigs, cows, chickens—a whole farm, in fact—and a lovely vegetable garden and a flower garden where the ladies could work if they felt up to it. "So much more human than the tragic one-room existence, cheek by jowl with people of a much rougher nature, which is the fate of most governesses when past their work in England," as Tiny wrote.

Kurt Hahn, one of the great modern educators, who raised the Duke of Edinburgh, among others, at his school in Scotland, told Tiny once that he considered the nursery education he had observed in English homes of the past far the best yet invented. Up to the age of seven or eight, the children led their own lives under the superintendence of the old-fashioned nurse and away from the activities of the rest of the house. "Nothing is so bad for young people," he said, "as to live the 'life of their parents' unless the parents are willing to do what is probably best of all—give up their lives, whilst the children are small, to training and being with them. This entails so much self-sacrifice and self-control that few parents are either willing or able to do it." Many great men—Winston Churchill among them—admit that it was to their nannies, rather than their mothers, that they owed everything. Churchill's Mrs. Everest and Edward Sackville-West's "Simpson" are famous, but thousands of no less devoted nannies remain unsung.

On Tiny's return home from school, she said, "I felt frightfully nervous as the butler ushered me into the drawing-room, for I had not seen my mother and father for a year and a half, as they had been in Syria all winter." (Her parents had returned in March, and on March 14 at Windsor, Queen Victoria knighted Mountstuart, who thus became a Grand Commander of the Order of the Star of India.) "They and my elder brothers were there, and we went through the usual rather chilly family greetings, and then a fifth person came into the room, a slight, pale man with dark hair and moustache. 'Your cousin Hermann,' said my mother stiffly." He was the son of Tiny's Aunt Alise, who had married the Swiss physician, had left him, and lived with her sons in Weimar. "We looked at each other, and I suppose from that moment made friends. His visit had not been a success; he had come over full of enthusiasm for England and excitement about his new-found relations, but he was a Continental, absolutely un-English from every point of view, and he reacted on my father's nerves, I think, and very much on those of my mother and my brothers. I do not suppose they had ever seen a foreign artist before. Diplomats and rich men get a sort of superficial resemblance all over the world. The become cosmopolitan, and it is easy for cosmopolitans to rub shoulders together. Hermann found it as difficult to get on in England as many an English boy finds Germany difficult, though I think on the whole there is more simple kindness on the Continent than in England; people are less afraid of giving themselves away.

"After lunch we went on the river. In those days the river was absolutely quiet all week. On Saturdays and Sundays there were a good many people but they behaved well, did not yell and scream, and generally took trouble to hide the evidence of their picnics. There were no howling gramophones, and people seemed to enjoy themselves without shouting the latest song. It was only on Bank Holidays that it resembled what it is today. On those days the residents carefully shut themselves up in their own gardens. We had tea on one of the many little islands. Hermann saw that it annoyed Evie to attract any kind of attention, so he climbed up into a tree and barked like a dog. For once I sympathized with Evie—in spite of the fact that Hermann was being extraordinarily funny and a really good mimic. Then one day he was going over the house, he walked into my room and saw there pictures of Shelley, Keats, Wagner, Mozart, and the other people I cared about, and suddenly realized from the very look of the room that here was somebody who thought as he did and who wanted the same things he did. That evening after tea we had a long talk, and I saw that he and I were strangely alike with the likeness that comes in families. He was unhappy at home and wanted freedom, and I wanted freedom too; we neither of us had a cent in the world so could not go our own way for the moment. Both of us were trying to develop, and at the same time live with people who wanted us to be quite different from what we were. It was an immense consolation to me, and I think to him too, to feel that there was someone in the family who so completely and absolutely understood. Our friendship was cemented. Hermann told me that he was unhappy during his visit because he felt the extraordinary difference between England and the Continent. He realized that it was impossible to make my family understand all that he wanted to see in England.

"After dinner he went out alone into the garden and suddenly he began to whistle *Parsifal*. It was the most astonishing thing I ever heard. No professional I have listened to could compare with him. He could whistle and somehow convey the sense of an orchestra. If he had not had such a passion for sculpture, he could have been a great musician. On our speaking of Wagner before Evie on that visit, Evie closed the discussion with the remark, 'I don't think any decent girl should know anything about Wagner.' Hermann went back to Germany, and I heard a few months afterwards that he had quarrelled violently with his mother and was working in Paris by himself. He told me when we met later that he was earning his living by cleaning out other men's studios for fifty *centimes* a day; he lived on that and did his sculpture in the evenings. His mother wanted him to be a doctor, but he fainted the first time he went into the dissecting room, and realized that for him it was an impossible profession."

Tiny never got over her devotion to Hermann, and it even later colored her educational and political views. Because Hermann's culture was German (though he was of Swiss-Scots parentage) she brought up all her children to speak German as their first language, gave them German children's books, soaked them in German literature, and herself was a pacifist in World War I and a Nazi in World War II out of sympathy for Germany. Music, which was her greatest love, was purely German for her, and her deplorable taste in art—the Pre-Raphaelites, Max Klinger—came from Hermann.

Edmund Gosse and Austin Dobson stayed at York House often for the weekend, and Tiny was introduced to both men's work. Gosse bored her terribly as a poet, though later on *Father and Son* became one of her favorite books. She adored Austin Dobson's writing. He was a shy, charming fellow, modest and attractive, whose light lyrics Tiny found enchanting. That summer they saw a lot of Count Szapary, a nice Hungarian at the embassy. Also of Monsieur Jusserand, who wrote an admirable life of Tiny's many-times-great-grandmother Joan Beaufort called *Le Roman d'un roi d'Ecosse*. Jusserand was a delightful man of letters and diplomat and a witty and brilliant talker. He gave Tiny many books and prints. He was always hungry and always quite frank about it.

One evening, when Cardinal Manning was among the guests, there was a lull in the conversation and suddenly the Cardinal boomed, "I'd light the fires of Smithfield again tomorrow if I had the power and I could thereby save one heretic soul." The whole table stopped talking at his allusion to the burning of heretics under Mary Tudor; then Tiny's mother said in a shocked voice, "Oh, Your Eminence, you can't mean that literally," whereupon Manning struck the table so that the glasses rang and said, "I mean it exactly as I have said, quite literally. It is far better that people should be burned in this world than that they should lose their souls in the next." Tiny never forgot the horror of so cruel a judgment.

Many diplomats visited—some of them having rather strange ways. An American, Mr. Kennedy, had the habit of thinking aloud and would murmur condescendingly, "Very good soup. Not perhaps a party soup, but an excellent family soup. Really, they do things very decently." Tiny had to study menu French and get it correct; had to order the food; and also had much to do with the making up of house-parties, seating guests, and so on—very good training.

Soon after Tiny's return from school her mother gave a garden party to introduce her to neighbors and friends. Tiny wore "a pale blue silk dress covered with cream-colored lace, and a bonnet to match. Bonnets were really over for girls, but I pleaded to have one, as it seemed to me more grown-up than a hat." There followed a party for many of the people who were attending the Alexander Pope celebrations; Pope had been born in 1688, two hundred years before, and Mountstuart was a member of the celebration committee.

Later Tiny and her mother made a round of visits, culminating in Tiny's introduction to two Duff residences in Scotland. She wrote of her initial impression of Delgaty Castle, which afterward she loved very much: "The old keep, rising straight out of the earth like a huge cliff, the windows put in haphazardly like martins' nests. Delgaty is immensely individual, and the oddness of the inhabitants seemed to me to make the whole thing like some strange dream of Ibsen's. On this first occasion my Uncle Ainslie and Aunt Fanny alarmed me exceedingly, and it was a most unhappy visit." There was a large dinner party, and Tiny went down with Captain Urquhart of Craigstown, the brother of Mrs. Duff of Hatton, to whom she made a remark which he, not hearing properly, took to be uncomplimentary, and thereafter his manner was very chilly. She hadn't the courage to explain. The man on the other side was a Mr. Udny, equally terrifying, and Tiny was speechless with misery. After dinner she was somewhat cheered by the kindness of her cousin Rachel Grant Duff, then a lovely girl of sixteen. But when bedtime came Tiny was scared to death and couldn't sleep, for Delgaty was the most haunted house she had ever stayed in. Altogether a dreadful visit.

They took the little train on to Banff and at last saw Eden. When her uncle was a boy, there had still been one big room of the old castle standing, where the tenants used to have their dances and meetings, but now it was falling to pieces. The house itself, with a Palladian porch, stands beautifully on a hill over the Deveron, which curls below it before flowing, three miles farther on at Banff, into the sea. Anne's son Richard—Tiny's grandson—bought back Eden in 1965, ninety years after Mountstuart had sold it. It has now to stand empty, as Richard otherwise would have to pay taxes on the house. "It is a romantic place," Tiny wrote, "but I can understand my mother's horror when she was taken up there directly after her marriage in April—bitter weather, insufficient heating, probably an awful cook and, to crown other disabilities, an election in progress."

Tiny and her mother then visited Aberdeen, where they were invited to dine with the dear old family lawyer, Mr. Hunter. On James Grant Duff's death Alise Obrist—*née* Grant Duff—had inherited the property of Auchterlies near Aberdeen, and Mount-stuart managed it for her. Later it passed to Hermann's two daughters, and on their death to Andrew Campbell of Cawdor. Mr. Hunter's law firm still acted when the property was transferred to Andrew Campbell. The dinner was at four o'clock, served on a polished mahogany table with beautiful little lace mats, an old style that has since been revived but then was quite unknown except to antediluvians. They had an enormous meal, complete with Bordeaux and brandy, which Mr. Hunter insisted on Tiny's tasting (alcohol was not then considered proper for young girls), and as a result she felt very sleepy.

The visits over, mother and daughter went back home. But before long, Tiny was off again—to her first dance. Accompanied by her brother Evelyn, she went to the Goschens' at Seacox Heath and thoroughly enjoyed herself. And more balls followed—two in Cheltenham, where she stayed with the Chamiers and walked over one morning to Lansdowne Villa as an "old girl," flaunting a man on each arm. On to her godmother, Lady Henley, for the Pytchley and other balls in the neighborhood; always further delights in store. Tiny, now grown up, began collecting admirers.

She says of this period: "After Christmas we made preparations for going up to London. My mother, after looking at several houses, chose 13 Great Stanhope Street. Like so many London houses it was excessively dirty and inconvenient but in a good position, and it had a big room which could be kept as a ballroom, so was suitable for one's first season. We went up in February and my mother took me to Cresser [then the "in" dress designer] to choose my Drawing Room dress: though presentations at Court were then held in the daytime and in the Palace Drawing Room (instead of the Ball Room), full evening dress was worn. Mr. Cresser looked me over calmly for a moment or two in complete silence, and then said, 'I think a *ceinture sauvage* would suit Miss Grant Duff.' My mother gasped, for it sounded as though there were to be nothing else. But he made a lovely dress of white satin, covered with white chiffon and ornamented with a *ceinture sauvage* in pearls around the hips and another around the bodice.

"I forget what minor royalty died that winter, but I seized on the opportunity of court mourning to procure for myself a slinky frock of black and a hat of similar hue with a falling lace veil that completely covered my face. Seeing me in it for the first time, Lady Sligo asked why I chose to appear as a lovely French widow. Lady Sligo was at that time one of the most charming hostesses in London and one of the wittiest women I ever met. She had that extraordinary logic and common sense which are perhaps the most remarkable gift of the French. Always amusing, she also showed a great sense of justice and benevolence. I remember my first visit to her, a very shy child of eighteen. She turned to my mother and said, 'Julia, I hope she flirts.' My mother said firmly that she hoped I did not. Lady Sligo's response was to turn to me and say, 'My dear, do not in this matter listen to your mother. If you do not flirt you will never know what sort of man you will want to marry.' On another occasion a certain great lady was bemoaning that her son should want to marry a nobody, whereupon Lady Sligo leaned fatly across their intervening chairs and, slapping her on the knee, said, 'My dear, if nobody married nobodies where would you and I be?'

"Lady Sligo's sister, Madeleine de Peyronnet, was even wittier than Lady Sligo. My father's diary is full of the *bons mots* for which this talented family was noted. Their mother was an extraordinarily able woman who wrote for both *The Nineteenth Cen-*

tury and the *Revue des Deux Mondes* when those periodicals influenced public opinion."

The fashionable London districts were well defined: Grosvenor Place and Portman Square, Pont Street and Lennox Gardens were considered good addresses. But not South Kensington; Tiny's mother felt that were she to take a place there she would jeopardize Tiny's matrimonial chances. Tiny wrote: "We were always at home on Sundays, and endless men came to call. There was a rite about this, as there was about everything else, and the man who was intimate enough to leave his hat in the hall felt superior to the man who had to carry up his hat and wrestle with it and his gloves and his teacup. The rule was, roughly, that if you were alone with your hostess and her girl, and another man turned up, you could stay because the ratio would be two to two, but if you were with your hostess alone and no one else came, you were supposed to leave at the end of ten minutes.

"No one danced during Lent, but there were a good many quiet dinner and evening parties, and my first Drawing Room. It was a terrible ordeal, and made worse by taking place in the morning. It requires courage to face one's sovereign almost naked at twelve noon on a wintry day. Upon arrival in the presence of Her Majesty, young men in uniform seized our four-yard trains and pulled them out; we realized we had to make five curtseys and withdraw backwards before they would be safely tucked up on our arms again. I knew that what the queen disliked most was having the back of her hand knocked by the lady's nose as she arose from her curtsey, and my agony was such that I almost fainted with terror. But I managed not to touch the august hand with my nose. The Prince of Wales shook hands with my mother and me and we then backed out. It was all far less beautiful and more frightening than the courts were later, with their warm rooms and pleasant party-ish atmosphere, but the old Queen herself was such an impressive figure that I am glad I saw, in its most frightening aspect, the 'Divinity which doth hedge a King.' There were absurd aspects, too: a small boy of our acquaintance taken to see Lord and Lady

Kimberly dressed for a Drawing Room, burst into floods of tears, sobbing, 'Grandpa looks like a drummer boy, and Grandmama's naked!'

"My mother gave a ball to, as it were, produce me. We had Liddel [the equivalent of Peter Duchin] to play for us, and I suppose about two to three hundred people. In that remote age hostesses knew each other well and would exchange their lists of debutantes and eligible young men, so it was somewhat less formidable. Also, most affairs were far less crowded, and dancing was generally comfortable. But the hostesses were not as forthcoming with introductions. If one was unlucky, one usually found a girl one knew who was equally unlucky, and could pair off with her and go and sit down and talk and have an amusing enough time, though hardly the reason for attending a ball.

"Many members of my father's staff were at my own ball, and I was especially glad to see Captains Evans, Bagot, and Cavendish. After dancing in India I was a little contemptuous of the London standard, which I thought pretty poor, but soon, by dint of never accepting a bad dancer, I had a collection of men around me who were really good and upon whom I could rely at balls, since a reputation for taking only good partners produced invitations from good dancers. After I married I gave small dances to which none but good dancers were asked, and they were great fun.

"The first time I danced with my husband I was terribly afraid it would turn out badly, since he was distinguished and brilliant, and most intellectual men do not care to dance. When I found he was an absolutely perfect dancer, I said to him with delighted surprise, 'But you really dance quite divinely!' He replied very crossly, 'Well, I don't see why I shouldn't dance divinely.' "

Soon after Hermann Obrist left, Tiny had resumed work as her father's secretary, finding it highly interesting. "His was an extraordinarily alert mind for an old man, and he had a great sense of humour. My mother, too, was an unusual woman, still very beautiful. And even Evelyn was a great help to me, unconsciously, because he knew French well and had a large collection of French literature which I devoured. He had good taste and real feeling for style and, though I think he would have been horrified if he had known I sampled his library, his comments on it to my father and mother at meals made a very deep impression on me.

"We were all expected to be down in time for nine o'clock breakfast, and father often had a party, as the Breakfast Club was still meeting. Even when it was not a day for the Breakfast Club, somebody would occasionally turn up, especially when we were in London. On these days the talk was extremely good. Father never appeared at lunch—he never ate it—and rarely for tea. Sometimes we had tea in the drawing room and oftener, when there was a young party, we had a nice rowdy time in the schoolroom upstairs, leaving the old people to themselves. For dinner we all dressed as though we were going to a party, even when there were no guests, not only in London but at York House.

"In those days Twickenham was practically a village. There were a lot of big houses mostly along the river, often beautifully furnished, inhabited by quiet, staid people. The dinner parties were always the same; an effort was made by the hostess to put the young people together, and after dinner one of us was invariably asked to play or sing. The level was not very high, but sometimes one of us would show real talent. Nearly everybody played Chopin waltzes or preludes, choosing the easier ones. Occasionally someone recited, and there was a great deal of mild flirtation, always very decorous. Most of us had house parties from Saturday to Monday, so that in an unexciting way there was a lot of change. The songs we sang were not outstanding from the point of view of either music or poetry; but compared to the ballads of today they were as different as the cooking of a first-class from that of a suburban hotel. As a child I listened with sentimental joy to the songs of Claribel and Milton Wellings, and by the time I was seventeen it was Goring Thomas and Theo Marzials. 'Ask Nothing More' was one of my *pièces de résistance*. Everyone sang Gilbert and Sullivan, Irish melodies, and Scottish and Irish folk songs. Most people with a smattering of musical taste knew the most popular songs of Grieg, Lassen, and Franz. And those whose voices were a little better tried Schubert and Schumann. Comic songs with jolly rollicking tunes were also popular: 'You're not the only pebble on the beach,' 'You should see me dance the Polka,' 'The man who broke the bank at Monte Carlo,' 'We sat upon the baby on the shore.'

"We dressed very simply. In each wardrobe there was a black evening dress, a white, or if a girl was lucky two whites and a coloured one, and we rang the changes on these for the winter and then if we were fairly affluent had another set for the summer. Very few of us could afford stockings to match our dresses, but we compromised with bronze-coloured ones. We also had, on every occasion, to wear gloves; no girl could possibly have clasped a man's sticky fingers. And men also wore gloves and did not put their hot hands on a silk dress or, as is now the case, on a bare back. Those of us who were impecunious wore their gloves very dirty; they were always of kid and costly to clean.

"Nobody had electric light, but there were oil lamps or, for very special occasions, quantities of candles. The latter was a very becoming light and somehow made women sparkle in a way that electricity does not. Our great preoccupations were our complexions and our figures. None of us was allowed to use any kind of cosmetic, in fact no well-born woman could possibly have done so, so we had to have good skins. And endless were the receipts and literature we exchanged on the subject. Quite early in my girlhood I came across the excellent and charming work by Baronne Staffe, the *Cabinet de Toilette*, which, in spite of thousands of later books, remains a great classic. When I told a friend that it stood on my bedroom bookshelf between Baltasar Gracián's *Art of Worldly Wisdom* and Thomas à Kempis's *Imitation of Christ*, Evie, who was sitting near, remarked with a faraway look in his eyes, 'I always say that it was written by the pious author of the *Imitation*.'

"We played a great deal of tennis, and Mother gave me a horse which I immediately christened Félise, being at that moment steeped in Swinburne. Félise carried me very well for six years, and I finally sold her on my marriage. She went on for some time after that. I used to ride, followed by a groom, in Richmond Park, Bushy Park, over Wimbledon Common, and sometimes over Hounslow Heath. The traffic along the road was never too bad and a well-trained horse rarely shied, though they never seemed to get used to perambulators or wheelbarrows. We would drive long distances to pay calls; society at Twickenham was much more county than suburban then.

"No one who has not lived on the Thames can know what an immense part it plays in the lives of those who do, and how one gets to know the river in every kind of mood. Everybody used it, even the old ladies who lived in the big houses along its banks, a boatman rowing them to pay calls. I remember one lady who must have been at least sixty-three, meeting my mother on the river. She had a small plant standing on one of the seats of the boat, and my mother, next time they met, very naturally asked, 'I suppose you were going to take the plant to somebody?' Whereupon the lady said rather shyly, 'I wasn't going anywhere, but I think that since it would not look very well going for a row by myself with a boatman, I always put a plant in the boat so that anyone seeing me should think, as you did, that I was dropping down to pay a call!' I never went out in a real racing skiff, but constantly in a tub, that is a boat holding only one person, with out-riggers which one steers oneself. These were very dangerous. If you let go of an oar you caught a crab and were almost immediately in the water, but we learned to manage them and could go frightfully fast. We also had a Canadian canoe and knew every islet up as far as Shepperton, and most days in the summer took our tea on the river, one of us staying to look after Father. I never could manage punting, I was not tall enough, and I always loathed steam launches. There seems to be no pleasure in a mechanical thing on the water.

"Twickenham Ferry was still extant, and in my youth everybody sang the song of that name. The old boatman with a wooden leg who took everyone back and forth was a most dreadful old ruffian, but there was no other means of getting across. We very occasionally went sailing, but, as none of us knew how to sail, it was somewhat frightening. I recall one awful day when Arthur, who was even more incompetent than my other brothers, very nearly capsized us. We kept going round and round and I was seized by that terrible manifestation—an uncontrollable fit of laughter. I laughed and I laughed, and Arthur got angrier and angrier and at last went for me with an oar. By this time a crowd had collected on the bank and was cheering on the two combatants. When we realized this we waived our mutual resentment and concentrated our efforts on getting to the boathouse.

"Lady Huntingtower and her sister used to receive at Ham House. It was, and I believe has remained till now, quite unspoilt, and the room where the Cabal sat was precisely the same as when it deliberated there. It was an eerie, haunted place with secret staircases, and I don't think I should have liked to sleep in any of the rooms.

"An astonishing amount of beauty has disappeared since I lived in Twickenham; the lovely old houses and the villages which have been destroyed or covered by the jerry builder. Of all centuries in the world's history, I suppose the last hundred years have seen the most destruction."

While leading this worldly and superficial life, Tiny still kept her interest in religion and the interior life. She rather fancied the Catholic Church. "I had leanings," she wrote. But she went to stay at Newnham Paddox, a great Catholic house, shortly after she came out. The place, where the Denbigh family had lived since 1622, was in dull country near Rugby; Tiny had been asked for some local hunt balls. There were six men and twenty-four women staying—and three of the men were priests. "The atmosphere was painfully Roman. A Miss Henslow tried to convert me, and in the servants' hall they tried to convert my maid, who was very indignant. I disliked it all intensely." At the first of the balls, a young man Tiny had known in London (slightly) rushed at her and cried out in delight, "Miss Grant Duff, how marvelous! Will you dance?" She drew herself up to her five feet three and said, "My name is Joans—Jones with an a: Joans." The young man apologized but did not become less attentive. At the next ball, Tiny's mother appeared and Tiny introduced her without a flicker of an eyelash, as "My mother, Lady Joans." Tiny's mother was not amused. Returned to town, the young man sought out Tiny at the very next ball. "Oh, Miss Joans, oh, Lady Joans," he cried. Tiny froze him with "My name is Grant Duff and this is my mother, Lady Grant Duff."

Tiny often returned to Newnham Paddox but never again behaved quite so badly. Mountstuart had loved the Denbighs from Oxford on; the eighth Earl was his contemporary, and Tiny grew fond of two of his children, Lady Winefride Elwes and Everard Feilding. Everard was interested in psychic phenomena and told Tiny how once, in midwinter, he was staying with a friend in the wilds of Hungary who said he could, like Faust, produce anything desired. So Everard said, "I'd like some strawberries." They were sitting alone in a big dining hall after midnight; the servants had long ago gone to bed. The man looked up and said a few words in a language Everard didn't know, but it wasn't Hungarian. A big basket (not bowl) of strawberries materialized on the table. The two men ate nearly all, but Everard managed to smuggle one up to his room and put it in his bed-table drawer; in the morning the drawer was empty.

After her first visit to the Denbighs, Tiny went in London to the three hours' devotion on Good Friday and heard a certain Mr. Bennett preach in an Anglican church. She was "terribly impressed. I locked myself into my room when I got home and cried and cried. The awful reality of the Crucifixion had at last come home to me. But it was not for many years that I became a Christian, though I went to church perfunctorily as occasion demanded. When I was with Nono at Smithills, I had seen that there was something which people called conversion, but I had not got it, and Christianity shocked me intellectually as a negation of beauty and order. I suppose I really was a pagan, for the pagan system seemed to me much wiser and more human. The Greeks had touched, I felt, the highest point of humanity, and everything, after that, was something of a comedown. I didn't then realize the amount of cruelty that underlay the sunny wisdom of the Greeks, and that Christ was the first person to protest torture and ill-health."

Tiny's ambivalence toward Christianity lasted all her life. She early taught her children Swinburne's lines:

> Thou hast conquered, O pale Galilean,
> And the world has grown grey with thy breath,

and she fed them (and herself) chunks of Nietzsche; his complete works were close to her boudoir desk. She regarded *Also Sprach Zarathustra*, of all the books she ever read, as "the one which has given me most help, and even when I read it now [1930], it gives me something new to think about. I suppose it has modelled my outlook and character more than any other book has done. It is the only publication that sufficiently brings home the importance of every action, however small, and the fact that we are responsible for the next generation, and that the next generation owes us anything only in so far as we have given it something worth while."

In spite of a new-found sympathy for Christ, Tiny loathed Saint Paul, then and always, agreeing with Matthew Arnold that he was the first Protestant. She always thought of the Church of England as Catholic; on one side of it were "Roman Catholics, who were fussy; on the other, Protestants, who were Philistines— cruel, cold, concerned with morals rather than mysticism, and, generally, lower-class." She disliked both Rome and the "sects" more and more, and deplored the conversion of her friend Una Birch, later the well-known writer Dame Una Pope-Hennessy. "Blinkers," she would tell Anne. "Poor Una's put on blinkers. Now they tell her what to think." She brought up her children, how-ever, to respect religion wherever they found it, and in the even-ings during the children's hour, while they sat in drawing room or boudoir, close to the fire on specially small chairs, making pen-wipers for Christmas presents or knitting socks for soldiers, she read to them from the *Bhagavad Gita*, the *Ramayana* of Tulsi Das, the *Upanishads*, the Buddhist legends, as well as from Greek legends and Icelandic sagas. She would quote to them over and over her beloved Nietzsche. "They say—what do they say? Let me say." And would add his: "This is my way; what is your way? *The* way does not exist."

VI

First Season

"There was much less excitement in my youth than there is for youngsters today," wrote Tiny, looking back on her first season, "but on the other hand we were gayer and enjoyed our pleasures much more acutely. When we came out we were told that we must not dance more than three or four times with the same man, but all the same we managed quite comfortably to get in eight or nine whirls with one partner whilst our chaperones were down at supper or talking to elderly friends in corners. It was merely a question of arranging to slip on to the dance floor unobserved and return unobtrusively to one's mama. The same thing happened at Ascot, the Derby and Henley, so one could see an enormous amount of whichever man in the party was the current favorite. That year was the only time I saw the Derby, and the extraordinary silence of the monumental crowd when the race began was an unforgettable experience.

"Ascot too was great fun. We wore, as people still do, curious trailing dresses which were no earthly use for any other occasion, but I still think it is one of the liveliest of all occasions. With the summer came the big garden parties at the House of Commons and Syon House, and Lady Jersey's and other houses close to London, and there again were endless chances of talking to one's lover of the moment without the supervision of the maternal eye. All the men wore top hats and frock coats with a gardenia or pink carnation in their buttonholes; sometimes a few would come deliberately got up for tennis, but that was considered just a little odd, and it was not until the end of my girlhood that people began to wear less conventional dress.

"I rode every morning in Rotten Row. Everyone was carefully clad, and the aspect of the Row was a great deal more attractive than it is now with people in blouses and skiing clothes. A friend called Florence Bishop and I were known as the galloping girls. The crowd walking by were also carefully turned out; and walking through the Park from eleven-thirty until luncheon one was bound to meet many friends. On Sundays church parade was from twelve to one, and most people turned in there at that time. Pretty, very well-dressed women sat in their carriages between three and five talking to friends, and church parade often resembled a big garden party. All the well-known beauties paraded, and I have seen men in top hats running like hares down the Row to see the Duchess of Leinster ride past on her big black horse. In those days people cared less for smartness and more for actual beauty—represented by women such as the Duchess of Leinster and her sisters, Mrs. Langtry, Lady Ormonde, Lady Listowel, and a host of others. Not one was aided by paint, and if a woman was pretty you knew she was pretty under any conditions. Except for a few outstanding leaders of fashion, the dressing of the women was not really good, but the men were generally impeccably attired, and they were astonishingly good-looking. Arthur Bagot, Sir Derek Keppel and George Keppel, Sir Harry Stonor, Philip Harbord, and Bill Franks were the ones I best remember as outstandingly handsome, but there were heaps of them, and the general level of dress made them look even more attractive than they naturally were.

"Dinner parties ranged from thirty people at big houses to nine or ten at smaller ones, or sometimes merely a *partie carrée*. It was said that no dinner should have less than the Graces or more than the Muses in the way of *convives*. But that was when guests talked across the table; when I started to attend dinner parties, the fashionable thing was to put on the table a sort of hedge, often made of beautiful flowers but almost concealing the people opposite. Dinner was *tête-à-tête* with the men on either side. If the partner on the left was occupied you could flirt your head off with the one on the right, and vice versa. Nobody knew anything about it. In fact, Lord Peel once proposed to me at a dinner party, and only my hostess, who was some way off, was unoccupied, and had very keen ears, heard. The hedge down the middle was usually arranged by a florist, often with mould and moss and such things, in which case a stray earwig would sometimes attack: it took all one's self-control not to scream whilst one's partner imprisoned it under a champagne glass.

"Dinners were very long, and one might sit for two hours. There was a clear and a thick soup; a white and colored fish; two entrées; roast meat; a bird of some kind; often a salad and then two sweets, hot and cold, and dessert savoury to follow. [Some of the favorite savories were (and are!) angels on horseback (slices of bacon around prunes or oysters); Welsh rabbit; éclairs filled with anchovy cream; stuffed eggs; herring roe on toast.] The younger people could not get through all this, and we used to amuse ourselves by betting on whether the guests opposite would eat all the dinner. Whosever protégé ate the most won the stakes. I remember a terrible episode once when, getting very excited because my old gentleman was not eating well and seeing him pass the sweet, I leaned forward and begged him to have some. He happened to be the Dean of Westminster. The whole table stopped talking and watched and could not imagine why I was so impertinent. I, of course, got scarlet, and my poor neighbour was convulsed. The Dean said, 'It is very kind of you, my dear young lady, but I am not so young as you are.' My mother was very cross.

"We invented a great many dodges for making dull people talk. I am supposed to have coined the immortal question, 'Do you like string?' And I think it was I who invented the alphabet game, in which one began, say, 'Do you like apples?' and had to get the conversation to badminton or the Balearic Isles without being observed. One made round pellets of bread for each letter achieved."

Tiny wrote down for her daughters "exactly how women were dressed, as I see such remarkable statements in certain books about the underlinen of the Victorian age. First, in winter a woollen and silk combination. Some women wore plain woollen, but these tickled. Then a white batiste chemise, with or without lace according to the taste of the wearer. I wore my chemise short, halfway up to my knee because a long one bunched, but many girls wore the long French chemise then in vogue. Then stocking suspenders shaped to one's waist or suspenders on one's stays and white drawers, and here again there were several schools. I wore mine short, folded over behind, not buttoned. Many girls considered this indecent and wore theirs buttoned round the waist and most girls wore stays, rather tight. And a flannel petticoat often trimmed with lace and insertion, and finally a black or white silk petticoat and a white petticoat bodice. The flannel petticoat and the combination were, of course, discarded in summer, and daring spirits (with much money) had petticoats to match their frocks."

She had an allowance of £100 a year (then about $500) but out of this she had to pay for Court dresses, riding habits, small visits alone from Saturday to Monday, tips, and all her pleasures such as concerts and theaters when she was not with her family. It was a tight fit, and she often had to refuse invitations because she could not afford them. Many other girls were in the same condition and sometimes lent each other clothes: Dot was horrified when Tiny wore a friend's gown at a party.

"Dresses are a great deal more decent now than they were. Most women were reasonably modest, but there were always half-a-dozen at a party who wore their dresses so low that they became 'Lelyesque.' I don't think it was pretty even with young and beautifully made women, and, as it was often the aged dowagers who wore their clothes slipping off, the effect was grotesque. There was a rhyme which used to be quoted at parties where such aged ladies were seen:

> The older she grows
> The more she shows,
> And God only knows
> What further revelations are in store for us.

At one dinner my partner was John Singer Sargent—Puritan Pagan. The lady next us apparently had nothing on above her waist except a slight curtain of lace, hung together on the shoulder by a bead. Sargent kept looking at her askance the whole time he was talking to me, and at last I said, 'What will you do if the bead gives?' 'I shall throw my napkin over her and run round to my hostess for protection,' was the reply.

"When I first came out I was not allowed to go anywhere by myself; a maid or a governess had to accompany me. And there was one dreadful scene with Father because he met Dot and me with our German governess Fräulein Ihlefeld in Piccadilly. Dot was then twelve and Fräulein at least thirty-six, but Father raged and said that no respectable woman walked along Piccadilly without an elderly chaperone or a man.

"At the beginning of May came the picture shows, and I went to all the private views. At the New Gallery Lettie Hornby introduced me to Mr. Llewellyn, later Sir William, who became President of the Royal Academy. He was a most beautiful young man, exhibiting a picture of a lady in green which I thought exquisite, and I was immensely impressed. Nor was my introduction to Sir Frederick, afterwards Lord Leighton, any less impressive. He asked us to his studio one Sunday afternoon, and thereafter I went many times to sit at the feet of the handsome, wise old painter.

"Watts was another painter whose studio I visited. He talked about his pictures, walking round the studio with his arm round me, kissing me at intervals. I remember one story he told me about a picture known as 'B.C. —— ' which represents two beautiful nude savages. He said that when it was exhibited a very earnest lady wrote to him and said that she had always found such teaching in his pictures, but that she and her friends had looked at this one with immense care and discussed it at length but they could not understand the meaning. Watts replied saying that he had been studying certain effects of sun and shadow and that the picture represented the reactions that would be caused by the first introduction to the oyster. The lady wrote back in great fury and said she was shocked that Mr. Watts would stoop to anything so frivolous and she could only suppose that B.C. meant 'Before Clothes.'

"When I look back over that first season, I realize it was clouded over by my constantly meeting the man I had cared so much about as a child. When I first saw him again, I asked him: 'How could you have made love to me like that?' He answered, 'God forgive me, I was so madly in love with you that I did not know what I was doing.' Now, wisely, he knew that only a rich marriage could help him and I was penniless. It never entered my head that I could marry him, but I was always trying to meet him, and my mother, equally naturally, trying to prevent it. At last, one evening my partner did not turn up and he, passing, saw me waiting and asked me to dance. We went off to a sitting-room and talked, and finally agreed not to see each other any more. I got up; then he said hesitatingly, 'Perhaps you had better go back to your mother alone, you know she hates to see you with me.' I don't know why, but that infuriated me: I saw he was frightened of my mother. I looked straight at him. 'Yes,' I said, 'I will go back alone.' I didn't shake hands with him; somehow I no longer wanted ever to see him again. I went back to my mother. She looked hard at me, 'You're very white,' she said. 'Do you want to go home?' 'No,' I said and I went on dancing. I never spoke to him again."

Exit from Tiny's life one Captain Evans-Gordon.

"I was happier," Tiny wrote, "when this affair was finally settled, but saw no one to replace him in my thoughts though there were many nice men." One of them was Maurice Fremantle, who was to die slowly of cancer in Hong Kong, devotedly nursed by a lady who afterward became the Princess Doria. Years later, Anne, when she became engaged to Maurice's second cousin, made friends with Maurice's mother, who welcomed her warmly into the Fremantle family, and also with Princess Doria, who told her of Maurice's sad and lonely death. Among Tiny's other prospects were George Goschen, Monty Erskine, St. John Coventry, and, of course, Arthur Bagot, who remained her greatest friend and incomparable standby and counselor. And there was an odd little Spaniard at the Spanish Embassy who was in love with her and always wooing her. He used to preface most of his remarks with: "*Je ne suis pas beau garçon comme Bagot, mais je ferai un mari dévoué. Je ne suis pas beau garçon comme Bagot, mais je passerai ma vie sur mes genoux devant ma femme.*" Several older men paid her a good deal of attention, and Tiny wrote: "I suppose I could have married my first season had I wanted to. But marriage without real attraction on both sides seemed to me unthinkable. I was quite aware of the importance of money and position, but could never have married a man who did not physically attract me.

"It was the fashion for a man who admired a girl to send her a bouquet if he knew she was going to a dance that night. Poor dears, it must have been an extravagant custom. They were usually sent anonymously. Occasionally two bouquets arrived and the unhappy girl was in a terrible quandary; she might easily wear the wrong one. An agonizing choice. In that way I lost a lover I was really attracted to.

"When a young friend recently asked me to describe the difference between the attitude of girls and men to each other in my youth and in my daughters', the first thing which came to mind was that then chivalry was still in mode, though it was often only skin deep. No young man, however badly he behaved in private, would have boasted of maltreating his wife or mistress. As a girl I fought against the 'good pal' posture which many girls demanded of men, and consequently was never regarded as such, though I always had many intimate men friends. A man now expects his woman to grovel—and often she does. Yet I think we had quite as many 'love affairs' as girls have now, though we were more reticent about them and carried on our flirtations with a certain amount of *tenue*. It is very depressing to those who have always been feminists to see the way the greater freedom of women has not led to greater self-reliance.

"It seems to me that the great 'love affairs' which were so notable in my youth are a thing of the past. I once saw a friend held firmly by two others at a ballroom door because he was going to rush to speak to a girl whose parents were marrying her to another man. And three other men of my acquaintance shot themselves because of women. Now they fall in and out of love quite comfortably and none of them appears particularly jealous of his successors.

"Also it is very difficult, from the social point of view, to say whether it is a good or bad thing that the *demi-monde* has almost disappeared. It seems to me more peculiar that a man should think he can take as mistress a girl whose house he visits as a friend, than that he should take his mistress from a different class.

"Amongst the people I recall my first year as constantly coming to the house were Sir William and Lady Gregory, he funnily enough in those days considered the more important of the two, whereas he actually was merely a charming old gentleman and a good raconteur. One of his stories concerned a large men's party, one of the first he had been to. Everybody got fearfully drunk; he was bored to tears and thought that if he could slip down under the table he could worm his way towards the door and escape. Accordingly, he slipped down as if overcome by drink and got under the table. His throat was immediately seized by a man whom he believed to be throttling him, and he fought fiercely. Suddenly a voice whispered, 'Arrah! Your Honour, don't take on so, I am only after loosening your stock!' In whispers he told the voice what he wanted and was allowed to escape. He discovered afterwards that someone of the sort was always

kept under the table to prevent old gentlemen being choked after
their potations.

"Lady Gregory was then a witty and friendly person, immensely fond of Society and with a highly developed social
consciousness. Nobody could have believed that she would develop into the genius that, long after middle age, she became. She
was one of the most curious instances of dormant talent I have
seen. At that point she detested the idea of Home Rule—but she
lived to write *The Gaol Gate* and to become the Egeria of the
Irish literary renaissance. It was Mr. Yeats who changed her so
completely.

"Henry Doyle, head of the National Gallery in Dublin, came
often. I had been brought up (as were all children of my generation) on Dickie Doyle's fairy books, and my enthusiasm for them
made Mr. Doyle a friend at once. Mr. and Mrs. William Lecky
also stayed. Mr. Lecky was a great friend of my father's of whom
I was very fond, in spite of a somewhat grotesque appearance.
I would often dine with Mrs. Lecky. There was a big screen in
her room, at the top of which Mr. Lecky's bald head appeared
as he came in. Later she told me that after he died what really
broke her courage was waiting, when the door opened, to see his
head appear, and then suddenly remembering.

"We sometimes went down to Oxford, staying with Miss
Smith—daughter of A. L. Smith, the master, who succeeded
Jowett at Balliol—and at Merton with Edith Brodrick, who was
entertaining for her uncle, the old Warden. He and his brother,
Lord Midleton, were two of the kindest but oddest men. Lord
Midleton, who was nearly blind, was once driving in a hansom
with his niece Alba, afterwards militant against England in the
Irish troubles. The horse bolted and fell over. A crowd collected
and someone shouted, 'Sit on 'er 'ead!' referring, of course, to the
horse, which was struggling to get up. When order was restored,
Lord Midleton was found inside the cab trying to sit on Alba's
head.

"Another time Lord Midleton suddenly began to tell me a most improper story, whereupon Lady Midleton rushed from the other end of the room saying, 'My dear, my dear, it isn't Maurice Fremantle, it's Tiny Grant Duff.' Of Lord Midleton also is told the tale about some new neighbours who had been asked to dine. Whilst waiting for their arrival, His Lordship went to look them up in what old Mr. Lowther called The Book. He came back to the drawing-room and, not seeing that the strangers had arrived, said cheerfully to Lady Midleton, 'You are quite right, my dear, the ———s are nobody, nobody at all!' "

His brother, the Warden of Merton, was also very eccentric. After Tiny married, she and her husband went to visit him and, getting very sleepy after dinner whilst her host discoursed on English literature, she was suddenly galvanized into life by hearing him remark, "Yes, my dear lady, I think if I had applied my mind to it, I could have written any of the shorter poems of Byron and Shelley." It was on this first visit to Merton that she saw, for the only time in her life, a bookworm in the great library there. The librarian showed it to her, a most unpleasant-looking creature.

Sir Donald Mackenzie Wallace was another intimate of her family's. After writing his book about Russia he was taken to a small literary club in Edinburgh, where conversation fell upon his book and he ventured to contradict a criticism that a young man made of it. Whereupon the young man said, "Well, I really must contradict you again because I have just been reviewing the book and I know I am right." "Pardon me," said Sir Donald. "I have just been writing it." The young critic was Robert Louis Stevenson.

Tiny wrote: "We became friendly with the Willie Tyrrells when they took a small house in Twickenham in Zion Row, an old row of houses that overlooked York House garden. Willie, afterwards Lord Tyrrell of Avon, was on the Foreign Office staff, already showing the immense promise he later achieved, culminating in the fulfillment of my father's prophecy that he would be appointed Ambassador in Paris.

"From Twickenham they moved to Brompton Square, where I would often stay with them. Brompton Square was then considered terribly improper, and my mother had qualms of conscience about my going there, but Maisie Tyrrell was so respected, and my mother was so fond of her, that she permitted it. When Willie's chief in the Foreign Office heard that Willie had gone to live there, he sent for him and remonstrated: 'My dear Tyrrell, when one is a Catholic and a respectable married man and in the Foreign Office, one does not live in Brompton Square.' But Willie did." And Tiny later bought a house there, from which her daughter Anne was married.

"Of the older men," Tiny wrote, "I remember best Sir Alfred Lyall and Walter Pater. They both came often to stay at York House and in London too. Sir Alfred was like an old troubadour, but at the same time had something extraordinarily boyish about him, and his chuckle was most infectious. I frequently visited them, and Bobby and Alfred, his two sons, were both friends. Sir Alfred was very kind about vetting my poetry and, though brutal in his criticisms, always encouraged me to go on. Sidney Colvin, who was also very kind, was much more complimentary but said that he did not think I had any real talent, only a facility for writing verse. Sir Alfred's own verse—now completely forgotten—is vivid and vital, in the tradition of Macaulay, and it has caught the atmosphere of India to a remarkable degree.

"I was so much influenced by Walter Pater's books that I am never quite sure that I did not read into his personality more than most people found. With his huge moustache and pale blue eyes, he looked strangely unlike one's image of the author of *Marius the Epicurean*. Precise in speech, always apposite, he was extremely shy. We used to go for walks along the towing-path at Twickenham, and I blush now to think how I aired my views about life and literature to this great man, he always courteous and forbearing and never snubbing. I only once saw him lose his *sang froid*. I forgot how, but the conversation turned on death. Pater jumped up and began walking up and down the room.

'I hate death,' he said. 'It is horrible to me even to think of it. I cannot bear even to come across a dead bird on my walks.' How glad I was, when he came to die, that his passing was without premonition and without pain, sudden and instantaneous.

"Vernon Lee told me that when still quite a young woman she received an invitation to stay with the great writer, and was overwhelmed with joy. When his sisters and she retired to bed she was much too excited to sleep and there was no book in the room. She recalled that she had left the book she was reading in the dining-room, so (it then being about two) thought she would be safe in creeping down to retrieve it. She opened the door cautiously and to her horror found herself in a lit room, a white cover on the table and, seated at the end of it, in pyjamas, in front of an enormous cheese—Mr. Pater! She stared and he stared and then he said sepulchrally, waving a huge knife, 'Have some cheese.' Vernon fled. What an opportunity missed of discussing life with Walter Pater at two a.m.—fortified by cheese!

"I used to stay a good deal with Lady Collyer, widow of Sir George Collyer, who had rooms at Hampton Court. It was a pleasure staying in the old Palace; the river there was quiet and lonely. A niece of hers and I would play cricket in the cloisters, and the sentry used to field for us, which I imagine was not in accordance with Her Majesty's regulations. Sometimes there were dances at the Palace, when we would have the lovely moonlit gardens to ourselves."

The wounds—leaving India, breaking with Captain Evans-Gordon—were healing or had healed, on the surface. Tiny was an extraordinarily vulnerable person, the more so because she was so good at concealing this fact.

VII

Second Season

During the summer of 1890 the Grant Duffs were again at their rented house in Great Stanhope Street, and Tiny's second season was very much like the first, only since she knew many more people she enjoyed it more. That summer she made friends with a family called Newman, who had a splendid house in Mayfair and an equally splendid one in the country. One of the sons, Herbert, a tall dragoon, paid her very marked attention, dancing with her constantly at every ball, and she and his sister, Ethel, rode together nearly every morning. Tiny began to think about him a good deal, and all that year he was the person who most attracted her.

When the summer ended he came to York House, and during the autumn she went to one or two houses where he was staying, and Herbert began to obsess her too much for her peace of mind. At a ball at the John Walters' (of *The Times*), where they were both staying, she realized that she cared very much, and after dancing with him nine times was sure that he cared too. About a fortnight later she went to his home for a visit. He showed her the gardens and farm, introducing her to the old retainers and behaving as though it were merely a question of time before he proposed. He was to come to a ball at her people's the month after, and she was supremely happy. The ball came, he sent her a huge bouquet, danced with her all night—and during their last waltz told her that he was shortly going to India, expressing the hope they should meet again some day. She was only nineteen, and her face probably showed her misery, for he said cheerfully, "We've had a nice time together, haven't we?" She said, "Yes, I do hope we'll meet sometime again."

He left next morning. Tiny was so unhappy that Ethel Newman, she was certain, noticed. Ethel was staying on two days longer than her brother, but said nothing. Herbert's attentions had been so marked that everybody knew Tiny's situation and was tacitly kind and commiserating.

Then a chance meeting changed Tiny's whole life. After her unhappy experience with Herbert, she threw herself into a disastrous flirtation with a man she did not care for, who was not at all a nice person. She did not heed Arthur Bagot's serious warning, and her father and mother, who were in some ways very unworldly, asked the man to the house frequently. It is often difficult for older people to know what is common knowledge to the young. Anyway, he was able to influence her, although she had no fondness for him. Then one day Tiny was asked to go to a ball at the Graham Robertsons'. Graham was an artist-illustrator, and they had interesting friends. Tiny went, and what happened to her there is best told in her own words.

"I had known by sight for some time, and immensely admired, a man who was always about with Graham Robertson called Jim Cagney. He was a doctor and I think the handsomest man I ever saw. Kathleen introduced him and we danced several times together and then went out on the balcony and talked. He saw that I was at a loose end, miserable, bitter and, above all, reckless. And in his quiet voice he talked to me more frankly and dispassionately than anyone else had ever done. He made clear how reckless women ended, how desperately sad, how *dull* their lives were, and how hopeless a life that was lived without any standards. He was, I believe, a devout Catholic, but he said not a word of religion; he merely showed the waste and stupidity of lives such as I was preparing for myself, and made me realize the necessity of entirely altering my outlook. We were a long time on the balcony and when we went back the ballroom was emptying. I said good-bye to him, thanked him from my heart, and went home with my thoughts full of him and my new good resolutions.

"I begged my mother to ask him to a ball we were giving soon, but she absolutely refused—he was a doctor, he was in a Bohemian set, no one knew him, and so on. Some days later we met in the park and talked again, but I couldn't be with him long, for I was with Aunt Fanny and Rachel. I felt he must have thought it strange that I did not ask him to call, which was the usual thing if a man and a girl who had been introduced liked each other.

"After I married, we met again and I asked him to come and see me, but four or five other people came in and we could not talk. He dined once but bored my husband, so I did not renew the invitation. A couple of years later he died of typhoid. And that is all I know of the man to whom I owe probably more than to any other person who ever crossed my path."

One of the few pleasant incidents of that winter was the visit of an old violinist, Reményi, whom Mountstuart had known years before in Hungary. Reményi had suddenly tired of Europe, where his reputation was considerable, and disappeared. He had the pleasure of reading his own obituary notices. He had gone to Java and remained there for ten years, learning the language and living like a Javanese; he told Tiny of the Happy Valley, where he had lived, and where no one had ever been known to commit a crime or to be unkind. He said it was like being in heaven. He played divinely and said to her father the nicest thing Tiny ever had said of her: "She is so lovely—when I saw her I gave a jomp."

The winter dragged on and on. As Tiny was still miserable, Lady Malmesbury, a friend of her mother, offered to have Tiny with her in Florence for a visit of two months in February and March. Tiny's relief can be imagined. She had been scarcely any-where on the Continent, and the invitation seemed too good to be true. Her mother's cousin, Mrs. Combe, who was going to Rome, would drop Tiny in Florence on the way. They arrived at six on a bitter winter morning, and Florence was colder than any-where Tiny had ever been except Edinburgh. She went straight to bed and was later awakened, to streaming sunshine, by a Ber-saglieri regiment going past with its wonderful little pipe-and-fife band. She never heard that sound again without a thrill; for her it had all Italy in it.

Lady Malmesbury was a conventional woman with little appre-ciation for art, but she was kind and conscientious about taking her guest to see the right things, and Tiny got to know the gal-leries and churches pretty well. They went to one or two small dances, and to the Shrove Tuesday Masked Ball at the Opera House. The wonderful symbolic rite which used to take place at midnight on Shrove Tuesday had died out; many Florentines remembered when the clergy, in a procession headed by a great cross, drove out the maskers and shut the doors.

The Florence of those days was still very largely the city of Ouida's novel *Friendship*. The people mentioned in it had grown older and more battered, but were still there. Tiny used to go out to tea with old Miss Forbes, and Ouida was still driving about. She had a villa outside the town, was quite plain and utterly unlike the lovely lady in *Friendship*. Mrs. Ross, the heroine, was still an invigorating though rather rough personality. When Tiny lunched with her, she sang songs in dialect to her guitar, and one could imagine how very attractive she must have been twenty years before. She used to keep a prie-dieu at her dressmaker's to try the effect of her clothes in prayer. The three old Misses Murray were exactly as depicted in *Friendship*, and their brother, Colonel Murray, took Tiny out in his *baroccino*, allowing her, as a great treat, occasionally to drive. Tiny thought it the nicest kind of vehicle—to ride in it was almost like being on horseback, so light was it, and one could go very fast indeed.

With Lady Malmesbury, Tiny went to Prince Corsini's Mon-day parties—dreadfully dull. The married ladies sat together, the girls sat together, and the young men stood in a corner. But Tiny realized the parties were very grand. Then there was a nice little American Princess Torrigiani, with whom Tiny sometimes lunched, and a pleasant American couple, the Mordaunts, who had taken a villa. Mrs. Mordaunt, poor woman, always looked haunted. When Tiny asked Lady Malmesbury why, with all her wealth and an adoring husband, Mrs. Mordaunt appeared unhappy, she was told that kidnapers had threatened their children in America. This had frightened them so much that they now lived permanently in Europe.

Tiny had been provided with a trotter—a woman chaperone who "trotted" around Florence with young girls—to take her out when Lady Malmesbury was tired, and noticed that the trotter was spoken to much more than she was. One beautiful cavalry officer used to follow them for hours at a time and, to the fury of the trotter, Tiny insisted on taking him for long walks over rough roads until the officer's feet must have ached in his shiny boots. However, he never gave way and always followed at a respectful distance. One English girl, who had been told she could not circulate freely as she did in England, nevertheless went out alone, was immediately followed by an amorous soldier and tried to get away by walking faster and faster. She got lost and found herself on the outskirts of Florence, still followed, and then, becoming really frightened, she went to a *guardia* and asked him to beg the gentleman to refrain. The *guardia* looked at her with admiration and said, "I quite understand his feelings." The girl finally found a cab. The second time Tiny was in Florence two years afterward, she insisted upon going out alone and was never molested. By then the Italians realized that English girls were allowed to go out by themselves and didn't bother them, though they often followed the girls for a while.

Tiny went occasionally to Lady Hobart's Villa on Bellosguardo and to Mrs. Scott's, where Queen Victoria also had visited, at the Villa Capponi, Arcetri. (Years later Anne spent two happy weeks there, staying with Henry and Esther Clifford: he a curator at

the Philadelphia Museum of Art, she a distinguished scholar and
author, and godmother to Anne's son Hugh.) Lord Ampthill was
at Florence with his mother and sister, and Tiny saw something
of them. Like all other Russells, he was a shy young man with
charming manners.

Lady Malmesbury, rather a cynical woman with a hard, matter-
of-fact point of view, was good for Tiny at this time, especially
in making her realize the value of "Society" and the usefulness of
standing well with it. Tiny had Bohemian leanings and would
have preferred knowing only people who amused her, but Lady
Malmesbury made her understand that she had to live in a mixed
world and that it was stupid to be eccentric in small things if she
wished to be allowed her way in big things.

The two months at Florence passed like a dream. All her life
she remembered—as she had of India—the agony of leaving Italy
for the distasteful cold north, and she firmly resolved that somehow she would go back.

It was at Lady Malmesbury's in Florence that Tiny first met
Monsieur and Madame Jakob Blumenthal, who were celebrated
for having what was London's nearest approach to a *salon* after
Lady William Russell's death. Their house at Hyde Park Gate
was quite small, but Madame was a very rich woman, witty, well
read, and a good talker. She had been a Miss Gore and inherited
a large sheep estate when very young, as a result of a tragic accident in which her whole family was drowned. An aunt, Mrs.
O'Connell, brought her to London, where she took music lessons
from Monsieur Blumenthal, then at the height of his fame as a
teacher and writer of songs. They fell in love and married, and it
was a consummately happy union in spite of the fact that he, born
a Jew, was a complete agnostic, and she was a devout Catholic.
To have been invited to sing or play at the Blumenthals' was a
credit to any musician. Monsieur never paid a cent to artists, but
the Blumenthals' kindness to professionals who needed it, and
their generosity were unbounded.

Monsieur's songs "The Requital" and "My Queen" had been

almost forgotten when Tiny came out, but they had been extremely popular and sung everywhere a decade before.

That summer the Blumenthals asked her to go out to their
chalet, on the Lake of Geneva, which played a great part in
their friends' lives. The favorite friends were admitted as "chale-
tains." Monsieur was Grand Master and Madame was Grand
Mistress of the chalet, and all were given little silver badges in
the shape of a chalet to be worn at Monsieur Blumenthal's best
parties. The house itself was one of the most enchanting places
Tiny ever stayed at, excessively comfortable but not pretty.
Madame was passionately fond of the scents of certain flowers—
bouvardia, datura, stephanotis, and lilium auratum. She always
had some of them in the house, and the scent of lilium auratum
always called up for Tiny the drawing room, with its tightly
closed windows, almost dark—for Madame hated sunlight—and
drenched in scent. Madame loved a good argument and used to
encourage her guests to spar and think out debatable points.

Two very nice boys, Lord Crichton and his brother, came to
stay. They were undergraduates and not even faintly interested
in girls. Madame, describing the party to a friend in London,
wrote, "Tiny, between those two young men, reminds me of a
small carnivorous animal in a cabbage patch."

She was a remarkable letter-writer and wrote to Tiny after her
first visit:

> The summer has gone, gone to join all the other summers.
> The Peloponnesian War is not more dead. Are you yourself
> living? You know the shops have an operation they call stock-
> taking? I like to take stock of my year and of the good and
> evil it has brought me. Evil, sometimes with a laughing face;
> good, with stern sad eyes. But to every woman over forty, if
> she be worth her salt, life is vicarious; actually or potentially
> she is a mother, burdened with the troubles of her children,
> glad with their joys. Some of my children are very interest-
> ing, especially those on whom I have even betting. Don't

you find each year brings you its message? Its crystallized
truth that remains when all that is accidental evaporates? The
years are God's preachers.

It touches me immensely that you cared to be here, and it
makes me feel that I had misunderstood you. I had thought
that your device would be that young device, "*J'écoute
venir.*" But here there is nothing to listen to, only a great
silence, the mountains who know, and will not say, therein
being like God. And God is so silent when one is young, no
doubt because:

> "Heaven to those no grace imparts
> Who hear not for the beating of their hearts."

Altogether it was a wonderful visit. And at the end Tiny's
father came to the Blumenthals' too. He and Tiny visited French
cathedrals on the way home—Sens, Beauvais, Soissons, and others.
Then on to Boury, which had been the home of Comte Auguste
de la Ferronays and is frequently alluded to in the *Récit d'une
Sœur*, by his daughter Pauline Craven. It was a dark, dismal house
and Tiny felt that the churchyard close by, where so many of the
de la Ferronays were buried, was depressing, as French country
churchyards often are. The proprietor of the house seemed to
have great feeling for all the family, and to the Grant Duffs it
was a privilege to be where so many saints had lived. They stayed
for several days in Paris on their way back, and before returning
to York House made a pilgrimage to the house where Mrs. Craven
had lived. She had died the summer before.

The second time Tiny went to the Blumenthals' country house
in Switzerland, Monsieur was writing a lovely set of songs that
were later published in two volumes as *Chansons Intimes*. Some
were in French and German, and she was to translate many of
them for him. Madame's gifted cousin Vera Wolkoff would sing
them. She had a tiny voice but was a good musician, and later she
too wrote delightful songs. The long, hot summer mornings, the
lake shimmering among the trees, the air heavy with heliotrope,

and the bees droning in the datura blossoms, with Monsieur improvising on the next balcony, remained among Tiny's happiest recollections.

The Blumenthals' butler, Stokes, wore enormous sidewhiskers and a mustache. He was invaluable, knew everybody, was careful to admit the right people and turn away the wrong ones; he was with the Blumenthals for many years. But Tiny never forgot the awful day, long after she married, when Monsieur suddenly came to her, looking quite ill. He said in an agonized voice, "Stokes!"

"Stokes is not dead, is he?" she asked.

"No," said Monsieur, "much, much worse." He sat down heavily in an armchair and recounted how they had discovered that Stokes had three establishments, all fed and clothed by Monsieur, the cook being also implicated in the nefarious transactions. Stokes was got rid of, and a darling fat butler came, called Ailie, whom Tiny liked much better and who stayed with them until the end.

Tiny was always aware of her friends' retainers, who, in many cases, became friends also, as did their pets. When Tiny had children, before taking them with her to stay with friends she would describe the people, the house, the garden, and the staff, so that the children too could enjoy such old friends as Bachelor, her mother's maid. When, after Tiny's death, Anne and her husband became American citizens, she missed, in the American nuclear family (father, mother, one, two, three children—rarely more) the multiple extended family that she had enjoyed while growing up, and that Tiny had enjoyed to an even greater extent. For nurses, cooks, butlers, maids, governesses, tutors, grooms, and chauffeurs were all real friends—or real enemies, as the case might be—enormously increasing one's range of understanding and affection.

VIII

Settling Down

Tiny, deploring the nonsense she felt was written about the hideousness of Victorian decoration, described York House as it was when she was twenty.

"To begin with, we had five bathrooms in the house. The two small girls slept in a large nursery with the nurse, on the other side of which was the schoolroom, both furnished with good old furniture and very little of it. The pictures were Arundel prints and a fine replica of Delacroix' Christ. I was allowed to do what I wanted with my own room, and my mother painted the furniture for me in pale yellow with designs of poppies. The walls were panelled with wood. I was scrupulously tidy and always had fresh flowers and a sort of altar with a little replica of the Venus de Milo, for I was in those days still rather anti-Christian, I think mostly under the influence of Douglas Ainslie, my cousin, who disliked Christianity with an intense, undivided hatred. [He became the translator of Benedetto Croce and later spent some time with Sri Ramana Maharshi in India.]

"To go back to the furnishings of York House. The spare rooms were most comfortable—one papered with a delightful Morris design of daisies and one with cherries; one simply painted in pale blue and one in salmon color. They were all gay, fitted with beautiful cupboards and very warm. The drawing room was Moorish in character, with a fine arch in squares of gold and red. Most of the furniture had been brought from India, so the whole room was rather Oriental. My father's library was upholstered in violet velvet, the dining room in pale yellow. There was not much furniture and all of it very good, mostly old pieces, later inherited by my brother, Arthur Grant Duff. We did not have yellow pots indiscriminately dumped about, as is commonly described in novels of this period. My mother's taste, apart from rather silly little ornate menu cards and calendars that she occasionally bought, seems to me to have been strikingly good. She was not so clever about clothes. In general, very beautiful women are rarely good at clothes.

"At the beginning of November we went to the Derbys' at Knowsley in Lancashire for a visit. It was awe-inspiring. Forty people were staying and the house was run in the great old manner. Lady Winifred Gardner was there with her sister Lady Margaret Herbert, Arthur Balfour [later (1902–1906) Prime Minister] and various other people. Three excellent *partis* were provided for our inspection: Mr. Cazalet, Mr. Jim Baillie, and Mr. Hamilton Russell, but none of them looked at the three girls present; they all immediately attached themselves to the most enchanting Lady Winifred. It was a pleasant party, and Lady Derby and Lady Margaret Cecil were so kind and interesting that one never felt shy. There were marvellous things in the house, too, of which I remember best the Holbein drawings.

"The end of the party was spoilt by a wave of influenza, my mother and three other guests being too ill to move. We younger ones, already infected, struggled on and got home to collapse in our turn; it was most unpleasant.

"The winter saw the first long visit to York House of my cousin Douglas Ainslie, when he stirred me with his enthusiasm for French literature. I would go to bed at ten and read till two: Balzac, de Musset, Stendhal, Flaubert, Alphonse Daudet, Verlaine,

Guy de Maupassant, Maurice Barrès, just entering on his great fame, and Maeterlinck. Though I don't think they did much harm in the long run, the immediate result of such books was to increase my love of luxury and make me more positive that life without beautiful things, lovely dresses and comfort and leisure, was not worth living.

"It was rather a hot-house atmosphere that winter of 1890. My mother, ill and in her room a good deal, did not want anyone with her, except in the evenings when her head ached and I used to massage her. Father had a secretary and was putting together his diaries, so did not need me to read to him for more than a couple of hours a day, and as Mother was ill we did not have many people to stay, so I was dependent on Douglas and on my sister's governess for amusements. Fräulein Ihlefeld, a woman of strong personality, was very musical, and when I wanted to sing she played my accompaniment by the hour, often while I improvised strange words of my own invention. We had a great music room, called the salon, where we could make as much noise as we liked—my little boudoir opened out of this.

"Fräulein and I used to go up to London for concerts, and since we could not afford any but shilling seats we went very early and took our lunch with us. But we were both so keen on music, we did not mind the discomfort. I had already heard many of the great players at Cheltenham: Sarasate, Norman-Neruda, Hallé, Joachim, Mark Hambourg as a little boy, and all the other infant prodigies, and in London I remember hearing all Grieg's concerts. We knew enough musical people to give me the chance of hearing the very first-rate singers at private parties. I heard Patti, de Soria, Sims Reeves, then very old, and Christine Nilsson at private parties, and, later on, most of the best artists at the Blumenthals' house.

"Douglas hired a horse, and Dot or I rode most days with him, and whoever didn't went to Kew or somewhere with my father. Then there was tea, and Douglas and I read to each other until it was time to dress for dinner, or until my small sisters came down to the boudoir to be told fairy tales. I had an immense fund of these, mostly invented, and the children loved them.

"I always got on perfectly with my sisters and we had absurd little nicknames amongst ourselves. They called me 'Little Eldest' because I was so small, Dot the 'Perfect Second' because we all admired her so much, Lily 'Extraordinary Middle' because she had such flaming red hair and was so eccentric, and Iseult 'Insane Youngest' because she had such odd ideas.

"Douglas and I were both writing a great deal of poetry, which we read out to each other with mutual applause, and we also recited pages of the Olympians. I can still hear myself shouting:

> *Je suis belle, ô mortel comme un rêve de pierre,*
> *Et mon sein, où chacun s'est meurtri tour à tour,*
> *Est fait pour inspirer au poète un amour . . . ,*

And Douglas matching this with:

> *Carmen est maigre—un trait de bistre*
> *Cerne son œil de gitana*
> *Ses yeux ont une lueur sinistre*
> *Sa peau—le diable la tanna . . . .*

How we wanted to go straight off to Paris and live in the Quartier Latin surrounded by painters and poets, and how dreadfully we should have disliked it! We were neither of us prepared for privations.

"Our own poetry was pretty bad. Mine was downright and not the least original, most influenced by Browning and Swinburne. Douglas' verse, on the other hand, was archaic, sombre, and difficult."

Mr. Richard Hutton, the editor of *The Spectator*, gave Tiny reviews to do. In some ways his taste was uncertain. When she was in Florence for the first time, an American woman had lent her two books, one Ada Negri's poems and the other Emily Dickinson's. She was thrilled by both and wrote reviews of them with copious extracts for Mr. Hutton. He took the one on Ada Negri but returned the Emily Dickinson with the comment, "I like your review and you have done your best for the lady. But the verses are too bad!" It is incredible that a man of letters should have felt that. (A few months after, Emily Dickinson became famous as the subject of a panegyric in the *Nineteenth Century*.)

"But in spite of Hutton's occasional want of perception," Tiny commented, "he was a wise and influential editor, and *The Spectator* rose to a height under his able guidance which it did not retain after his death." Tiny went on: "In the summer of 1891 Angelo Gubernatis, the old Italian *homme de lettres*, came to stay with us and asked me to do an article on Watts' pictures for his periodical. I also wrote a certain amount for a little paper called *Woman* and had poems in various weeklies and magazines. I wrote enormously but had the sense to destroy a great deal, although I wish I had been less diffident about my own powers. However, my father and mother were both so much more gifted than I was that they thought nothing of my attempts. And I lived amongst brilliant people who thought everything but the best a waste of time."

Tiny's mother wrote competent poetry and sketched very well. She had never had any training, but she had an inherent gift. Certainly art was the great interest of her life, and whenever she could she would leave everything and go off for a whole morning's or afternoon's painting. She was also published in many periodicals, and Tiny thought one poem, "A Night in the Mediterranean," worth preserving. It tells of a night journey from Algiers to Marseilles and the reflections of one of the passengers on a man whom she had seen leaning disconsolately over the rail, and who next morning had disappeared.

> As he leans over the vessel side,
>   Watching its track of sapphire and snow,
> Does he muse and wonder what might betide
>   If he sought for peace in the depths below?

After that plunge comes a Saviour's breast,
  Or the Depths of Hell, or unconscious rest.

An accident—the priest was kind
  And Masses said for the stricken soul,
The philosopher talked of an unstrung mind
  And a spirit beyond its own control.
To neither—perhaps—occurred the thought
  Of a wearied child whom the Father sought.

Worn with sorrow and stained with sin,
  Was he not wise to seek that door
Where alone a new life might begin,
  Where alone the past could be wholly o'er?
Who knows? Like a child in the night he cried,
  And the storm and darkness alone replied.

The following was written by Tiny in 1890.

Forget that I was worthless of your care.
Between us two there lies
No longer life's glad questions and replies,
But Death with sad blind eyes,
And silence deeper than all questions are.

Forget I halted in the path you trod.
Forget I could not climb the starlit heights
But sought the well-remembered sounds and sights,
The flowering valley, full of dear delights,
You, who have gone to God.

Dear, had you said: For my sake do this thing,
Leave life's unworthy struggles and its joys,
The prizes that the angels hold but toys
I had left all the jangle and the noise
And gone unmurmuring.

But in your grave blue eyes the light shone pure,
My Parsifal, who pointed out the Way,
Asking not whether I would go or stay,

Shewing me only how to fight and pray,
To struggle and endure.

Forget my purpose vain and wavering will.
I lay these lilies on your cold, dead breast,
And when you wake you will forget the rest,
Knowing I gave you all I had—my best,
And fain would give it still.

IX

Coming of Age

Of 1891 Tiny wrote: "In the spring we took a house in Great Cumberland Place, belonging to the traveller Theodore Bent. It was this year that I went to Commemoration Balls at Oxford for the only time, staying with the Lyttelton-Gells and then with Beatrice Max Müller. Commem Week was, and I suppose still is, the most enchanting experience a girl can have. A ball each night, breakfast in some college, a morning idling on the river, garden parties in the afternoon—a debutante's paradise. Added to which, on this occasion, the weather was lovely and the gardens beautiful.

"I went to stay two or three times a year at Ightham Mote, supposedly the oldest inhabited house in England, with the Colyer-Fergussons, where private theatricals were popular. On one occasion, George Harris brought down a quiet, self-possessed man who manipulated his eye-glass more cleverly than anyone I had ever seen. He was cast, on that first occasion, as my father in a comedy we were acting. It was John Galsworthy, and, charming as he was, we didn't suspect that as a writer he would reach the heights he afterwards attained. I never quite understood his reputation. He seemed to me a person who had learned his craft perfectly, but who had extraordinarily little to say. As a human being he was remarkable indeed, and I don't wonder his friends cared for him as they did. One of the most delightful dinner parties I remember was at the Granville Barkers. Mr. Galsworthy and Mr. Bernard Shaw were there, and it was an exhilarating evening, the men waxing enthusiastic about films, which were just then beginning.

"I had met Gertrude Bell that summer at the Ridgeway, and we made great friends at once; she often came to York House and was much cleverer than I was, which was a pleasure. For me, the last word about friendship was said by a later friend, Lily Millet, who remarked firmly, 'My equals ain't good enough for me—I want my superiors.' Gertrude was enchanting, her gaiety infectious, and her good fellowship warm and endearing. She was an ugly woman but had great strength and the grace that goes so often with physical strength."

T. E. Lawrence later told Tiny a delightful story about Gertrude Bell. While he was in the Arabian desert, she appeared on an exploratory expedition. Naturally he had to offer her the hospitality of his tent, share his food, water, and equipment with her. After a few days she left, and he felt he had to explain her arrival and departure to his Arab servants and to the local sheiks. She had come out, he told them, on approval as his bride, but he had decided she wouldn't do and had dismissed her.

Two of the people Tiny liked best were Logan Pearsall Smith and Alys, his sister. They were both fine dancers and extraordinarily high-spirited and delightful people, both good-looking. (Their father, who had been a well-known Evangelical preacher, was said to have seduced young converts in a tree.) She later married Bertrand Russell. Alys and Bertrand are described in Beatrice Webb's *Our Partnership*. Beatrice and Sydney Webb ("the Webbs") used to stay for months on end with the young Russells, who were then living in Friday's Hill, a house that had belonged to Alys's parents, near Haslemere, in Surrey.

"The Russells are the most attractive married couple I know," Mrs. Webb wrote of them in 1901. "Young and virtuous, they combine in the pair personal charm, unique intelligence, the woman having the one, the man the other in the superlative degree.

Romantically attached to each other, they have diverse interests; Alys concerns herself with social reform, Bertrand with the higher mathematics." And she goes on to describe them separately: "Alys is . . . charming to look at, tall, graceful, with regular features, clear skin, bright blue eyes and soft curly nut-brown hair, always smiling, often laughing, warm-hearted and sympathetically intelligent." Bertrand is "a slight, dark-haired man, with prominent forehead, bright eyes, strong features, except for a retreating chin, nervous hands, and alert, quick movements. In morals, he is a puritan, in personal habits almost an ascetic . . . but, intellectually, he is audacious . . . he indulges in the wildest paradoxes and the broadest jokes."

Tiny stayed a good deal with the Maxses. Admiral Maxse had the cold logical atheism of a Frenchman and was a great friend of Clemenceau. He once mentioned that when in Paris he had told Clemenceau, "You know I am no lover of the Germans, I cannot abide them. But if your countrymen go on as they are, we shall be driven to join the Triple Alliance."

"*Dieu merci,*" Clemenceau replied, "*c'est la paix.*"

Louis Mallet and Tiny started the Pessimist Society at this time. One had to be invited to join; there was no subscription, and the only stipulation was that you must accept its motto: "We believe in the folly and vanity of attempting anything." "We had a magazine," Tiny explained, "*The Mausoleum*, and I recall one advertisement: 'Why Buy New Coffins when We Have a Vast Number of Misfit and Secondhand Coffins at Reasonable Price?' The motto on the front page was:

Le Printemps adorable a perdu son parfum.

And lower down:

Nous avons en parfaite horreur les utopistes, les philanthropistes, et tout ceux qui prétendent changer l'invariable nature et l'agencement fatale des Sociétés.

"Most people understood that it was a huge joke, but one or two old ladies and some rather stodgy younger people wrote me extremely priggish letters saying that Life was such a splendid thing—all opportunity—and happiness was a duty. These of course filled Louis and me with joy.

"Louis wrote an amusing article explaining that *The Mausoleum* was not a resting place for manuscripts which had been refused by other periodicals. I think our magazine was probably inspired by one started by J. K. Stephens a couple of years earlier, called *The Reflector*.

"In September 1892 the brilliant Miss Cornelia Sorabji, who had been a sensation at Oxford when she first arrived to study law, was with us a good deal. I have rarely seen a more beautiful woman. I asked her once what she was going to do, having experienced both Indian and English civilizations, and she replied, 'I am going back to India; I think on the whole that civilization is the deeper one.'

"Many distinguished people came that year to York House, for an Oriental Congress was being held in London. With Angelo Gubernatis, on his second visit, came Prince Teano, a son of the Duke of Sermoneta. Old Sir Henry Howarth arrived too; he had with him a curious dagger, a Japanese one, smelling strongly of scent. You could wash it and wash it, but nothing altered its perfume, and apparently even in Japan it was a great rarity and nobody knew the secret of the scent. He told me that shortly after he wrote *The History of the Mongols* he was next a young lady at dinner who, as they went down, said, 'You know, I have been dying to meet you.' 'You overwhelm me, my dear young lady,' he said, 'but why?' 'Oh, I heard Papa say that you had written a history of Mongrels and I just adore dogs!' "

Tiny at last achieved her ambition to return to Italy. "My grandmother had left me a little legacy and I asked if I might go to Florence for the winter to continue my singing lessons and learn Italian, so it was arranged that I should go to Miss Letty Lambert, a sister of Lady Hylton. Lady Dufferin, then Ambassadress at Rome, offered to take charge of me; and I stayed the first fortnight in Rome with her, after which my brother Evie, who was at the Embassy, took me on to Florence. I knew her daughters and liked them both, so it was a charming plan. Rome is too overwhelming to see much of in two weeks, but Evie took me to a lot of his friends: beautiful and charming women. The ones I remember best were all great beauties: Duchess Nicoletta Gracioli, Donna Elena Rospigliosi and the Marchesa Theodoli, of whom it was said that when she came out of church after her wedding, the crowd knelt down, thinking it was the Madonna.

"Miss Lambert was an Irish old maid, living at Piazza d'Arno. She had written nice letters and I went off in great hopes, but she was even nicer than her letters. Amusing, cordial, understanding, and with the vein of eccentricity which is lovable when joined with other pleasing qualities. We got on famously from the first moment. I had a funny little bedroom with a table in it where I could work, and Miss Lambert hired a good piano. She fed me well, and I was supremely happy with my lessons and visits to galleries.

"After ten days, to my great excitement, I had a letter from my cousin Hermann Obrist to say that he was coming to Florence to take a studio. He arrived the following week, thin and shattered by the awful privations he had suffered in Paris but now, from his mother's estate—she had died recently—with enough money to live comfortably. He worked hard but we always spent a couple of hours a day together, and I am still grateful for everything he taught me.

"I saw a good deal of Charles Leland and his wife—Leland was the well-known American who wrote as Hans Breitmann. A delightful old gentleman over six feet tall, with a long white beard, he looked what he was, a great necromancer. He was also amusing, befitting the author of the *Breitmann Ballads*. Mrs. Leland was a quiet, douce creature, sometimes terrified by her husband's stories and remarks, but she never offered more than a startled 'Oh

Chawles.' He knew a tremendous amount about witches and warlocks and ancient superstitions. One day when we were walking together we passed a dirty, rather ugly old woman. As we went by, Leland bent down and said something in her ear. The woman stopped dead, stared at him, and then broke out into wild prayers. 'What did you say to her?' I asked. 'I told her,' he said quietly, 'I know she is a witch, and I *do* know.' The woman watched us the length of the Arno, terrified.

"Shortly after I arrived in Florence, a young German, a friend of Mr. Leland, appeared on my horizon. His name was Hans von Wulffen, he was in a smart Guards Regiment, he fell for me— and proposed almost immediately. I, obsessed by everything German, accepted him. But my heart failed me after two days' engagement and I rushed to Hermann to extricate me from this difficulty. A terrible time ensued, in which Hermann tried to explain to Hans; at last he was convinced and gave me my freedom, and left Florence infuriated with the English. He was a nice creature, and I had never had so many violets in my life.

"I had been taking singing lessons for four or five weeks, when Hermann asked to come with me to my lesson. I was nervous, but consented. My lesson over, we walked away. Hermann was silent all along the Lung'Arno, and then he said, 'I am going to say something which will make you feel very miserable: it is not worth your while continuing. Your voice is too small, you haven't a strong throat, and though you have a good ear, you will inevitably fail. If you want to do something in art it must be supremely good, or else it is not worth your time and money.'

"We had by this time got home and, more dead than alive, I went in without saying good-bye. I trusted him so absolutely that I knew he wouldn't have said anything so wounding unless it were true, and I also knew that he had lived all his life amongst musicians, so there was nothing for it but to accept. Except for when I left India, that was the most miserable day of my life.

"At about half past eight the bell rang and Hermann came in. He said, 'I knew you must be utterly wretched, and I came back to see you.' I was most touched and told him I had accepted what he said, but couldn't possibly discuss it then, so he left.

"Next morning I wrote to my singing master and told him of my decision. He was angry, but I think Hermann was right. My voice would never have got strong enough to make my lessons worth while.

"In the middle of January I had an attack of influenza and was dreadfully ill; for two or three days my temperature reached 105. At last Lady Alba Hobart Hampden brought Doctor Baldwin, a remarkable American doctor, to see me. Doctor Baldwin averred that when he came into the room I was quite delirious and in a high fever, saying, 'What on earth do you come here for? I hate America, she has no literature.' Letty Lambert was as ill as I, so the doctor installed a little Italian nun as nurse.

"When I was beginning to sit up and read, Doctor Baldwin suddenly one morning arrived with his arms full of books, which he dumped on the bed. 'When you have read these,' he said firmly, 'you can tell me whether America has any literature, or not.'

"I was so weak after this illness that I could not go back to London with Evelyn, who was leaving the Embassy at Rome, so Lady Alba kindly asked me to stay at the Villa Montauto. As I got stronger, we went sometimes to nearby villas, notably those of Madame Zoubhoff and Lady Paget. Madame Zoubhoff had a handsome black-haired savage-looking niece with whom we often went to tea, and one day we found with her a fair woman, with the loveliest figure and clothes, her cousin, Comtesse Fleury. In the course of the afternoon the two women had a violent row, shouting the most awful French epithets at each other, but it was so funny and the scene so unlike anything known to Alba or me that we were both in fits of laughter.

"Madame Fleury and I became very intimate, and I saw her most days: I was immensely flattered by the notice of the older and much cleverer woman. What I contributed to this friendship I never knew, since we viewed most subjects very differently. Anyway, fast friends we became. I introduced her to Hermann, with whom she fell very much in love. He was extremely amused, but not in the least in love with her, maintaining that artists like nice placid women who do not make demands.

"Alba was a real resource. She had great humour and was one of the noblest-minded of women. We used to go on long walks together and explore the country round. The spring was just beginning. One day in February Vernon Lee asked a Miss Macdougall I knew to bring me to lunch. We went to her villa, and there I met for the first time, though I had often seen her, Flora Priestley, Sargent's favorite model. We four lunched together, and at intervals a door was opened and food passed through to Vernon's mythical brother, who never appeared. I felt I was seeing life but did not know enough to realize how brilliant was Vernon Lee, nor how beautiful Flora Priestley. To me only the carefully groomed women were worth looking at, and Flora was untidy and always wore the wrong clothes."

In 1935 Tiny lunched with Flora Priestley, who said she needed £20 for some charity; would Tiny buy a little six-by-eight-inch oil painting that she had been given by Cézanne one day when she was in his studio? It was of a cup and mug, subdued in color. Tiny said she didn't care for Cézanne, she liked only the Pre-Raphaelites, but she had a daughter with advanced tastes. She told Anne, who said she'd love to buy it, but possessed at that moment only £17 she could spare. Mama said she would make the sum up to the £20, and Anne hung the little painting in her Gloucestershire mill. Everyone laughed at "Anne's Cézanne," until Anne's husband found the picture listed in Venturi's catalogue of Cézanne's paintings. Anne sold the tiny picture for £250 when she wanted to go to the United States; it was bought by Dr. Albert Barnes for his collection.

Had Tiny known that friends of Hermann wanted a nursery governess for their small child, she would have offered herself. But her money was exhausted, so there was apparently no alternative to making for home. She had learned so much, and had had such a full and wonderful time, that it was less dreadful going

back to England than it might have been. But it was terrible saying good-by to Hermann.

England was cold and dreary, and she promptly came down
with the German measles, which was prevalent that spring. As
soon as she was up, Fräulein Ihlefeld took her away to an awful
place called Felixstowe, on the coast, where the cold and food
were terrible, and she felt worse and worse. Bracing air never did
suit her. At last her mother, who wanted a change herself and
wished to see Arthur at Stockholm, decided that she would make
the journey that summer and take Tiny with her.

"During the voyage at the beginning of June, a nice fat Swede
fell in love with me," she wrote, "and took us about at Gothen-
burg; he was very kind." Tiny always perked up when someone
fell in love with her. "Later he turned up at Twickenham. Arthur
had taken a dear little house for us at Drottningholm and had engaged a first-rate cook; Mother had brought her maid, so we were
comfortable, though primitive. My bath was a narrow water-butt,
in which one day I stuck—and couldn't get out of the cold water.
After several desperate attempts I felt the only thing to do, as
no one was around to call, was to turn the whole affair over and
pull myself out by the legs of the bed. And at last, rather scratched,
got out. After this I soaped myself before getting in, so as to slip
out more easily.

"We went to Uppsala and Trollhättan and down the big lakes
Vänern and Mälaren. It was captivating and I, innately greedy,
adored the delicious Swedish food—such cream, such bread, such
butter, the wild strawberries, the tasty salt things for smorgasbord,
and good food to be had even in station restaurants.

"I would spend hours rowing on the big lake. The boat was
heavy and the oars clumsy, and although I was a good sculler I
was used to well-balanced oars. This boat was all right if there was
no wind, but I had a few nasty experiences. Once a sudden squall
got up and drove me into a bank of reeds and the water was so
rough that each time I got clear I was driven back, till I was so
exhausted that I could scarcely hold the oars. Then, also, I used

to bathe, though the water was too cold to be very pleasant. Mother sketched all day and Arthur was in Stockholm at the Legation, so I had to amuse myself. We did not see many people. Our Minister was Sir Hugh, afterwards Lord Gough, and his wife, Lady Georgina, a nice comfortable woman. He was a queer character. Sitting shyly by him one night I asked, 'Do you know many nice Swedes in Stockholm?' He looked at me gravely and replied, 'I do not see much of the Swedes. I always say that a British Minister is there to look after his own nationals; it is not necessary to cultivate the people of the country.' I noticed that Lady Georgina chuckled and Arthur had some difficulty in remaining solemn, and was told afterwards that this was one of his chief's favorite tenets; that he was celebrated in the Service for his odd opinions. They were kind, friendly people and I stayed with them years afterwards at Lough Cutra in Ireland.

"Mother returned to York House, and Arthur and I went on to Copenhagen, en route for Bayreuth. I had just enough money for four performances and the journey and cost of rooms, and I had to be *very* economical. In Copenhagen we went to a sort of outdoor music-hall and I felt I was seeing life. And, of course, we paid our respects to Hans Andersen's grave.

"From Berlin we went via Nuremberg to Bayreuth. I was thrilled by Nuremberg, and Longfellow's poem was the most perfect guide book, though he does not mention the Torture Chamber, which Arthur insisted on seeing. I looked at the Maiden but when the woman guide said, '*Dann wird der Mensch langsam zerquetscht*' ['Then they were slowly squished'] I rushed outside.

"At Bayreuth there was a letter from Comtesse Fleury, saying that she was at the Fantaisie outside the town, and that Arthur and I must come there. So we got rooms over a local carpenter's. They were crude but we didn't mind, we were both young and carefree.

"The ten days that followed were most dramatic. Giovanni Costa—*le beau* Costa—whom I had known at Florence, arrived and fell violently in love with Madame Fleury, who liked his personal appearance. Unfortunately she already had a train of adorers, including the Marquis de St. Phalles and a poet whose name escapes me. These were much annoyed by the strange English people who barged in and whom Madame Fleury welcomed with passionate enthusiasm, neglecting her other guests. At the first supper, in the restaurant outside the theatre at Bayreuth, I was sitting next Bébé [Fleury] when George Causton, an old acquaintance, was sitting at another table. When he saw me he rushed to our table, knelt down beside it, and engaged me in a long conversation. I, of course, introduced him to Bébé, with whom he fell in love. At yet another table Hermann and Aloys turned up. Bébé had been in love with Hermann four months before and was not quite over it, so there we were, with these complicated tragicomedies seething round the harmless Piggie [Arthur] and me.

"Of my first *Parsifal* it is impossible to speak. I was so overwhelmed that when I came out from the first act I could not have said who or where I was. But *Parsifal* is a play that can only be seen at Bayreuth; anywhere else the mood is wrong, it must be a great religious ceremony or else it is nothing.

"This is what I wrote to my mother:

We saw *Parsifal* yesterday, I cannot say anything about it, as there is nothing more to be said. But I think if one were ten times an atheist, it would make one believe in God. It is a great thing to have seen the best in the world.

Madame Fleury is here, though not in the same house. She is very wonderful and has *ravissantes toilettes*. George Causton is here also. I have introduced them to each other, and when she gets over being shocked at his extraordinary manners, I think they will be good friends.

I am sorry I didn't come here five or six years ago. There are quantities of idiots who pass irrelevant remarks and spend the time in the *entractes* cavilling over little scenic details. But even they daren't move during the music. I hope to be taken to see Madame Wagner tomorrow, but don't know if it can be managed. [It was.]

"It was wonderful being there with Hermann and Aloys. They knew Bayreuth and everything about it so intimately that they were able to show me things which nobody else could. It was the richest experience of my life, second only to my time in India as a child. And I am glad to say that after I married, my husband and I went often; he was *the* perfect companion at Bayreuth.

"I owe a great deal to Bébé Fleury. She was the first person to give me any inkling of how beautiful clothes might be. Clothes, at the time I write of, were, especially in England, fussy and ugly, and Bébé, who had a lovely figure, had her clothes cut so that they did not detract from her beauty. To watch her put flowers in a vase taught one the art of arranging flowers. She had no real means of expression; her writing was poor, though her novel *A Quoi Bon* (published in 1892 under the pseudonym of "Ossit") had a certain *succès d'estime*. Her paintings were also not distinguished, but she was an intense personality and influenced all her friends. I couldn't understand why Hermann was not in love with her, as she with him. But I suppose in Paris he had known many women of her type. Most men fell before her and became her devoted slaves. She was generous and never the least catty, and I was grateful for her friendship. We quarrelled when she insisted on knowing my people—for Bébé was not for families.

"We had an enchanting time at Bayreuth. And when I was not with Hermann, I was observing with amusement the dramas that were being played around me. In the end Bébé was becoming difficult about George Causton, constantly asking me if he was in love with me. At last, in despair, I asked Hermann's advice, which was 'My dear, you can do nothing but bolt'; and I told Arthur we must go directly after the last performance for which we had tickets. Hermann helped us, and we went off to Nuremberg that night, arriving very late.

"Next morning, before my coffee was brought, an agitated waiter came up and told me that a very odd Englishman with wild hair was enquiring for me downstairs. My heart sank, for I knew it was George Causton. How he had tracked us down I do not know, but there he was and with us he remained, unable to pack, shrieking for Arthur and me at all moments. But he *was* a most interesting companion.

"We did not take a house for the season of 1893; when we wanted a night or two in town, we went up from York House to comfortable lodgings in Albemarle Street. That summer I first met Mike Stannard, whose people and mine knew each other well. He came to lunch at York House; and we went on the river and came back intimate friends. Except for Hermann, his was the greatest friendship of my life with anyone my own age. He was like someone out of the *Morte d'Arthur*, a romantic of romantics, but also the *moyen homme sensuel*, clever, amusing, good at all games, a born gambler and always infatuated about some woman.

"I went down to Ripon to his people and adored Lady Stannard straightaway. Soon Mike and I couldn't be parted, he wrote to me every day, sometimes twice, and spent with me every moment he could get away from his regiment. But we neither of us had a cent and knew that we couldn't marry. We had that out early in the proceedings. 'But that,' as Mike said firmly, 'doesn't prevent my caring for you more than for anyone else in the world.'

"After this visit I wrote in my diary: 'He is a real *trouvaille*, charming, sympathetic, clever with all the qualities of an Englishman and none of the defects. I would prefer a second-rate foreigner to a second-rate Englishman; one does not so keenly realize the vulgarities of another nation, and the foreigner would certainly have more sense of humour. I go home tomorrow, and am glad to have stayed here. They are dear people, and Lady Stannard is just the sort of woman I want to be when I'm forty—motherly, kind, absolutely simple, and yet able to talk well if she wants to.'

"I had a large number of regular correspondents, Marie von

Bunsen, Loulou Radziwill (later Princess Blücher), George Harris, Ernest Bonus, Mabel Cartwright and Gabrielle Borthwick, who all wrote letters which would have been worth keeping, and I am sorry now that I destroyed so many. But I kept this from Mike:

A steady course of Balzac, says your friend Oscar Wilde, reduces our living friends to shadows, and our acquaintances to the shadows of shades. This is a statement for the truth of which I can vouch. I have lately finished *Le Père Goriot* for the second time, and I feel quite dazed still, and convinced I'm moving in a sham world: to keep up the delusion I've embarked on 'Une ténébreuse affaire' which promises well. Have you read any of Maeterlinck's plays, you minute devourer of literature?

Coming in, I ran into Aubrey Beardsley of *Yellow Book* fame, who had been taken in by a friend of mine. He is a weird-looking creature whom she has the sense to dislike. What is interesting is that his drawings are quite genuine, and not mere affectation of style to suit the morbid taste of the day. It's very odd that it should be so, I don't know if you've ever looked into his drawings but the abominable sort of oriental depravity mixed with a Hogarth-like kind of substratum of truth is curiously revolting. One can't help being struck by the falseness—the evil of it."

Tiny made several pleasant visits during August. In those days visits were longer. One settled and became part of the household, accepted its rules and regulations, and did not assert one's own individuality. In houses where no one smoked, one did not smoke; in houses where Mrs. Grundy was an honored guest, one did not air one's views about such writers as Guy de Maupassant or Baudelaire. "In fact, as my father put it," Tiny noted, "one 'kept one's beasts in separate cages.'

"It was sometimes difficult, for I never liked telling lies. One day at lunch with Lady Reay, they were discussing the latest scandalous novel, called *All That Was Possible*. Arthur Milner turned to me and asked, 'Have you read it, Miss Grant Duff?'

Lady Bantry on the opposite side of the table interrupted in shocked disapproval, 'I should *hope* not,' and all eyes turned to me. I summoned my courage and said casually, 'It's the book about a South American Republic, isn't it?' There was a general sigh of relief. Lady Reay said hastily, "No, no, it's about something *quite* different,' so I was saved.

"I went again to the Blumenthals' at their chalet at Vevey that summer and was as happy as before. There were constant changes of guests, but my favorite was an old Monsieur de Gautard and his son, who lived at Vevey in a delightful house, full of fine Swiss furniture. Monsieur de Gautard told me a great deal about the Switzerland of his youth, including a fearful description of the last public execution, at which not only was he himself present, but there were in the crowd numerous women and children."

This from Tiny's diary at the Blumenthals' chalet:

"Went for a long walk—the sunset was wonderful. This place makes me sick at heart in spite of the beauty, it is so like Ootacamund. It is horrible to be hurt, still, like that. After all these years, a scent or a puff of wind will make me see it all again, and bring the tears to my eyes. I wonder, shall I ever love any man, woman, or child as I loved Ootacamund? Hardly. Never mind, I will go, as I have always determined, out there the moment I can—for good! And leave all the rest. Oh, for £500 a year! Say my life is to last fifty—I would sell fifteen years of it for £500 a year."

X

Engagement and Marriage

On May 28, 1894, the fiftieth anniversary of Mountstuart's first "start for the Continent," Tiny's father and mother went, via Milan and Venice, to Greece. Mountstuart was on a government mission, with two other delegates. He was, as usual, most reticent in his diary about what he did, making, as he put it, "the very slightest reference to it which is in any way possible," while listing every single plant he met. Meanwhile, Tiny was left in charge of York House and her two small sisters. "It was," she wrote, "an extraordinarily happy time. Miss Ihlefeld, the children, and I were the best of friends. Mike Stannard came down three or four days a week and we spent lazy days on the river, sometimes with the children and Fräulein and sometimes alone. We rode together, read in the garden, or played tennis. And fell more and more in love—yet knew it couldn't come to anything; and there were spells of misery when we were determined to be together and talked about going off to the colonies. But love in a cottage was not for us, though we cared intensely and were so happy together; we both hated the thought that such a life might spoil our enchantment. And so the summer passed—terribly happily and terribly miserably. Then my father and mother came back from Athens with Dot and we took up life as usual.

"In September Dr. Baldwin came to stay and regaled us with stories about a clinic he had had in the Apennines. One day a man came to him with all the symptoms of having been bewitched—as described in Burton's *Anatomy of Melancholy*. He told how he had fallen foul of some old woman and how she had cast a spell on him. 'She takes my food' he said, 'she takes my sleep.' And in truth the man was emaciated, exhausted, and appeared to be dying. Dr. Baldwin talked with the old woman, and promised her that if she would remove the curse he would alleviate her rheumatism. So she took a bit of cord tied in a circle, muttered some words over it, and gave it to Dr. Baldwin for the sufferer to sleep with under his pillow. He did so, and appeared at once to revive and, aided by diet and medicine, completely recovered.

"Colonel Leigh Hunt, a grandson of the poet, came to lunch one day and told us that the peasants near Viareggio say that they sometimes see the ghost of Shelley wandering along the shore looking out to sea.

"We moved back into London to Prince's Gate in December and began giving small dances. It was great fun having Dot out. She was much prettier than I, but we were so different it didn't really matter. We both had heaps of men who liked us, and our girl friends were different, for I was six years older than Dot.

"On the eleventh of December in bitter cold weather, I was due to dine with some people called Tremaine, whom I did not particularly like, and I didn't want to go. I asked Dot to take my place, but she was dining elsewhere, so, much against the grain, and in a bad temper, I dressed and arrived twenty minutes late. The dinner had already begun when I arrived. I slipped into the only vacant place; a man I knew called Cobb was on my left, and a tall, fair stranger on my right. I talked to Mr. Cobb until my neighbour turned. After dinner we all went on to a theatre, where I found myself next the same man and discovered that his name was Jackson and that he had been at Balliol.

"When I got home, I went upstairs and found Dot already in bed and asleep. I woke her up and said, 'I have met the man I am going to marry.' She, very cross and sleepy, said, 'What's his name?' 'Jackson,' I said. 'Damn Mr. Jackson,' she snapped. 'Go to bed!'

"He told me later that he went home and told his mother the same thing, but he had said, 'I must go and call on Mrs. Tremaine on Sunday and find out who she is, for I did not catch her name.'

"The next morning when I came down to breakfast, I said to Father as I was helping myself to eggs and bacon, 'Father, if it is any comfort to you, I have done fluctuating, I have met the man I am going to marry.' Father, very bored, asked his name and woke up in the most excited way when I said he had been at Balliol. He told me that some years ago, when he was staying with the Master, he fell into conversation with a man who was quite young. The butler later told him that the young man was Mr. Fritz Jackson of Balliol. Father said that even then young Mr. Jackson impressed him as one of the most brilliant people he had ever come across."

Frederick Huth Jackson (always called Fritz) came from a background much different from Tiny's. Whereas she was landed gentry and British on both sides, Fritz's grandfather William Jackson had left his father's farm in Cheshire during the industrial revolution and had gone to work in Liverpool, where he rose in the world. William went into coal, into shipping, into real estate, and prospered. He became a Liberal Member of Parliament and briefly was in one of Gladstone's Ministries (Education). He was made a baronet. He married a Welsh girl called Hughues and through her came into Guern Castle in Flintshire. His eldest son succeeded to the title; his youngest son, Thomas, inherited the simple square house William had built around 1820, simply called the Manor House, Birkenhead. Thomas had been rejected by every insurance company when a young man, as out of some sixteen siblings only his elder brother, one sister, and he remained; all the others died of tuberculosis. Thomas lived to be ninety-nine and used to chuckle at how much he had lost the insurance company.

Thomas married Hermine Meinertzhagen, whose family had left Bremen in 1826. They came from a village called Meinertzhagen, and stemmed from Tilman Meinertzhagen, whose death in Cologne is recorded in 1473. He left a will and was a man of substance. Many of his successors were mayors of Bremen, and named Daniel. The present (1970) Daniel Meinertzhagen, a director of the Bank of England, is the fourteenth in direct line. Hermine Meinerzthagen's mother was a Huth, whose father had fled from Hamburg when the French came there under Napoleon. Frederick Huth and Company had been established as a banking house in Hamburg in the early eighteenth century. In 1808, when Napoleon invaded Spain, the then Frederick Huth was a young man in the firm's Madrid branch. He was personally so highly regarded that the Spanish royal family, before fleeing, confided their jewels to him. He took them, and the girl he was courting, Maria Teresa Mayfren, and fled home to Hamburg. But "Boney" soon followed. Frederick fled again, with bride and jewels, to London, where he opened a branch of Frederick Huth and Company at 12 Tottenhouse Yard, on the security of the Spanish crown jewels. After Waterloo, he returned the jewels intact, with interest on the security they had afforded him. As a result, his firm was invited to the Spanish possessions in Latin America.

In 1810 Frederick, accompanied by his Spanish wife, set off in a chartered ship for Chile, with goods on board worth £200,000 sterling, half from England, half from Europe. He was told to trade in Chile and return with £400,000—or else! When he arrived in February at San Antonio, the port of Santiago, everyone was delighted with his wares. But the local would-be purchasers told him they could not pay until the end of June, when the harvest was to be sold and they would have ready money. Young Huth was in a quandary; if he gave credit, he had no security, and everyone might default. On the other hand, if he returned to Europe he could hardly get back to Chile before the end of June, and he had been told to sell his wares. He decided to trust and to sit it out. So for four months he waited, growing ever more anxious. Finally, on the last day of June, when he had determined to kill himself rather than return home empty-handed, he saw, coming over the hills, a seemingly endless procession of mules, heavily laden. The Indians were returning with the gold to pay him. Not one had defaulted, and young Huth, having got his £400,000, came home. So pleased were the English and European merchants who had entrusted him with their goods that thereafter they used Frederick Huth and Company's good offices all over Latin America. And the South Americans were no less pleased at having been trusted.

The company, having established branches all over South America, stayed on when the young republics threw off the Spanish yoke. It flourished until after World War II in England, North America, and some twenty Latin American countries. Frederick's younger brother Henry was a collector of pictures, of porcelain; above all, of books. The Huth library was world-famous, and when Tiny's and Fritz's daughter Anne was working in Washington in the British Embassy in World War II, she found a Shakespeare first folio in the Folger Library that had been in the Huth library along with many Elizabethan first editions.

Fritz, like Tiny, was one of eight children (two others had died in infancy). He was the eldest of five boys and three girls. He was musical, and at sixteen, while still at Harrow, trained a Welsh choir from around Guern and took them to the Crystal Palace, where they won the top gold medal. Fritz himself won music prizes at Harrow for singing and composition, and also played the piano. At Balliol he helped found the Balliol Musical Society, which still organizes Sunday-evening concerts. He was devoted to his mother, who, with her European background, was civilized, musical, and sensitive. His father, two generations from the plow, was almost illiterate and a selfish Victorian male, inconsiderate to his wife, uninterested in his children. Fritz left home at twenty-one, after getting his degree at Balliol, and went into

Frederick Huth and Company in London. He never accepted a penny from his father thereafter, though they always remained on good terms.

Having decided, in that first moment of meeting Fritz Jackson, that this would not again be, as with Mike Stannard, just a "love affair"—as such fallings in love were then called—but that she would marry him, Tiny prepared her strategy. "I went down to Ightham after Christmas," she wrote. "George Harris and Hubert Hamilton and Mike Stannard were all asked as friends of mine, and we went to a lot of balls. I told Mike that I felt I had to marry that year. My sister was out, and it is a great drawback for a girl to have an older sister who, in some ways, attracts more attention. I was in a cleft stick, and at the same time I felt from the very first moment that Fritz Jackson was the only man I had met who could possibly hold me. He was immensely attractive, both physically and mentally, and he also showed a very non-English tenderness, which came no doubt from his German mother. I am sure Englishmen generally are good husbands, but to be called 'old girl' and to be dragged off to play golf or to hunt or whatever it may be, when one was not feeling in the mood for it, because one's husband wished it—these things would not have suited me. It doesn't matter where the wife is prepared to give up her individuality, but it doesn't always do.

"At Ightham, Mike and I said good-by. He was terribly unhappy, but saw that we were right, and knew just as well as I did that marriage for him would be a tragedy. We went to the loveliest ball at Knole—the house with 362 rooms, 12 courtyards and 7 staircases about which later Virginia Woolf was to write *Orlando*. All the women had powdered hair and the men were in uniform or facings. When it was over, we parted in the old chapel as we went up to bed, and later he wrote me the following letter:

> I have come home—why, I wonder, with the instinct of a hunted beast—hurt to death, seeking to die alone, away from its kind—and at home: and how much worse off. I know I shall not die, that nothing will happen—that though life is

changed to me, all will go on as before: the frost will go on, and the trains will go on, and on Sunday I shall take a party to church. There will be no difference outwardly, though I seem to be a different person from the creature who wore my name and semblance last week. I have called to the mountains to fall upon me and the high hills to cover me, but who cares?

Darling, I know that Time, the great consoler, will intervene. When you stood on the stairs in the rambling house with the candle in your hand, and your dear, dear hair falling round your face and shoulders, I wanted to come to you and kneel and kiss your feet in pure worship. I am glad now you went away: had you let me come I should have worshipped, but besides that I love you humanly, passionately, with a man's passion, strong as death, strong as the faith of a mediaeval saint, stronger at times almost than the devotion, the almost ecstatic purely spiritual Love I felt for you at that moment.

Now we have got to a double road, and each leads into a bank of fog: we have turned off on separate paths, as far as we can see they do not meet again, but we know nothing. We have faced that fact, and we've said farewell. It's not been easy, but it's been done.

And now, darling, I've written much to little purpose. I've been setting in order, and reading your letters, and I feel that I must say Goodbye. The last time I read them was on Leith Hill the day I went for a long, lone ride, years and years ago. The letters, the picture, a photo, two books, and a few flowers and a small, small shoe, they're all I have of you, almost all I'm ever to have."

A little later Lady Malmesbury asked Tiny down to Bournemouth and, without consulting her, asked Mike too. She told her she had done this and asked, "Is there anyone else you would like?" Tiny answered, "Yes, Fritz Jackson."

Tiny commented: "We went through it all again, Mike and I, and I was almost desperate with the strain of the whole thing. Fritz came down every Sunday and brought his sister Evie, a charming, good-looking girl. The third Sunday he proposed, and I accepted him. I said, 'You know, you mustn't think you are marrying a sheet of blank paper, I've been engaged two or three times and had a great many love affairs.' 'My dear child,' he replied, 'I am marrying your future, not your past. I have probably had a good many love affairs too, and we can both tell each other about them later on, if we want to.' That has always seemed to me the sanest way of looking at marriage."

When Anne was a girl, Tiny told her that Fritz had had, between Oxford and his marriage, one mistress (he was thirty-two to Tiny's twenty-four when they married). Tiny also said that once she was walking alone in London and noticed a woman staring into a flower shop whom Tiny for a moment mistook for Fritz's sister Winifred. The woman observed Tiny closely. When Fritz died, Tiny received a most beautiful wreath with no indication of the donor, and wondered. . . .

Commenting on her engagement, Tiny added: "Another thing I have felt all my life is that marriage is 'for keeps' and that the question of 'being in love,' save that of physical attraction, is not very germane to the matter. I have known a few, but very few, marriages in which the man and woman fell desperately in love at first sight, and were in love all their lives. But I think the old gentleman who said, 'My dear, it is the ladies men do not marry who are canonized—not the ones they do,' was right. The fact is that married life is to most men and women a bit of a strain, and it takes good temper, sense, and tact to make it prosper.

"And my own marriage was an unqualified success. We were supremely happy, and were devoted lovers as well as devoted friends.

"About a week after my engagement, my father, who knew me very well, was lunching with Lady Grosvenor. There was a large party and father was heard to say, to the amusement of the table, 'Yes, Lady Grosvenor, by some immense bit of luck, Tiny has become engaged to the only man I ever saw with whom she would stay for more than a fortnight.'

"My engagement was received with great enthusiasm by my family; my small sisters exclaiming together, 'Thank God, then *one* of us won't be an old maid!'

"A couple of Sundays afterwards, when we went to church to have our banns called, Iseult, who was a child from whom no secrets were hid, said, 'I knew Tiny was terribly frightened, for she swanked more than usual,' which was true. My father, I think, liked my husband more than he had ever liked any young man and they became very, very great friends. Mother liked him too—in fact all my family were pleased.

"Two days after the engagement Fritz's mother came down to London and from the moment I saw her I realized what friends we would be. She was a remarkable woman, extraordinarily able and a good talker and extremely musical. She had the best kind of German culture, but this, in the northern town (Liverpool) into which she had married, had no scope and she was somewhat starved intellectually, though she had a happy family circle. My husband worshipped her and wrote to her every day of his life, both before and after he married; after our marriage she told me what a terrible anguish his engagement had been. She had felt that everything had come to an end, and then, it appeared, he loved her more than ever. Our friendship was a blessed thing.

"We were engaged only six weeks, and though we had to start carefully, there was enough money to get along. I wanted to be married in London, but Mother, quite rightly, I realized, thought it better to have the wedding at York House.

"We were married at St. Mary's Twickenham on the eleventh of May, 1895—a white wedding; all white silk and lilac. The night before, Cosmo Gordon Lang—then, like Cardinal Newman sixty-five years before, Vicar of St. Mary's Oxford, later to be Archbishop of Canterbury—came down to marry us. Old John Farmer, the musician who had written a march for the fairy prince in *Cinderella*, played it at our wedding. We also had 'Praise the Lord, Ye Heavens Adore Him' and the great Chorale of Leuthen. My bridesmaids were Rachel Grant Duff, Edith Bonham (who afterwards married my brother Evie), Amy Gaskell, my sister-in-law Evie Jackson, Margaret Stanley, and my sister Dot.

"I slept late, and when my maid came to tell me it was time to dress, I suddenly lost my nerve and felt I couldn't go through with it. I said to her, 'You must go and say there is not going to be any wedding, I can't possibly marry.' So she, terribly distracted, flew to my friend Clare Macpherson, who was staying, and told her the predicament. Clare came to my bedroom with a huge glass of champagne and, in a tone with which one would speak to a naughty child, said, 'Now, Tiny, drink this down and don't let's have any more nonsense.' She stood over me whilst I dressed and delivered me into Father's hands on time. Fritz and his best man, on the other hand, had been denied access to the church because they had no tickets. Fritz parleyed with the church official and then said, 'There cannot be *any* wedding without me.'

"We walked from York House to the church and there was a solid phalanx of people on either side of our path. I literally do not remember anything about it, except that I heard Charlie Shaw, the boatman, say as I passed, 'I taught her to row, I did.' When I got into the church I saw no one except Lady Stannard, and as I walked up the aisle I suddenly felt the most terrific pull on my train but went on: afterwards I was told that the two small pages, Max Colyer-Fergusson and Hugo Tyrrell, had started happily but young Tyrrell, who was very fat, had fallen down, and clutching my train was dragged up the aisle. He said to his mother, when retrieved, 'I cried, but I did not let go.' In the vestry I remember the Duchess of Albany bearing down upon me and kissing me cordially, and then we went back to the house and all the wearying fatigue of a wedding party."

Mountstuart's account, from his diary, is as follows: "Clara was married this afternoon to Mr. Frederick Huth Jackson, junior partner in the house of Frederick Huth & Company. The six bridesmaids were able, thanks to the absence of anything like a possibility of rain, to form a procession at the door of this house, and walk straight to the church, which was filled with white flowers."

Tiny's account continued: "The thing I minded most was saying goodbye to Dot, for we had been so very close and happy together. And then we were in the carriage going to Guilford, where Fritz's friend Mr. More Molyneux had lent us his adorable little house for the honeymoon.

"The first morning I woke early and lay in bed listening to the birds, when my maid brought in my bath. I was faced with the problem—what was I to do? Fritz was asleep still. Should I have my bath? Or should I wait and send him to his dressing-room? I lay and thought. Then I said to myself, 'You have never had the faintest feeling about nudity, why should you start it now?' As I slipped out of my nightgown I heard Fritz rouse himself. But I got quietly into the bath, and proceeded with my toilet.

"Long afterwards I asked him if he was shocked, and he said very simply, 'No. All I could feel was wonder that there was anything so lovely in the world.' "

A Georgian Child

XI

Savoy

Mama's bedroom was at the top of the tower. One window looked onto the lake, the other into the branches of the great catalpa, beyond which the ground fell away, five hundred feet down to the foot of the hill of Tresserve. On the night Anne was born the nightingales were shouting in the full moonlight. Mama had had a huge mirror hung opposite the catalpa window, so she could look into its reflection. She lay there, not moaning, though the pains were coming regularly now at two-minute intervals. Between then she smiled, for tonight the nightingales could yell unmolested. Last night she had been unable to sleep for their song, and to silence them she had fired her revolver down into the ivy that grew over the tower. Marie-Louise, the housekeeper, had been delighted, for she was always afraid of the "bad lots" who came up through the woods from Aix, "up to no good"; the shot must have scared them good and proper.

Dr. Holman, Mama's Sussex doctor who had come with the family from England, was readying his chloroform and mask. When stage two of Mama's labor was reached, he would do all he could to ease her pain. It was twelve years since she had last felt those corkscrewy pangs, when Konradin was born, yet she recognized them instantly; perhaps she had never really forgotten.

She considered praying; she had, being High, a great devotion to Our Lady, but since Roman Catholics declared according to the new-fangled doctrine of the Immaculate Conception, that Mary had been protected from the consequences of Eve's sin—that is, from the agonies both of birth and of death, Mama decided she would not bother her, since she wouldn't know what one was talking about. As for God, who had fastened such horrors upon women, Mama was certainly not going to give Him the pleasure of hearing her whine or grovel; nothing would please the Eternal Sadist more. So she lay there silent, tangled in her heavy cloud of brown hair.

In the morning there was a small bright-redheaded daughter beside her, and she was content. She had installed a goat, for she had been unable to feed her first two children. And Anne throve on goat's milk in the Savoyard sunshine.

The tower where Anne was born was Saracen, built of clumsy rough-hewn blocks of stone, six feet or more thick. It was square, three stories and three steps tall. The three steps led nowhere. Mama's predecessor, Lady Whalley, an ex-lady-in-waiting to Queen Victoria—the Queen had stayed in the house in 1875—had built an L-shaped annex onto the tower and had put a roof over the three steps. *Her* predecessor had tried to build onto them, but had shortly thereafter committed suicide. Not for nothing was the house called La Maison du Diable. Tradition had it that on that spot a man had been building himself a house. Morning after morning he found his work undone, like Penelope's web. Staying awake one evening, he saw the devil, who offered to build the house in one night, in exchange, of course, for the customary fee. The man agreed to hand over his soul, and the house was built, but when the sun's first rays struck the cross that stood on top of nearby Mont Revard, the devil fled, leaving unfinished the staircase of three steps, and a curse on whoever would complete his diabolic edifice. When the devil came to collect his wages, the owner was taking a siesta. The man's wife quickly stuffed the family black cat through an opening in the kitchen wall (still visible today), and off the devil went.

All rubbish, said Henry James, who came up to visit in a victoria. The Saracens, he explained, being paynim, were naturally considered to be devils by the locals. They had held that part of Savoy for only some seventeen years, around 780. Then they quit in a great hurry, after a Frankish victory, leaving their fortress unfinished. Mama accepted both versions, though she preferred the Satanic to the Saracen, in spite of the fact that the cross, Croix du Nivolet, had not been erected until 1890, in memory of some climbers who fell to their deaths thence.

Only part of the Lac du Bourget—the biggest lake in France, nine miles at its widest, and eleven miles long—was visible from the Maison: the southern end, above which the gentle Mont Colombier rose about the hillock on which, heronlike, perched the castle of Châtillon. At that end, too, was a reedy plain across which ran a canal that joined the lake to the river Rhône. To the south could be seen the Mont du Chat, its even razorback summit spurting up into the rocky peak called the Dent. This south side of the lake used to be Italy, and if a man had murdered in France, he was safe there. The Mont du Chat, which once was the boundary between two countries, is still a country boundary: north is Ain, south is Savoy. Hannibal crossed the Mont with his elephants—have not their bones been found on the pass? Though the skeptics say mastodon, mastodon. Hautecombe, a long white building, glimmers in the lee of the Mont. A Benedictine monastery, it is still Italian, for all the Dukes of Savoy are buried there, even since they became Kings of Italy, and there the monks might still wear their habits even during the days of Combes. Exactly opposite the Maison du Diable is Bourdeaux, a square building, probably also Saracen, from whose terrace pebbles can be dropped a hundred and fifty feet straight down into the lake.

Papa had bought the Maison for Mama because he hated hotels and they both liked to take the Aix waters in summer. Unfortunately, across the road at the end of the drive was the Hôtel de Bois-Lamartine, whose owner, M. Escoffier, was a furious Anglophobe. He detested Lady Whalley, had insulted Queen Victoria when she visited, and when Mama arrived tried to cut off the spring that rose on his land but gushed out in a fountain on the road below the Maison—a fountain used by all. He had reduced it to a trickle, which, as the Maison had town water and three bathrooms, did not worry Mama as much as it did her poorer neighbors. But for their sake Mama went to law in Chambéry and, to everyone's astonishment, won her case: Escoffier was forbidden to tap the spring and indeed was ordered to protect it with a fence and allow access to it by everyone. This was just as well, for the only alternative public water was the Tillet, a malodorous stream that ran along the bottom of Mama's property, full of garbage, tin cans, dead cats, sewage, trash, and typhoid germs. In this women scrubbed their laundry on wooden boards, and when Escoffier halted the spring, they dipped their pails in this and carried the filthy liquid home to drink. The tower of the Maison du Diable and its Victorian annex stood in some eighteen acres of steep land, part garden, part natural woodland. There were walks paths, bamboos and cedars, box hedges and banks of wild strawberries. There was a big fruit and vegetable garden, to which Mama would lead guests, urging them to sample the currants: "The white are sweeter than the red." There were beds of melons; once Anne ate *all* the young ones, thinking they were tiny squash. There was a huge wistaria vine all over the tower, bee-loud in April, and other vines ran along the annex wall, providing white and red grapes to be picked in September if one leaned out of the upper windows. There were balconies in back and front of the annex, with blue hydrangeas in huge tubs, and on the slope of lawn flame-colored begonias and a great tulip tree. Around the back of the house were planted marigolds, zinnias, or asters, according to the season. Here later Anne kept snails, fenced in, but the village boys stole them.

The house was always full of guests, as Aix seemed to be on the way everywhere. The Rome expresses thundered through twice daily; it was only fifty miles from Geneva, and it was also on the direct route south to the Riviera, and, via Perpignan, to Barcelona. Train buffs came who rose at two a.m. (or kept their hosts up), and the problem was never to get guests to come, but rather to persuade them to leave. For the Maison was an enchanted place, and when Anne's turn came to ask friends to stay, friends would bring friends, and they friends of friends. Anne's husband would rise at five to avoid them, go out with easel, canvas, and paints, and return only at night for supper. One male cousin who came in sin left the girl behind; she stayed on and on, finally had to be taken and put forcibly on a train.

One of Anne's earliest memories was the journey to Aix. First came the dull bit from Vitcoria Station to Newhaven or Dover, then the channel—Mama always took the girls down to the ladies' cabin and made everyone lie down; it was smelly and stuffy and Anne longed to be running about on deck. Then the three-hour train trip to Paris, with a lovely restaurant car with *pervenche* blue china plates and huge windows looking out on orchards and cattle. They played a game, counting one for each horse, cow, sheep, or pig. A cat looking out of a window won the game. Paris was crossed in a taxi that still smelled of horses; then came the long night journey. And in the dawn, suddenly, the mountains. For at Culoz it was already getting light, and one could see through the misted windows the great hills crouching around the train: each year finding them still there was a new miracle. Then at last the lake, with its low edging hills curling at the trains passing, like cats that arched and rippled their backs when stroked. As the lake widened, the line of hills on the far edge grew higher, corpse-pale, with pine trees growing like black stubble about their cheeks. Then sunrise over the snow-covered Belledonne Mountains on the other side, beyond Mont Revard. When the train stopped at Aix they would get out—Papa, Mama, the girls, whatever nurse or governess was with them, and sometimes Marie-Louise too, though more often she had gone ahead to open up the Maison. She had been nurse, now was housekeeper, and perhaps—as Konradin told Anne years later—was also more.

Papa, whom in London or Sussex the children saw only in the evening in pale blue or red silk pajamas, playing solitaire while resting in bed before dinner at eight, at Aix appeared every day for lunch, to which generally, when in France, the girls were allowed to come down. Yet he remained a remote and somewhat alarming figure, although the girls took turns pushing him up the Tresserve hill to Mass, which he followed in a blue book called *An Anglican's Guide to High Mass Abroad*. Dr. Holman always accompanied the family to Aix and with his stethoscopes plugged into his ears would listen to Papa's heart. The girls were allowed sometimes to listen too. Papa had injured his heart running with a large suitcase to catch a train, when going to Bayreuth to hear Wagner the year before World War I. "He broke his aorta," Mama would say, shaking her head gravely, and the girls had to be very quiet in the morning, tiptoeing past his bedroom door.

Anne, sent to fetch fresh water from the Tresserve spring, once broke the big carafe. Papa said, "How careless," and she never forgot her terror at his censure. But he liked taking the girls in a hired Daimler up to Chambotte, to the very top, where an old Scotswoman kept a restaurant at which there were real scones for tea. He would take them also on a little cogwheel railway up to the top of Mount Revard, where there were masses of blueberries; the girls would eat so many that when they came down adverse and sarcastic comments would be made about their early-British appearance, with woadlike stains on lips and chins. They would ride donkeys, too, sitting in little basket panniers and followed by a nurse on foot, going to tea with Mama's friends up the Tresserve hill.

When Anne was six months old, Mama weaned her from her goat and took her to England. Arthur Rackham painted Anne naked, holding a seashell to her ear after being carried to England's shore by mermaids and sprites, who welcomed her to golden sands.

XII

Possingworth

Papa had just inherited Possingworth, a neo-Gothic mansion in Sussex, from his great-uncle. A masterpiece by Sir Giles Scott, it had been built in 1874 for Louis Huth, and, as he died childless, it had gone to Papa. Mama thought it frightful.

It was thickly decorated with turrets and gilded iron crowns, gables and stone beasts, both real and heraldic, with angels and mottoes and every imaginable unnecessary ornament. Even the banisters were carved with oak leaves, rabbits, birds; the chimney-pieces were a riot of stucco embellishments; the fireplaces were tiled; the hall windows were all of stained glass; the gardens were full of statues, stone seats, urns, also of box and yew titivated and manicured. With Possingworth, a mile away, went a lovely Elizabethan manor that had belonged to Sir Walter Raleigh, with a formal garden of cypresses and ilexes, and a plain oak staircase whose banisters ended in huge polished balls of darker oak. This house Mama loved, and she retired to it whenever she could find tenants for the mansion. In London, Fritz had bought 64 Rutland Gate, a house opposite that of some of his cousins, where Beatrice Potter had refused Joseph Chamberlain. Fritz at thirty-two was a Director of the Bank of England, and by the time Anne was born he was senior partner in Frederick Huth and Company, Sheriff of

London, and President of the Institute of Bankers. In 1911 he refused a peerage, and later he also refused a baronetcy; he did not believe in hereditary honors. Tiny and Fritz, a year after their marriage, had had a son called Frederick Huth (Fritzl), like his father, and two years later they had a daughter called Konradin, because Tiny loved all things German and because Hermann had called her by that name—a Hohenstaufen Emperor's name—for he said Tiny was a mixture, part royal, part ragamuffin. "Fritzl" the boy was called; he looked Spanish—he was small, had black hair and blue eyes, was musical like his father, and had a fatal fascination, as he grew older, for women, and a no less fatal passion for gambling.

Konradin, when she was four, contracted bovine tuberculosis; Tiny's doctor told her she should not have any more children, as there was such a history of tuberculosis in her husband's family. But when Konradin was twelve the same doctor affirmed her completely cured and told Tiny she could have more children if she cared to. Longing for a second son, Tiny and Fritz promptly had Anne. Disappointed, they had one last try. Another daughter was born in London when Anne was two. She was christened at Waldron, the parish in which Possingworth was, and to celebrate the occasion Fritz gave the tenth-century church a bell, which still bids:

> Clare Annabel Huth
> Ring out the false, ring in the truth.

In the 1238 Close Roll, Poselingwurth was the place where Posell's people lived. For Anne and Clare, Possingworth was home for the four summers of World War I, and for spring and fall too, and Christmas holidays, until they were eleven and nine. The house was the setting for marvelous games. Mama had invented the best one of all, Pigs, which they played together each evening, together with any guests who happened to be staying. The girls would go down to Mama's cedar-paneled boudoir at six p.m., or to the big bay-windowed drawing room, and Pigs began. Each participant made an agreeable sty of chairs. All day the pigs are pleasant creatures looking for acorns or truffles; but at day's end, when the clock strikes eight, every pig must be in its sty, for then the wolf appears. But worse than any wolf, your best friend and boon companion may prove to be a werepig, that is, may turn into a wolf at night and, having obtained access to your safe sty, will devour you. A terrifying game just before bedtime. Guests (always grown-ups; Anne has no recollection of any children invited to stay or play) played with passion. So realistic was Mama that Konradin told her once, "When we play pigs I forget you are my mother and think you are another child." Instantly Fritzl objected. "When we play pigs," he told Mama, "I *know* you are a pig."

The oak staircases and banisters at Possingworth were wonderful for sliding down; in their memory Anne still slides down the banisters at the New York Public Library on 42nd Street. Possingworth had a conservatory filled with huge camellia trees, orange trees, and a tree palm; Anne never saw another tree palm until she drove between Vera Cruz and Oaxaca in Mexico, where there were many. The conservatory smelled of green things growing and, in the winter, of orange blossom. It was next to the picture gallery, which was so long you could roller skate in it. Here Uncle Arthur's books were kept: the unexpurgated *Arabian Nights*, the whole of Scott (Waverley edition), *Daphnis and Chloë*, *Purchas His Pilgrims*. Anne read them all. In fact, the only theft of her life was a big illustrated book on tree and serpent worship which she took to the nursery and, when Uncle Arthur retired and collected his library, conveniently forgot to return.

The estate was a little over two thousand acres and comprised some twenty farms, besides the park, which consisted of landscaped meadows dotted with small groves of carefully chosen and planted trees, under which rhododendron and azalea grew, edged with nettles and thistles. Since there was only one telephone, handcranked, in the mansion, and wartime communications were slow, Anne and Clare would bicycle, walk, or ride to the various families living on the place, with messages glad or sad. Also they would ride almost daily to the keepers' to get rabbits or pheasants, ducks or pigeons, for the larder. They would be sent too with simple medicines to the sick, the convalescent, or new mothers. These journeys, which gave ample time for collecting, also gave time for recollecting.

Collecting was a wartime necessity. "Never come home empty-handed," Mama told the girls, and whether they walked, rode, or bicycled they carried a basket. She showed them how to pick the young nettles. Even, she declared, without gloves, if you grasped the nettle, haply it did not sting you, though in practice this never proved true for the girls. However, where there were nettles there were always dock leaves close by, and dock leaf applied to the sting cured it. This, Mama declared, was an example of the Providence of Nature. (The plucked nettles, cooked, tasted like spinach.) The girls also picked young bracken shoots, before the crooklike tops uncurled. These, boiled, tasted like (slightly furry) asparagus. They picked wild sorrel, of which a delicious soup was made. This, Mama told Mabel the cook, must never be followed by rhubarb, for the combination was a favorite French way of disposing of husbands, quite surely fatal to the partaker and safe for the perpetrator. The girls picked elder blossom, linden flowers, and wild mint for tisanes that one drank at bedtime to induce sleep and pleasant dreams: did not Hans Andersen's Elder-Tree Mother promise these? In the fall there were mushrooms and puffballs to be gathered, and also many kinds of toadstool. There were *Boletus edulis* and *Boletus granulatus* and poor man's beefsteak that grew in huge excrescences on trees, and *chanterelles* that grew deep in the woods and smelled of apricots, and fairy-ring mushrooms that made a circle on the lawn, within which one must never step, lest the fairies come at night and steal one away, and *cèpes* that could be distinguished from the deadly amanitas only by their undersides.

Mama had a book with all possible toadstools pictured in it, which at first she trusted implicitly, matching the specimens the girls brought in with the illustrations. Then she learned the author had died from eating toadstools he had picked. Thereafter she sent samples of each new-found variety up by car to the Natural History Museum in London, where it was identified and returned (often in unrecognizable condition, there being no refrigeration there) before the children were told to collect more of, or carefully avoid, the type of toadstool in question. In all, some eighteen kinds of edible toadstools were found to flourish on the estate and contributed variety to the dull wartime fare. Berries too were gathered: Konradin sucked yewberries, but these Anne and Clare were forbidden even to touch; sheep that ate them died. But Konradin spat out the seeds, and Anne and Clare too watched the birds eat the dangerous berries and learned that the deadly seeds passed through them and out. Hips and haws were collected and made into a sour jam; blackberries and crabapples were made into pies, and rowanberry made a glorious orange-colored jelly, which was eaten with venison. Anne herself made a dark purple concoction from elderberries, proudly named Annie's elderberry stout. Papa was sick all night after only sampling it.

If collection was caused by war shortages, recollection resulted from ethical ambivalence. The girls knew that disobedience was naughty, that picking one's nose was nasty. But life wasn't as simple as that. Sometimes it seemed to Anne that trying to avoid reprobation was as tricky as riding or bicycling down a lane during or after a heavy rainfall, trying to avoid the dripping branches or bushes on either side that soaked one's clothes or blinded one with spray.

Obviously a lie was bad. Anne's first had been that she had cleaned her teeth when she hadn't. Bessie, the nursemaid, a nutbrown girl with gypsy blood, had simply run her finger along Anne's toothbrush, said, "That's a lie, it's dry," and marched her down to the boudoir, where Mama, sitting at her desk doing the weekly books, was stern. And when Anne was sent with a bottle of delectable Parrish's Chemical Food—a flame-colored iron-compound tonic—to the Kenwards', a family of ten who provided nursery and scullery maids galore, and whose father was an undergardener, she drank just a little of it on the way. On her return

Mama said, "Iron stains the teeth. That medicine is therefore to be drunk through a straw. Bessie could see by looking at your mouth that you had been stealing."

"But it was *your* medicine I was taking to the Kenwards," Anne wailed. "I'm not stealing from you when I eat lettuce leaves from your garden, or your gooseberries." Her protest availed her not at all.

Clare, too, was punished for transgressions she did not understand. Anne wrote daily verses which were generally approved when she read them aloud. Clare wrote only two lines:

> "Too late, too late," said the rabbit on the plate,
> Which the gentlemen ate too late,

which caused pleasure, but did not cause anything like the pride that Anne's sentimental or pious verse gave. Then one day Clare suddenly produced a lovely poem, far superior to any of Anne's. It was much admired. But Konradin discovered the same poem in a book called *Mopsa the Fairy* by Jean Ingelow. Clare had merely copied it out. "I didn't take the poem away *from* anyone." Clare argued between tears. "I didn't steal it or even spoil the book by cutting it out with scissors." She gave up writing verse then and there forever.

Both girls suffered, while they accepted, an arbitrary distribution of roles: Clare was the pretty one, so charming and dainty that visitors had been brought to the nursery to see her, aged two, sitting up in her high chair eating her egg; Anne, with her pink eyelashes like those of a middle-white pig, and her untidy red hair—her husband later dubbed her a "permanent haystack"—was cast as the "clever one."

The war's coming had confused the children. Until then, they had spoken no English, though they lived most of the year in London or Sussex. They talked French with Mama and Papa, and with Peronne, Mama's maid, who brushed Mama's long hair morning and evening and once a week, when she had washed Mama's fourteen hog-bristle hairbrushes in ammonia, set them out to dry in the sun on their special stand made by Winchester, the estate carpenter. (Mama never herself once brushed her cloud of long dark hair from the day she married to the day Papa died.) With their beloved nurse Anna, who was Danish, the girls spoke German. Anna was so loved that each evening Anne, praying, thanked God for her. Even when Anna slapped her it was, Anne impudently declared, "only a friendly greeting." German too was what Sybilla von Würm, the governess, spoke. But the day war was declared, teen-aged Konradin, who almost never deigned to visit the nursery wing, climbed up there and, breathless, announced to her sisters, "Now, you horrid little Huns, if I ever hear either of you speak a word of German again, I'll tell the police on you." Four-year-old Anne and two-year-old Clare didn't understand her words, but her tone caused tears.

Next morning, Danish Anna and German Wormy had both vanished: in their stead came Bessie, and Eliza Honeybun, once a housemaid, was promoted to nurse. Bessie slept in a tiny room overlooking the leads, where one could climb for miles among the roofs. There was a tower opposite her windows, where owls lived. They came at night into her room, huge white owls like square-faced angels, bringing offerings of dead mice which they deposited on the end of Bessie's bed.

Eliza wore a stiff collar and highly starched apron; under it, she was cuddly and soft. She had two sisters, Emily and Jane, who worked in London. "We three girls," Eliza would say, even when all three were over eighty. Her young man had died from injuries incurred falling off a ladder; in his memory she would sing long, sad Moody and Sankey hymns, like "When the dewy light was fading" and "Now the laborer's task is o'er." She made the girls work hard. They had to clean their own black-button boots and brush their cloth gaiters—buttoned too, with a buttonhook. Anne had to make her own bed each morning. Clare, not yet liable to this chore, invented a family to help Anne. There were Gongia

Gooda, the Queen of Golden Fircone, and her sister, Sinny. Anne called, "Sinny, Sinny, come and help me make my bed," and each morning Sinny came.

Soon there was lots of outside work as well. The men disappeared from the estate, leaving boys like Freddy, who was fourteen and soon was taking care of twelve cows in the home farm, helped only by Mrs. Heddon, a Land Girl; Una Humble-Crofts, the vicar's redheaded daughter; and Konradin. Old men like Winchester, who had a fringe of snow-white beard and worked in a loft smelling sweetly of wood shavings, stayed too. He made furniture, and when he made a drawer it could be slid into the chest forward and backward; he also made miniature chests for the girls, of rosewood or cedar; he made wheelbarrows and ladders, mended the home-farm yokes and wheels, put new handles on pitchforks and brooms. For Anne and Clare he also made bows of ash or yew, with arrows tipped with hen or turkey feathers. The girls called the arrows for Caliphs—Omar, Ali, Hassan; for Chinese emperors—Hsuan Tsung, Su Tsung, Genghis Khan; for Roman emperors—Justinian, Julian, Valentinian, Valerian. Winchester also made Konradin a little cart for her fierce goat, Ferdinand, to pull. Ferdinand was quiet enough in harness, though careless; he would go over a bump or rut or the road's edge, upset cart and girls, and go on dragging while they, unable to stop him or get out, would be bruised and scratched. Out of harness he was the sleek black devil he looked and once ripped Konradin's thigh nine inches with his horns, after which Mama had the horns' tips cut off.

Konradin taught the girls to help. Clare fed the hens, dry grain in the morning, mash in the evening; Anne learned to milk and by the war's end was milking two cows morning and evening, washing the udders first, stripping them after, and preparing the feed for all twelve cows. It was delicious: linseed cake, of which both girls ate quantities, and sometimes dry bran mixed with molasses. Cattle ate far better than human beings.

When one sow had too big a litter to nurse, the girls brought two piglets home and raised them on bottles.

Anne and Clare learned how to separate; how to make butter, a long, heavy job that involved turning the heavy oak brassbound churn over and over, sometimes for an hour, if the weather was warm; how to make cheese, standing the milk in flat pans with rennet, then pouring off the whey and draining the curds in muslin; how to grade eggs by candling and then preserve them; how to slice turnips and mangel-wurzels and mix them with chaff for winter feed. They were responsible for their ponies too, feeding them oats—sparingly—once a day and fresh hay twice in winter; in summer the ponies were turned out to grass and got barrel-bellied.

Mama taught by example, working as hard as Konradin, as hard as Freddy. She had designed a uniform, trousers of dark green corduroy for winter, light blue cotton for summer, worn tucked into high boots, with a jacket of the same material to the knee. She wore it herself, made her daughters and the land girls wear it, and sent packing a pretty London ex-typist who insisted on feeding the pigs in a pink silk blouse and tight moiré black skirt. Mama worked all day, cutting thistles with a scythe bigger than she, sickling nettles, mowing lawns, trimming the yew and box hedges, weeding lawns and rolling them, besides coping with wounded officers in the mansion and Belgians living in the "policies."

In the house she would take the girls with her to the servants' quarters and there, in each stuffy bedroom with three beds—occupied by kitchen, scullery, and stillroom maid, or by three housemaids (there were twenty-two indoor servants)—would open the windows, pull the covers off the beds. The rooms and the beds smelled horribly. Mama explained, "It's because the girls don't wash. Here they have bathrooms, and I've told Mabel to see that they bathe, though it's hard to get them into good habits. But"—and here she looked sternly at Anne and Clare—"we're no different from them. If we didn't wash, we would smell as horrid."

Eliza, when this was retailed to her, confirmed Mama's view.

"Why, of course. That's why so many ladies use scent. All foreign women do. The French stink something awful, that's why they're so keen on perfume."

Mama insisted on putting a bathroom into every cottage that was built on the estate. She never pretended to like the "lower classes," as she called the poor. She frankly disliked them but wanted to do everything in her power to better their condition. They could change, she realized, only if their environment changed. Konradin objected that "they" would keep coals in the bath. "What if they do?" Mama replied, unruffled. "Their children won't."

She also took tremendous pains to improve the schools in the two villages of which Papa was squire. She chose the schoolmasters and encouraged the children, not only by offering scholarships to the secondary school in Uckfield but by giving prizes for wood carvings, offering models—a Chinese porcelain hippopotamus, a Copenhagen white china pig, a Japanese owl—to the children. She also made Anne and Clare take the lodgekeeper's daughter into their nursery when her mother had pneumonia, and when the child infected them with lice merely commented, "The poor child's not to blame. It wasn't her fault." Likewise, when Alec, a pantry boy, broke his thigh during a romp with the maids on the back stairs, she made Papa pay all his bills. Anne and Clare were puzzled at her double standard for gentle and simple.

One summer when the children got back from the seaside, their piggy bank was found broken open and the contents gone, including a gold half-sovereign each that Grandpapa had given them at Christmas. Mama's only comment was, "It's your own fault. You should not have left the piggy bank out in full view. You must never leave temptation around, lest the lower classes fall into it. In which case we have only ourselves to blame."

Anne, who was logical, early concluded that, by the same token, the last petition in the Lord's Prayer meant that whenever we fell into temptation it was really God's fault.

XIII

Balm in Gilead

Mama was High, Papa Low. Because he was patron of two Sussex livings, the family went alternate Sundays to Waldron, where in a stone Norman church the vicar (the twenty-eighth since the church was consecrated in 1087) read Matins at eleven, and to Cross-in-Hand, named for a halt the Crusaders made before embarking at Newhaven, ten miles away. At Cross-in-Hand, the curate celebrated Sung Eucharist at ten-thirty in a Victorian Gothic nonentity. In winter, they went in the dogcart or the milk float—directly descended, Mama declared, from the chariot in which Boadicea fought the Romans, scythes sticking out of its axles—drawn by Polly, a skittish white mare, who shied at shadows. Polly was "put up" during the service either in the yard of the pub across from the church or in the curate's loosebox. In summer, they would all walk the two miles across the park to Waldron, on a small footpath through the grove of Wellingtonias called the Twelve Apostles because there were thirteen; then across a trefoil-gold meadow, over the bridge that crossed the end of the lake near the boathouse, where baby rabbits could be caught by hand when they panicked (they never lived long in captivity); through open purple-heathered country to the keepers' cottages, where there were horrid corpses—of jays, weasels, the odd hawk

WALDRON

or owl—hung on wires as a warning to their kind; then down a sandy lane to the last half-mile, which was asphalt. Or they drove the four miles to Cross-in-Hand in the open Talbot—pale gray, with red leather upholstery and big brass lamps—driven by Papa, since neither groom nor chauffeur was ever called out on a Sunday.

Religion in any form was sheer delight. Papa read the lessons; he liked only the Old Testament and I Corinthians 13, saying the rest of the New was poor English. And, of course, only in the Authorized Version; no copy of the Revised was allowed to darken either church or Possingworth. Konradin, after she was married lived on the place with Arthur, who managed the estate for Papa. The words of the lessons sent shivers through the little girls: Jezebel thrown down for the dogs to lick up her blood, David lamenting his "brother" Jonathan, Elisha's bears. . . . And they loved the hymns, with their aching longing for the "other country"—Jerusalem the Golden, for dear love of whose very name of Bernard of Morlaix wept (as rendered by John Mason Neale)—with their promises that the tearless life is there, where the fair ocean has on shore, the bright day no time, and the Beatific Vision glads the saints around.

In Scotland, where they had a house at the seaside in Aberdeenshire, they went either to the small "pisky" (Episcopalian) church smelling of varnish, or to the fine kirk, whose dominie was a local antiquarian. Dr. Bruce would annually present them with copies of his privately printed, very long sermons. Mama believed all the branches of Christianity should be venerated and visited, though she did not believe she need, like the Queen, become a Presbyterian in Scotland, and she took Communion only in her own denomination, despising those High Anglicans who when on the Continent went to Communion in Roman churches, to make sure then, at least, of receiving a validly consecrated Host. But in France, when they attended Mass in the little village church at Tresserve, Papa was so attentive that once Monsieur le Curé commented on the "heretic in our midst whose behavior is so edifying he does not wait in the café playing *boules* until the sermon is over, like some we know who shall be nameless."

Mama, with incandescent memories of India, delighted in all forms of *puja*—worship—to whomever they might be directed, recalling with affection the magenta-powder-smeared sacred stones in the Nilgiri hills, with a few flowers, a joss stick, and maybe a small bowl of milk left for the guardian snake. She burned joss sticks in her boudoir in her London house before a large plaster cast of the Apollo Belvedere, and in her bedroom there, beside her bed, kept an altar with crucifix and candles, but on it also were two jeweled daggers. In town the pleasures of prayer included venerating a bronze Buddha, who sat in a corner of the roof garden, surrounded by scarlet geraniums or purple asters, and doing *puja* to a big green Ming vase in the drawing room. Everything was holy because inhabited—whether animal, like the guinea pigs Lenin and Trotsky, or vegetable, like the great camellia trees in the conservatory at Possingworth, or mineral, like the flickering coal fire in the night nursery, whose flames proved Loki, or Agni, present. In the country shrine-building—under a bay tree, to Apollo; in a flowering azalea grove, to Flora; under a cotoneaster where dead birds were buried, to Persephone—was the chief summer activity of the "children's hour," from six to seven, when Anne and Clare, in the saggy plain serge or cotton frocks designed by Mama, without belts, pockets, or other ornament, came down from the nursery to enjoy their mother's company.

They were also allowed down to lunch on special occasions— when a distinguished or celebrated guest was present. On such occasions, instead of going up the hill to Mass, they were sent to accompany the visitors to the summer-only Anglican church at the nearby spa, which was so low as to be almost "chapel." Here Lady Willingdon—later vicereine of India—shocked the girls by powdering her nose in church, and Lord Victor Seymour, a bearded clergyman Anne had mistaken for God at Clare's christening, shocked them no less by kneeling alone and ostentatiously at the "was made man" in the Nicene Creed.

Religion permeated every aspect of Anne's and Clare's lives. When Anne had be give up her bottle—she loved to lie on her back on a blue cushion in front of the day-nursery fire and suck— she was promised she would be given it back in Heaven. Learning that Judas was in Hell, she crept out of her white wooden crib to pray for him and was furious with her governess, Lutheran Sybilla von Würm, for deprecating the behavior of Pontius Pilate. "He did all he could," Anne wailed. "He tried and tried to save Jesus."

The nursery—indeed, the whole house—was the scene of constant religious controversy. Nanny Eliza Honeybun was Low and thought Cromwell right and Charles I wrong. Hair-brushing, one hundred strokes morning and evening, brought redheaded Anne the joys of martyrdom; while Anne argued, Eliza would pull her hair until Anne thought she was growing a halo. Papa next day inquired after her headache.

Clare, younger, prettier, plumper, looked like Luther. "And how is the Reformer?" Henry James asked one day at lunch. He had been brought over from Rye by Violet Hammersley. They had stopped to ask the price of seedling conifers at a local nurseryman's. "Conifers! Conifers!" the tipsy gardener had twitted them, poking Henry James suggestively in the ribs. "That's not what's on your mind this noon."

World War I continued, and Belgian refugees had been installed in every available cottage, incurring everyone's dislike—including Mama's—because they invaded the gardens, thinking it their right to walk therein. They also caught all the trout in the lake and hung their laundry not on tidy lines behind their dwellings but spread out on japonica and forsythia bushes and on the grass. "B-Belgians," said Henry James sympathetically. "S-such a b-b-bunchy p-people. You never see them s-singly, like g-grapes." Anne and Clare, who had never before heard a stammerer, thought him wonderful.

For the Belgians, and later for some of the convalescent wounded who filled Possingworth, a priest would be fetched in the Daimler from Mayfield, where there was a Catholic convent and a girls' school attended by the daughter of Read, the Scots head gardener, who came from the Western Isles, to which the Reformation had never penetrated. Read was a tremendous ally, willing to allow Anne and Clare into the apple rooms to sample as many russets, golden pippins, Coxes, Oranges, McIntoshes, or Jonathans as they could eat. He would scrape raw carrots for them and pull down onions from the bundles hanging in the potting shed. Sometimes he would even cut them a few grapes or slip them a surreptitious nectarine or peach. He would let them loose under the strawberry nets, or at the gooseberries, and when it rained would talk in the the hothouses, while cutting freesias or tuberoses for Mama's boudoir, of early printed books. He gave Anne an old German missal with fine woodcuts, some terrifying, of death (a skeleton) coming to clutch the housewife, the child, the soldier. Read's wife was a sickly invalid, ivory-pale, and Anne thought her as inadmissible as most wives—Harold the chauffeur's Annie, for example, who refused to help in the house, or Marmaduke Pickthall's Muriel.

Marmaduke, a clergyman's son turned Moslem, lived on the estate. Muriel had remained his only wife, though Anne and Clare begged Marmaduke to marry them both. "After all, you are allowed four," they claimed. But he explained he had vowed, while a Christian, to "cleave to her only." She shared neither his faith nor his talents—he was a gifted and successful novelist—and seemed a meowing person, not happy in Sussex or later in India, where Marmaduke went to edit the Bombay *Chronicle*.

How much wiser, both Anne and Clare thought, were bachelors like Pink, the butler, who also had refused to marry Anne when, aged four, she had flung fat arms around his knees at lunch and proposed—"Most unsuitable, miss," he had said firmly—and who after Papa's death become a lay brother in an Anglican monastery. Or like Sir Roger Casement, who pushed Anne's pram in Hyde Park and died a martyr. The girls were awakened at six to pray for him while he was being hanged. Mama had done everything to get him shot. "Hanging is not a gentleman's death," she had objected in vain to the Prime Minister. Or like Mr. Yeats, who, though married, did not travel with his wife but with the adoring Lady Gregory. These two came all the way up to the nursery and gave the girls autographed books and told tales of the Tuatha De Danaan, as exciting as the Greek gods. Indeed, was not Aengus of the Birds an Irish Apollo, as Baldur was a Norse one?

Anne and Clare learned to write by copying the names of Greek gods and other mythological figures in Mrs. Robert Bridges' copperplate script: A for Aphrodite, B for Bacchus, C for Calliope, D for Demeter, E for Erinys . . . On winter evenings, by the boudoir fire place—tiled with scenes of Old Testament stories—Mama would read them the legends from Baldwin's *Pantheon*. The girls knitted, a lump of sugar inside every ball of wool to encourage perseverance.

In the hall, sparsely furnished with a Bechstein grand piano and an immense font of pink Carrara marble, the stained-glass windows represented various couples: Jason and Medea, Hector and Andromache, Ulysses and Penelope, Hero and Leander. These called for more stories, and what stories! How much more agreeable were pagan legends about comprehensible beings than the Old Testament stories about that bad-tempered person on Sinai telling people to dash babies to death on stones, and killing the kind-hearted who dared disobey and save one poor baby. He even gave His own son to be killed, or Himself killed Him. Anne, aged six, wrote firmly in her brown velvet-bound, embroidered blank-leaved book, "I hate God but love Jesus Christ." Aged seven, she would ride over to the Manor Farm to argue with the chief shepherd, Brown, while munching winter kale stalks (fodder for the sheep, but poor man's asparagus to her). Brown, Wesleyan, thought nothing mattered since Jesus loves us, this we know. But Anne insisted, "If Christ was God, He was responsible for Calvary—yes-no? He could have avoided being killed, since He was God, but since He didn't, He committed either murder or suicide."

Brown, gentle, weatherbeaten, only replied, "A pity you are not a Wesleyan, miss. We ordain women preachers, and you are sure argumentative. Once you were saved, you'd be the means of saving many."

Or Anne would ride on to the Pond House, where Marmaduke stood at his high desk, writing. She could always disturb him, for he loved talking of God. "How *can* He have created death! I wouldn't even kill Arthur," Anne said. (Her brother-in-law was her current enemy.) "He always makes it easy for us," Marmaduke replied. "And if you didn't have to die, life would have no meaning, just dragging on idefinitely. You must learn the sura that says, 'Say I take refuge in the Lord of the Daybreak, from the evil of His creation.'"

"But I don't," Anne said. "I don't think creation is evil. It's the Creator who is. And He can't prevent my hating Him."

"Oh yes He can, He can take away your reason," Marmaduke said.

"Then I'd say Omar Khayyám's words to Him: 'For all the sin

wherewith the face of man is blackened, man's forgiveness give—
and take!' "

"If your reason were gone, you wouldn't be able to," Marmaduke said, perhaps hopefully.

Anne saw the force of this, but thought a God whose followers
considered Him capable of such enormity even nastier than she
could have imagined.

On the other hand, life was heavenly. Riding, swimming, arguing—these were the three best things. Galloping on one's fat pony
along the mile-long stretch of Hawkhurst Common, the air gorse-
nutty, the bracken man-high at the woods' edge; swimming across
the mile-wide lake, flat on one's back, and staring at the cloud-
scudded pale-blue sky; arguing with Brown, with Clare, with
Eliza—all this suggested an agreeable deity.

It was death was the snag. The string of decomposing corpses at
the keepers', the hundreds of pheasants piled in the pantry after a
big shoot, with rabbits galore, these uncounted, the half-strangu-
lated rabbits caught in snares met with when out riding and
pharisaically passed by, since what could one do? The horrid fascination of watching a keeper's boy putting ferrets down a rabbit's
hole and the terrified furry creature rushing out of its second exit,
to be netted and its neck broken. These were daily reminders that
"death's fingers twine already in thy hair," as Anne and Clare
wrote in their copybooks, graduating from single names to sentences as they became literate. One morning they found ladders
propped against the house, and several gardeners cutting the ivy.
Dozens of tiny naked or near-naked birds, flung unfledged from
their nests in the ivy, were dying on the lawn. Anne tried to persuade the men to stop, but they refused to do so without orders.
Using the outside telephone for the first time, Anne got onto
Mama in London, who halted the clipping until later, when the
baby birds had left their nests. She was less successful in saving the
moles. When out riding, she and Clare would spring and collect all
mole traps they encountered and throw them into the lake.

Alas, Arthur arrived, furious, one morning in the nursery. "I will send you to your father!" he threatened.

"We will send you to our mother," they countered boldly. "She told us to save moles. She hates traps."

"But she has a fur coat made of dozens of Possingworth mole-skins all the same," Arthur said grimly, and it was true.

Yet death, however horrible, held great fascination for the girls. To the fury of their governess, they would often walk to Wal-dron, pretending to be collecting specimens of wildflowers or distinguishing between cirrus and cumulus clouds or identifying trees, until they arrived at the village, when they would dash into the churchyard, hoping for a funeral. It was the words they were after, and the drama—the slow lowering of the coffin into the ground, and the splendid, lugubrious final words of committal: "Earth to earth, ashes to ashes, dust to dust." They loved sad hymns, too: "Brief life is here our portion," and "When the fan of judgment shall winnow from the floor, the chaff into the furnace, that flameth evermore." Songs and stories had to end badly. One favorite, about a girl who jilted her lover, who thereupon went to sea and drowned, ended, "Perhaps I shall see thee and love thee again, when the sea giveth up her dead." Anne and Clare changed "perhaps" to "perchance," as making such a bourgeois happy ending less likely. Every night, prayers said, they arranged themselves with hands folded crosswise on chest, feet crossed like Crusaders, so that were "If I should die before I wake" to become reality, they would appear dignified, at least. Yet it was not death itself but the possibility of "something after death" that intrigued them. They would discuss the stench, the pain, the bitter end. "Bad smell do smell," Anne would tell Clare as they passed the keepers' charnel house. But how, except "through the dark door," could they reach "the sunlit land that recks not, of tempest nor of fight"? They read and acted *Pilgrim's Progress* and George Macdonald's *Lilith*, and Anne wrote to AE, the Irish poet and mystic, to ask how one reached Tir-na-nOg, the faerie country that was the pre-

Christian Celtic paradise. Was it necessary first to die? No, he replied, and wrote long letters describing a technique for getting there by emptying the mind before going to sleep, then gradually opening it to the single thought of that other country—more green, more golden, more flower-filled and rainbow-hued than any here.

The war complicated everything. Dear gardeners disappeared, subsequently to be prayed for. Fritzl donned khaki and, on leave, took them out in the Talbot, Harold driving while Fritzl shot right and left, killing or wounding rabbits and hares that scattered and screamed. Then he was gone, and the girls, listening to the guns across the Channel, would look out the night-nursery window to see Mama walking in the park in the moonlight, a ghostly figure in her white batiste nightgown, followed by the tame black lamb the girls had raised on a bottle after its mother died. Every day, there were casualty lists in the papers. When Lady Gregory came again, she was too sad to visit the nursery; her only son had just been killed in Italy and her nephew had been murdered in his Irish castle by the Sinn Fein. In revenge for such murders, the Black and Tans with their brutality and beastliness smirched England's good name. There was no end to it.

Mama had become a vociferous pacifist, a member of the Independent Labour Party, and Anne and Clare were turned out of Miss Vacani's dancing class in London because of their mother's heinous opinions. There was rationing, and nursery food, always bad, got even worse, for there was a religious feud between kitchen and nursery. Mabel, the cook, was a Plymouth Sister and had won the scullery maids to her stern creed—no dancing, theaters, movies—while Eliza Honeybun and Miss Rigby, the stiff spinster who succeeded poor Wormy, were Church of England. Rabbit stew, rabbit roast, as a treat rabbit mousse—always rabbit. Anne would detail the sufferings the rabbit had endured before it arrived on their plates until Clare cried and Daisy, the new nursemaid, gagged.

In London, at Rutland Gate, there were air raids, and Anne and

Clare, wrapped in blankets, would be carried down from the night nursery to Mama's room, where she would sing the *"Dies Irae"* in English over and over to them, while Papa and any guests would assemble in the basement, to be served light refreshments by Pink. Once the girls were carried out onto the balcony to see a burning Zeppelin, like some huge flaming cigar in the sky. Anne cried because there were people up there, but Miss Rigby said, "Serve 'em right," and Mama sighed and said, "It's their *karma*." In Hyde Park the girls watched boys with pink faces and fair hair lunging with bayonets at sacks of sawdust. Daisy gloated, "They'll be doing that to Germans soon." She was pregnant, and her young man was dead in Flanders, leaving her dishonored and alone.

Religion was more and more unsatisfactory. Canon Humble-Crofts at Waldron prayed, "God bless our brave men, strengthen our armies, bring us victory." But Mama said the German clergymen were saying the same, and Marmaduke was no help, for his Allah was for the Turks, wasn't He? And the Turks were pro-German and were massacring Armenians, and the Greeks—good Christians all—were massacring the Turks. Anne argued with everyone, becoming a frightful bore, as she knew the Gospels almost by heart and dished up pacifist quotations until one of her two godfathers, William Temple Franks, head of the Mint, got furious and said he would never again bother talking to a silly little girl except about suitable subjects like animals. "Then we'll talk about hunting," Anne said. "That's beastly too."

Since the Lord was so unreliable, Anne and Clare became very political. Religion, politics, and literature were the only subjects worth discussing, Mama said, despising those who talked of servants, babies, clothes, gardens, and sex. London was full of politics. Lord Carson was villain for Mama (he was against Irish freedom), hero for Eliza (she disliked the Papist Irish and the dissenting Welsh equally; both were dark, dirty folk). Asquith was nicknamed Wait-and-See, and Lloyd George (Welsh) was tricky; Eliza's farmer cousin had not called his best boar George, lest it disparage the King, or Lloyd, lest it insult the pig. Mama sewed curtains for the 1917 Club, and Anne and Clare put in the curtain rings; they accompanied Mama to the mass rally at the Albert Hall to celebrate the Russian Revolution. Anne wore bright green, for the Sinn Fein; Clare, red. They both canvassed the neighboring mews for the Labour candidate, running up and down slummy stairs shouting, "Vote, vote, vote for Mrs. Despard! Throw the old Tory down the drain!" Anne invited Ramsay MacDonald to her seventh birthday party, and he came, though Pink refused to pass him the potatoes, saying he would not serve a traitor to His Majesty. When Bertrand Russell came for his first meal out of jail—he had been imprisoned as a conscientious objector and had gone on a hunger strike, together with Clifford Allen and Noel Buxton—he described to Anne and Clare the horrors of being forcibly fed by a stomach pump. Anne turned to the man on her right, her father's boss, the Governor of the Bank of England, and politely asked if he too had just come out of jail. But no courage, even Bertrand Russell's, could make the war stop, and Mama said nothing would so long as the munitions-makers got their dividends and had to give just their sons, not their money.

So it seemed only literature was left. Words alone could cope. Even when one only wanted, like Job, to curse God and die, it helped to call Him by the great names: God of God, Light of Light, Very God of Very God. Anne learned chunks of poetry— the whole of Omar Khayyám, the whole of Gray's "Elegy"— and would recite them entire to embarrassed or bored guests or to the captive nursery audience of Clare and Eliza. She would climb the rungs of stile or ladder and preach fire and brimstone, directed *at* God, not purporting to come from Him, only reproving Clare when she wandered away to pick cowslips or kingcups. "Incarnate" was a favorite word, "incarnate by the Holy Ghost" a favorite phrase. Single words had power, too: P words, "pilgrim," "porphyry," "prophetic," "peripheral," "plenitude"; and short words, like "vain": "To my true king I offered free from stain, courage and faith, vain faith and courage vain."

On her eighth birthday, Anne woke to a perfect June day. She ran to the window. If she could see the sea, fourteen miles away, through a gap in the blue downs, she would have a happy year. She did not see the sea, but at the foot of an oak tree, shining red-gold in the slanted light, lay what must be the golden key at the rainbow's end. She ran downstairs into the garden, past the border full of asphodel and lupins, then across the meadow. The trefoil had all been eaten by the cattle, and the ground was bumpy from drought and dirty with droppings. When she reached the oak, instead of the golden key she found an ocher drainpipe upended against the tree trunk, burnished by the sun. She walked slowly back to clean out the guinea pigs (her morning chore) and put a clean copy of the *Liberator* on their floor. Then she went to her desk and opened her brown velvet book. No lessons today, in honor of her birthday. She read what she had written when Sir Roger was hanged:

> Ah, Sir Roger Kasment
> Dauntless knight of God
> Thou with glorious courage
> Tramped o'er death's light sod.

"Sod" was not accurate; Daisy had explained the mechanism of the trapdoor. Still, writing things down helped. Though the gods were powerless or odious—they either didn't or couldn't stop people making war, and anyway human beings murdered each other and had to die—though politics brought good men to jail, and though the golden key had turned out to be only a sunlit drainpipe, so long as the words came, everything was bearable. She wrote:

> All was calm
> The very trees sang a psalm
> The pigeon softly cooed
> My riam is done.

Here was Balm in Gilead.

XIV

Chaste in Timbuctoo

Mama insisted on the same religious instruction for the farm
and garden children as for her own. She had Daisy and May Kenward, as well as Ruby and Gladys, two of the kitchenmaids, prepared for confirmation with Anne by Cosmo Gordon Lang, then
Archbishop of York (later Archbishop of Canterbury). He had
been at Balliol with Papa, then had digs with him in London. He
married Mama and Papa, Konradin and Arthur, later Anne and
Christopher, Clare and Louis; buried Papa and Mama; and was
the nearest thing to a private chaplain and spiritual director to the
whole family that the Anglican Church allows. Anne loved him
dearly, and he would write her carefully printed letters, with
drawings of himself in his high archbishop's hat and pectoral
cross. At seven, she was the youngest child he had ever prepared
for confirmation, but she was already as tall as the nurserymaids
and scullerymaids. Later, when she became a Labour candidate,
she realized why. She could always tell what part of London she
was in by whether she—five feet six—was taller than the men.
She always was, in the East End, where there were only the poor,
stunted and undernourished and undersized.

After Christopher and Anne were married, they would celebrate their wedding anniversary each year, at Cosmo's invitation,

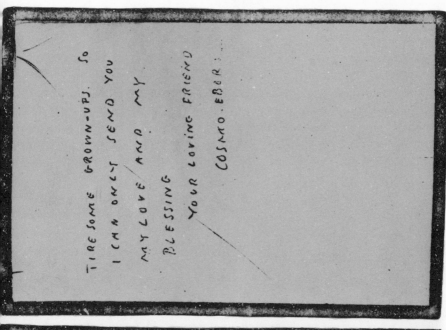

BISHOPTHORPE,
YORK. MY DEAR ANNIE.

MANY THANKS FOR YOUR NICE LETTER AND YOUR PICTURE OF ME I SEND YOU ANOTHER DRAWN BY ME WHICH I HOPE IS AS GOOD A LIKENESS I WISH VERY MUCH THAT I COULD COME AND STAY AGAIN AND SEE YOU.

BUT ALAS! I HAVE VERY LITTLE TIME TO SEE NICE LITTLE GIRLS LIKE YOU. I HAVE TOO MUCH TROUBLE WITH

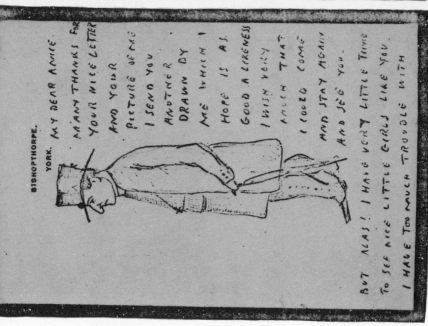

TIRESOME GROWN-UPS. SO I CAN ONLY SEND YOU MY LOVE AND MY BLESSING

YOUR LOVING FRIEND

COSMO EBOR:

by staying overnight in Lambeth Palace, receiving Communion from him in the morning in the chapel (where he also christened their sons), and breakfasting with him after. On an easel in his drawing room stood a superb portrait of Penelope Rich, the girl to whom Sir Philip Sidney wrote the greatest sonnet sequence in English written to a woman. Penelope had tawny gold hair and brown eyes, and her marriage, celebrated at Lambeth by Archbishop Laud after her divorce from Lord Rich, was the only thing of which Laud publicly repented on the scaffold. Yet he had always kept her portrait displayed, as Cosmo did also.

Christopher and Anne, breakfasting with His Grace on the morning of November 12, 1936, learned, by glancing at the American papers spread out on the side table, about the state of the king's liaison with Mrs. Simpson. WILL DAVID WED WALLY? ran the headlines. Like most British not in Court circles, Anne and Christopher had no idea how far things had gone, though Anne's cousin Harry, who was Lord Lieutenant of Monmouthshire, had complained that when the King visited the distressed areas there, he had insisted on sleeping in his train with Mrs. Simpson, instead of staying with Coz Harry as protocol required him to do.

The Archbishop, seeing Anne's and her husband's concern, told them the marriage must and would be stopped. "It would be the end of monarchy in England," he told them. He added that next day editorial silence on the subject would be broken—at his instigation—by a leader (editorial) in the Yorkshire *Post* which would alert the country. It did.

For Anne and Clare as children at Possingworth in wartime it was the question of guilt that presented problems. Right and wrong were clear enough. Obviously there were always two alternatives, and by virtue of being a human being one had always a choice between them. What was tricky was the spiral. Why was something for which Anne and Clare got punished all right for Daisy? Were there not other layers and levels always depending on background, income, opportunity, country, education, even health? The guilt in the choice made obviously varied. "Of course," Mama said, smiling, "of course it all depends."

"Depends on what?" Anne asked.

Mama replied, still smiling, " 'The crimes of Clapham chaste in Timbuctoo.' Surely that explains it all, doesn't it?"

It didn't. Not for Anne, or for Clare either.

Armistice Day, November 11, 1918, offered another example of such problems. It had been a wholly glorious day. Konradin and Anne (Clare was in bed with something or other; she was "delicate" and suffered from colitis, among other things) had ridden to every cottage on the place—even as far afield as the Moat Farm in Hellingly, all of six miles—to bring the glad news. Because of the Allied victory, Konradin had let Anne off keeping pennies under her elbows and between her knees and the saddle (if dropped, they came out of her allowance of sixpence a week). Then, as dusk fell, there was a huge bonfire on the terrace outside the mansion. As the flames leapt up, Konradin, the pantry boys, Borecomb the groom, and Harold the chauffeur (the former had TB, the latter had been invalided home from Gallipoli with endemic malaria) produced and threw into the blaze a huge paper effigy of the Kaiser, complete with horsehair black mustache. Mama was horrified but was unable to stop Konradin. Papa, who could have, was still in London.

Mama never had allowed Guy Fawkes celebrations. "It's the torture and death of a live human being you are celebrating," she would tell the girls. "Much better let all Parliaments burn than one human. Anyway, the House of Commons did burn at the turn of the century, and all that happened was that it was rebuilt." She had been a pacifist all through the war, throwing out the Little Willie dolls from each of which a black tongue would pop out when they were hanged, offered by patriotic aunts to Anne and Clare. She wrote to the *Times* objecting to the killing by similar patriots of their pet dachshunds.

Konradin declared (she detested her mother, who accepted it

calmly) that Mama was pro-German only out of an unsatisfied and uncomprehended love for her two male first cousins, Aloys and Hermann Obrist—above all, for Hermann, who survived; Aloys had killed himself before World War I. Whatever the cause, Anne and Clare were brought up on German children's books, German fairy tales, German poetry, and German music. Papa spoke perfect German; traveling round the world as a young man, he had been seconded by the German consul in New Zealand into interpreting for visiting German grandees. Anne and Clare were adults before they realized there was any serious music that wasn't German. Scottish folk songs, English hymns, and French nursery rhymes were all they knew outside of the great corpus of German music; never a word about Scriabin, Rachmaninoff, Fauré, and so forth, did they learn.

Music, to the girls, was a chore. At four Anne had been given a lovely book of Japanese flower paintings as a prize for learning to play a brief Bach chorale, and a great piano teacher had been summoned to listen. He decided she wasn't good enough for him to bother with, and a slew of governesses and countless hours of practicing confirmed his judgment. From four to fourteen Anne practiced daily for never less than an hour; at fourteen she thankfully gave up the piano and briefly studied organ, as her touch was so hard it would bring Papa, ordinarily gentle and courteous, out of his library or study in a rage. As there were several pianos in each house, Anne first ascertained where Papa was before venturing to practice.

Papa shouted no less often at governesses; only one, a Hungarian, had a touch that he approved. She was sexy and, the girls thought, smelled nasty, but she was also cuddly and lively, calling them her *chelas* and herself their *guru*, and acting *Kim* with them and *Hajji Baba*. After she went, Maria Reinshagen came. Her parents, Jewish merchants, had fled Lithuania in 1917 during the Russian Revolution. She proved no more gifted musically than her predecessors, but she was lazy and therefore lasted longer, since she never played herself. She taught the girls a smattering of

Tiny at the age of three on horseback.

A newspaper cartoon of Mountstuart.

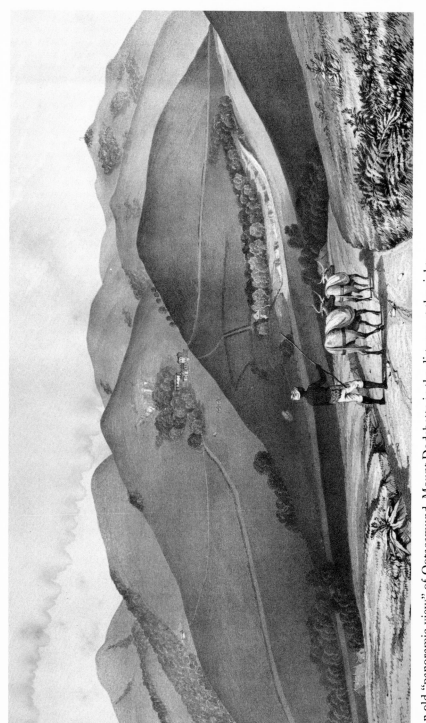

An old "panoramic view" of Ootacamund. Mount Dodabetta in the distance at the right.

Tiny's mother with Adrian (at the age of three) at Knebworth—painting by Arthur Hughes.

Smithills Hall in Lancashire.

Tiny at the age of
ten with her mother.

Mountstuart on his deathbed.

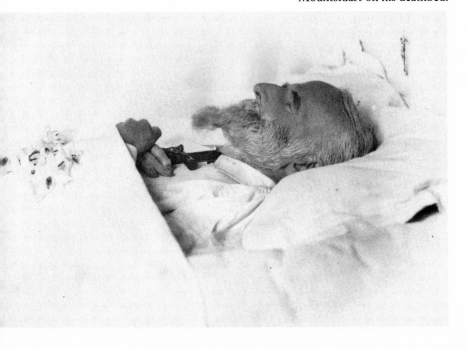

Tiny at the age of twenty.   Adrian.

Frederick Huth Jackson—by John Singer Sargent.

Anne, at the age of six months, delivered to the shores of England,
as pictured by Arthur Rackham.

Sargent's portrait of Tiny.

The Curé at Tresserve.

The Maison.

Anne at the age of three.

Mama with Anne and Clare.

Anne and Mama.

Anne at the time of her first communion.

Possingworth.

Possingworth Lake.

Mama with a snake at Aix.

Clare at the age of ten.

Pauline Palffy.

A postcard sent to Anne
by Gandhi in 1919.

Mahatma Gandhi महात्मा गांधी.

Bertrand Russell.

Anne and Christopher at Aix in the summer of 1930.

Russian and lovely Russian folk songs, but she also added to their moral incertitude. For on her first day at Possingworth, as Pink passed the peas at lunch, she seized the silver dish from his astonished hand and declared, "Mr. Pink, it is not correct for one human being to serve another. It degrades him who serves and him who is served. We are all equal."

Pink, scarlet, begged, "Please to remain seated, miss." Mama, in German, asked her not to embarrass the poor man.

Anne and Clare were used to Mama's socialism; no sooner was the war ended than she became a founding member of the Fellowship of Reconciliation, doing everything she could to stop the Allied blockade. But it never embarrassed the servants. Maria's communism was more exciting and more discombobulating. Everything, Maria explained, belonged to everyone and must be used for the benefit of all. So one day, when Maria had left her small gold watch in the bathroom, Clare put it on and refused to return it. "No," she told first Maria, then Eliza, who was called upon to arbitrate, "Maria tells us private property is wrong. I like the watch. I found it and will keep it."

Led downstairs, struggling and indignant, by Eliza, to Mama's boudoir, Clare explained her case. Mama said it didn't the least matter what Fräulein Reinshagen thought. " 'He [or in this case she] who takes what isn't his'n, when he's cotched is sent to pris'n,' " Mama quoted. "We keep our rules, whatever other people do," she added.

That the beliefs of a grown-up—and Maria, at twenty, was obviously a grown-up—didn't matter was a novel idea. That one had to behave to people according to one's *own* beliefs, not base one's conduct on that of others, was also novel, but less agreeable. Under duress, Clare returned the watch, but neither she nor Anne thought Mama was being either just or fair. Also, they despised Maria for accepting the watch back. "If you were true to your beliefs, Clare should keep it with your blessing," Anne told her.

In spite of this *contretemps*, however, both Anne and Clare became very fond of Maria, for she not only taught them folk

songs but also showed them that right and wrong can be totally
independent of any belief. For Maria believed in nothing, or
rather in no one, in no "power outside ourselves that makes for
righteousness." What made her tick was her own image of what
she wished to be, in the context of a society where everyone was
equally concerned with being and doing the best he could, for his
own sake—not for God's or the neighbors'.

One glorious summer day the girls had been let off lessons and,
having watered their gardens and their pets, decided to ride over
to tea at Konradin's, about two miles away. They saddled their
ponies and crossed the park, the wild hyacinths pools of scented
blue around every oak, the lime trees just beginning to give off
their bee-loud scent, the hedges white with strange-smelling hawthorn. When they arrived, they told May Kenward (promoted
now to be Konradin's parlormaid) that "the aunts have come,"
being very proud of their six-week-old niece. Konradin was up
at the pigsties, May told them, so they tied their ponies and
found Konradin helping the butcher load five pigs onto his trap.
Horrified by the squealing and the sight of terror soon to be pain
and death, they ran away. Konradin found them at the pond, collecting tadpoles in a jam jar. She told them gleefully, "I'm so
pleased. I managed to sell the butcher the tubercular pigs with the
other three."

"Didn't you tell the butcher they were ill?" Anne asked.

"Of course not, silly," Konradin replied. "If he can't spot a
sick pig, it's not my job to teach him. I'm just glad I got the same
price for every pig."

Riding home after a good tea (cucumber sandwiches and a
dripping cake), Clare said she thought they should tell the
butcher. "Better tell Mama," Anne said. Mama said the butcher
would discover when he killed the pigs whether they could be
sold for human consumption or no: it was up to him to decide
whether he would or would not sell the tainted meat. Anne and
Clare were shocked all over again.

When Hitler came into power, Mama's pro-German passion

applauded him. Since Hitler had obtained ninety-nine percent of
the German vote in the 1938 plebiscite, the Germans obviously
wanted him. He was against the infamous Treaty of Versailles,
which Mama had disapproved from the first; ergo, he was not only
what Germans wanted but what Germany needed. She joined the
British Union of Fascists, went to Sir Oswald Mosley's rallies, and
often had him to tea. Anne, who was Labour, used to avoid shaking hands with him when they met, bowing instead.

When World War II broke out, Mama, in her seventies, was
dying of cancer. Clare, whose husband was in the Army, was living with her, going daily to work in an armaments factory. Mama
went on seeing Mosley—and who knows whom else besides?
Clare felt she must inform the local police of Mama's goings-on.
"That's all right," they told her. "We had her name along with
the others. Most of them will be going to jail. Not your ma,
though. We'll not bother her, seeing her condition. We'll leave
her till the Lord sees fit to take her."

Anne, in the United States with two small children, had her own
moral problems that Mamas ethics were not much help in solving.
From 1942 to 1945, having evacuated her two small children to
kind friends in Tuxedo Park, New York, Anne was working in the
British Embassy in Washington, in the Indian Section, where her
boss, Sir Girja Bajpai, was pro-British. Anne was Research Assist-
ant. "Find evidence that Gandhi is in the pay of the Japanese,"
Sir Girja ordered Anne. "We are worried that so many Americans
are anti-British about India."

Anne could find no evidence—there was, of course, none—
and was censured for her inability to provide what was asked.
Later sacked, she was immediately hired by another department
of the embassy, the India Supply Mission, whose head, K. C. Ma-
hindra, was pro-Indian and passionately pro-Gandhi.

Gandhi himself, with whom Anne corresponded as a child—
he began letters "Dear young friend" and put them in small enve-
lopes addressed to "the little girl who loves India" inside larger
letters to Marmaduke—conjured up a small moral problem the

only time she met him. It was during the Imperial Conference in London in 1931, and he was at a party given by Victor and Ruth Gollancz. "I am a vegetarian," Anne told him, "but I eat eggs."

"Ah," he replied, "dear madam, someday you will see the fallacy behind the egg."

When World War II was over, Anne became a United States citizen out of conviction: here was a country that owned no colonies, that did not have territorial ambitions, that had saved Europe and produced the Marshall Plan to feed the vanquished. Then she learned that the Japanese had been putting out peace feelers before the bomb was dropped on Hiroshima. Soon the United States entered Vietnam. She went to Saigon in 1960 and found a full-scale war already going on. In her hotel she heard on the radio that the Vietcong had apologized for killing a French doctor and his two teen-age sons who had gone duck-shooting near the town. "We thought he was American," they explained. "If we'd known he was French we'd never have shot him."

Perhaps, however, the last word on morality is not that the crimes of Clapham are chaste in Timbuctoo (though they undoubtedly are), nor that, as Ernest Hemingway wrote, "morality is what you feel good after" (though this too is true), but that, as the *Brihad Upanishad* (the longest, and traditionally the most important) puts it: "As one acts and behaves, so does one become. He who does good becomes good; he who does evil becomes evil. An individual is made up of desires. As is his desire, so is his will; as is his will, so is his act."

XV

Friends and Relations

"Bless all friends and relations" was the last petition the girls said in their prayers. They approved not only this clear distinction but also the inviolable order: friends must always come first. Friends were people like Pink, the butler, solemn as an undertaker, whom no one had ever seen without his tails, yet who was constitutionally unable to handle his footmen, still less the pantry boys. Of Paul, aged not more than fifteen, he said, "Madam, he frightens me; he goes white with rage." Paul, a gay Savoyard imported from France, polished the drawing-room floor by sitting on a waxed cloth and sliding around, and polished the silver not at all. Of a wartime replacement Pink announced, "Madam, Mr. Heddon is home and is murdering Mrs. Heddon, and I dare not intervene." Mama dared.

When Anne's toy penguin Tojaccus was lost, after Anne and Clare had been visiting another friend, Mr. Saunders, who kept a shop on the lion pavement in the Brompton Road—so-called because eight stone lions stood at intervals on the broadest part— Pink was deeply sympathetic. The girls had been spending their sixpence a week in Mr. Saunders' shop. He sold semiprecious stones such as opal matrix, and chunks of chalcedony and sardius and amethyst, also fossils and blown ostrich eggs and shells. Tojaccus had been dropped on the way home. Next morning, retracing their sad steps, they saw Tojaccus in a lingerie-shop window. Some kind passerby had picked him up and put him there. Pink, informed, immediately telephoned Papa on his own initiative. A board meeting at the Bank of England, discussing the effect on the price of gold of the Russian Revolution, was in progress when Anne's father was interrupted by an urgent telephone call, to hear Pink's sepulchral voice announce, "The bird has been found."

Another friend was Charles Morgan, who wrote a long story for and about Tojaccus. He was then a young midshipman, and his first novel, a searing exposé of conditions aboard a man-of-war, *The Gunroom*—now a collector's item—had just appeared and been suppressed by the Admiralty. Charles and Fritzl were interned together in Holland, where Charles found the material for *The Fountain*, wherein Fritzl figures as Ballater. Fritzl, who had volunteered from Eton as soon as war was declared, had been ninety days on Hill 60 and was one of the few officers to survive. He transferred to the RAF and was shot down over neutral Holland and interned. Charles was taken prisoner of war in Holland and was similarly interned. Fritzl and Charles had met in a most agreeable moated Dutch castle, where they were held. Mama went to visit them, talking such rank socialism aboard the muffled ship on which she crossed the submarine-infested Channel that only the fact of her husband's being a Privy Councillor saved her from instant arrest. Charles helped Anne immensely when she began to write, sending her at one time weekly postcards inscribed "Read Milton *Read Milton* READ MILTON." He often took her to first nights; he was drama critic of the *Times* and his theater reviews were models. Once he took her to a play entitled *The Harlot*, and his comment was, "This, as its title indicates, is a play about a mother. Her only problem is whether to suffer a fate worse than death, or send her son to a school worse than Eton." Charles married a beautiful Welsh novelist, Hilda Vaughan, descended from Henry Vaughan the Silurist. Their daughter married into the nobility: Charles often referred to "my son-in-law, the Marquess of Anglesey."

Another much-loved friend was Sir Frank Swettenham, after whom Port Swettenham is called. Sometime Governor of the Malay Peninsula, he lived alone in a London house full of Chinese monochromes and bronzes, of ceramic Han figures and lush eighteenth-century Chinese faïence. He told Anne many strange stories; one was the truth of the story in Joseph Conrad's *Lord Jim*. The mate's real name was Andrews. He had come out from an Essex rectory and signed up as first mate aboard an old, old ship—the name *Patna* will do—that had peddled jute between Singapore and Dundee. Her owners, a syndicate of half-caste merchants, had insured her heavily for many years, with never any dividend on the insurance; she never as much as ran aground in a fog or collided with a tug in a storm. She had, in fact, been afloat more years than anyone (except the insurance company) liked to count. But she was definitely an antique, and finally the insurance people got sticky about those long three-month journeys, so her owners changed her cargo and her ports of call and signed on a new crew, as the old gang could not stomach the idea of remaining in the East all year round and lugging a lot of fanatical natives instead of nice clean jute. Andrews was glad to get the job; he looked and was young and inexperienced.

Eight hundred passengers came aboard the *Patna* as she rode anchor in Singapore harbor, all poor, all pilgrims Mecca-bound. Most brought their own food—rice or fruit—carried gourds of water, wore every shade of cotton and dirty silk topped with turbans or head veils. They slept all over everything; at night it was impossible to move without stumbling over a soiled heap of rags that resolved itself into a woman sleeping, a clutch of children, or a whining man. One night, for some mysterious reason never ascertained, the whole ship rose, lifted herself bodily, and went over "something awash, say a water-logged wreck." She went over the jump, as Conrad described it, "as easy as a snake crawling over a stick, then checked herself suddenly." Her engines stopped, the forebeak filled with water, and there was a big hole in the waterline. The aged bulkhead might give way at any moment, and the "damn thing would go down like a lump of lead." Andrews was asleep in his bunk. The skipper, the second mate, and all three of the ship's engineers got into one lifeboat and rowed across the still sea by the light of the gibbous moon, leaving Jim and eight hundred passengers to their fate—and two Malays at the wheel.

Andrews shouted curses after the boat, then went down to the engine room with the two Malays and shored up the bulkhead. It took till dawn. At daybreak Andrews, exhausted, went up and wearily told the pilgrims that there was no possibility of fitting eight hundred people into the six remaining lifeboats. The two Malays translated his speech, and those that knew told those who had not heard. The passengers did not stampede or rush the lifeboats or attack Andrews. Instead every man, woman, and child went down to the hold, where their pitiful belongings were stacked. Andrews ran up the ensign, Union down, at the main gaff, then watched the eight hundred reappear, in twos and threes. Gone were their colored head veils and bright cottons, their shoddy silks; everyone was now clad only in a shroud, from the oldest gaffer to the tiniest baby. They had all brought their cere-cloths with them, in case their felicity should be to die on the way to Mecca; now the moment had come, they would meet death, already ghostly and unafraid in the pale dawn, wearing their winding sheets. For five hours they waited patiently on the scorching deck for the ship to sink. For five hours Andrews scanned the horizon in vain for help. Not one of the eight hundred made any attempt to escape or uttered any complaint. They accepted death, as they had accepted life.

At noon Andrews saw a steamer and signaled her, a Blue Funnel passenger ship, bound for Australia. She put out a boat, and when she came up, her crew, after satisfying themselves there was no plague on board, signaled for men, and by nightfall the damage was repaired, the engines were started, and Andrews was loaned five white officers to help him take the *Patna* on to Aden, while the Blue Funnel's captain undertook to report the vessel safe at Singapore. Meanwhile the deserting crew had been picked up by a Marseilles-bound ship and deposited at Aden, where they reported the *Patna* sunk with all passengers, the native crew and one white officer. They wired the ship's owners, who lost no time informing the insurance company, and then returned to Singapore as passengers. The sensation in Aden when the *Patna* arrived, and the inquiry, have been magnificently described by Conrad. Andrews, besides being complimented by the court, was offered a good job on the Blue Funnel line, which he accepted.

Another strange story Sir Frank Swettenham told Anne was that of the death of the last Duc de la Trémoille. Anne wrote it into her first novel, *Come to Dust*, and years later, in Chicago, met the lady in the case. Sir Frank gave Anne a Chinese scroll with the story of Monkey. Decades later, she found the same story made into a superb color film in mainland China, with haunting traditional melodies which were played constantly on the radio in all trains, including the Trans-Siberian.

Yet another friend was Henry Yates Thompson, who had been Gladstone's private secretary. Anne inherited him from her dead grandfather Mountstuart, and she dubbed him her "beaver," for at that time in London there was a game played by all the young: it took two players; on sighting a bearded man, the first one to cry loudly, "Beaver," got a score—15, 30, 40, and so on, as in tennis. A red beaver or a female beaver won the game outright. Bearded persons often objected strongly, and Anne and Clare were occasionally reprimanded or chased. For it was essential to say the word loudly enough for the beaver to hear, and thus become aware of one's score. Luckily Mr. Thompson enjoyed being Anne's beaver, and delighted in showing Anne his treasures. At his house, 19 Portman Square—now belonging to the Courtauld Institute—he had Le Beau Dunois's missal, which Saint Joan may have used, and an early illuminated Dante, with the 33rd canto of the *Paradiso* illustrated by a painting of a pure white rose whose petals opened against blue skies, and many, many fabulous books, most of which he left to the Fitzwilliam Museum Library in Cambridge. He also had several Jean Fouquet landscapes, in which the azure medieval sky and green fields and cobalt hills seemed to Anne to recall the Celestial Country. Henry Yates Thompson gave Anne a thirteenth-century Book of Hours for her twenty-first birthday, which she sold when she came to the United States penniless (since she could bring out no sterling), with two small children, during the bombing of London. In his will he left her a little Elzevir Virgil, which she gave to Bertrand Russell's eldest son, then a young Air Force officer in Washington in World War II, who had confessed to Anne how much he loved the classics, because his father would not allow him to study Greek or Latin.

When Anne grew up, the dinner parties at the Yates Thompsons' in Portman Square were the most lavish she ever attended. They had no telephone and even in the 1930s used a carriage and pair. The invitations were delivered in this, by hand, about a week before the chosen date. Before dinner, light or dark sherry was served. Then there was caviar, on wooden plates with wooden knives, with vodka. Two soups, a clear and a thick, with which malmsey was drunk. Château Yquem was offered with the light fish, and rosé with the salmon; claret with the game—pheasant, partridge, guinea hen, capercaille, or grouse, according to the season. Burgundy with the joint. This was followed by an entremets, a mousse of chicken or rabbit, or an elaborate aspic, or a vegetable (e.g., peas) in a mold, with mousseline sauce. Then always an ice-cream bombe, with champagne. Either a savory or cheese, with port; then fruit and coffee with liqueurs and brandy. The company, though always agreeable, was cozy rather than distinguished, Mrs. Yates Thompson's nephew, Christopher Chancellor, being probably the most brilliant habitué. When only just down from Cambridge he had been sent to China for Reuters, learned Chinese, and rose rapidly to the head of that firm, and then of the Bowater Corporation. His mother-in-law, Lady Muriel Paget, also a frequent guest at the Yates Thompsons', was one of the most eccentric Englishwomen (quite a feat), having as her pet charity English governesses stranded in Russia by the Revolution. She visited them there, cosseted them, and begged for them. Her husband, Sir Richard, had theories about the way speech evolved which he illustrated at dinner parties by blowing on paper models.

It was Bertrand (Bertie) Russell, however, who proved to be the most enduring of the nursery friends. Anne knew she could always say anything to him, and the girls were always allowed down to lunch when he appeared. Bertie told Anne that *his* mother thought *her* great-aunt Beatrice Potter (later Mrs. Sidney Webb) flighty and frivolous; Anne, who considered the formidable author of the Minority Report on the Poor Law terrifying—though she kindly had Anne and Christopher to dinner shortly after their marriage—found this hard to believe.

Bertie was fond of Mama all his life, and when she was dying he wrote her a tender, stoic farewell.

Little Datchet Farm, Malvern, Pa.

My dear Tiny

I have just heard from your daughter the very painful news of your grave illness. It makes me very sad. There is not much one can say. I can imagine your perfect courage.

So many long-ago memories are associated with you—children's parties at your house and Pembroke Lodge and the Burdetts'—your father walking over by Twickenham Ferry on Sundays—his reminiscences of the Metaphysical Society dividing on "Is there a God?"—the times when I was barely grown up and used to come to York House and listen with admiration while you talked of Kater Murr, Verlaine, Dostoevsky, etc., most of which I bought in consequence. How difficult it is to live in the modern world when that was the world to which one's early habits were adjusted! I do not like exile, particularly because it means not seeing old friends. I hope to return to England in 1945, but that is too late.

Goodbye with most sincere friendship

8 July 1942   Bertrand Russell

Anne was at that time working in the British Embassy in Washington; her husband was in the (British) Censorship and could not leave England. Anne saw a lot of Bertie; she stayed in Pennsylvania with him and his third wife, Patricia Spence (Peter), a flaming redhead, whose son Conrad was the same age as Anne's Richard and very fierce.

Bertie was always very direct. When he and Peter came to stay with Anne in Washington she asked him, "Why did you divorce Alys, as you say you are against divorce?"

"Because she had madness in her family and I wanted children."

"Why did you divorce Dora, then?" Anne asked.

"Because I could not afford the children she had after we married which were not by me," he replied.

Discussing his brother Frank, Anne wondered that anyone would like to give pain to someone he loved. "I understand it very well," Bertie said.

While they talked, walking beside the Potomac, Peter was entertaining a "gentleman friend" in Anne's living room.

When Anne got compassionate leave to go to Mama, dying in Somerset, she offered Bertie and Peter her Georgetown house—with two small boys in it. Peter and Bertie, who had not been able to find a house in wartime Washington, accepted with alacrity. But when their plans changed, Peter left Anne's home, left also Anne's two sons, having first phoned the British Embassy to say the children would be alone. Anne arrived in Lisbon to find two telegrams: MAMA DEAD, said one from Clare; the other, RUSSELL ARRANGEMENT BROKEN DOWN, from the Embassy.

In England in 1951, Anne learned from one of her aunts (who was Bertie's first cousin) that Bertrand and his third wife were divorced, and that his first wife, Alys, had just died. Bertrand had been to see her, and they had spent a happy afternoon together. When he left, eighty-one-year-old Alys asked Anne's aunt, "I think he has come back to me, don't you? I don't think he will marry again now, do you?" Anne's aunt assured her she thought it unlikely. Twenty-four hours later, Alys Russell was happily dead; little more than a year later, Lord Russell had remarried.

When Anne's son Adam was seventeen and newly at Balliol, she went out to Richmond with him, and Bertrand gave them a wonderful lunch in his upstairs library, a pleasant room with a big fireplace—lit, thank God, on a bitter August afternoon. He had just married his fourth wife, and above the big double bed in their room was a huge painting of a dove descending.

Bertrand told Adam how unhappy he had been as a youth, and how Benjamin Jowett, the great Master of Balliol, had saved his life. "But you weren't at Balliol," Anne objected, wondering how Dr. Jowett could have reached out to Trinity, Cambridge, to save.

"No," he agreed, "but one night I went to bed determined to commit suicide next day. I dreamed that the Master of Balliol stood at the foot of my bed and told me, 'Don't do it, young man; don't do it; you will live to regret it.' Which was nonsense, of course, but when I woke up I was completely cured. I didn't commit suicide then, and I have never wanted to since."

They talked of his son, then Viscount Amberley, who had been in Washington, attached to the British Admiralty mission during the war. He had married an American, the daughter of the poet Vachel Lindsay. At that time the young people shared Bertrand's house with him; they have since divorced.

"And Kate?" Anne asked after his daughter.

"Last time I saw her she had her arm in a sling; she had fallen out of a tree or something. Kate married an American too, Charles Tait, a don, and they live near Harvard," he said.

"And Conrad?" asked Anne, adding, "Last time I saw him he had bitten his mother so badly she too had her arm in a sling." Conrad is Bertie's son by this third wife, Peter.

"He is a tug [scholar] at Eton," said Bertie, drawing on his pipe.

"Maths, I suppose?" Anne asked, remembering the child's startling brilliance at mental arithmetic when he was five.

"No, classics."

Anne was amazed. Bertie had never allowed his elder children to study either Greek or Latin, and John Amberley had taken to the dead languages as other children take to dope. When Anne had met him during the war, he was in uniform and shyly had drawn out of his pocket a little well-thumbed edition of Horace. And now Conrad was doing the same!

"Yes, classics," Bertie said. "It is odd; I suppose whatever one is forbidden is what one wants, and if only God had the sense to forbid us to be good, we all would be perfect paragons at once."

Bertie spoke then of his plane crash in Norway. A flying boat carrying him to a lecture crashed at Hommelvika near Trondheim. "I was sitting in the front part of the plane, and they wouldn't let me smoke. 'I must smoke or I'll die,' I said. If I hadn't smoked, I would have died," he told Anne, "for I was allowed to smoke at the back of the plane. When it crashed, I thought we were just landing and didn't realize anything was wrong until I found myself in the sea, in my heavy overcoat, instead of in a boat. I had to swim for ten minutes. I didn't know until much later that all the people in the front part of the plane were drowned—nineteen in all."

"How could you stand the cold?" Anne asked, remembering once—on the way to England on leave during the war—jumping off a boat in Halifax harbor in August and nearly dying of the shock of the cold.

"It *was* cold," Bertie said, "but after a few minutes I was fished out and dried. I remember it was hard to get any alcohol, and of course, under those circumstances, that was what I wanted most. They would not let me give my lecture, although I could perfectly well have gone ahead and delivered my talk."

Anne asked him why he didn't stay longer in America, where he had so many friends and admirers. "I prefer my own countrymen," he said. "The older I get, the more certain I am of that."

Anne asked if he minded the discomforts of contemporary England, but he said no, he found he could detach himself from them. "Holy abandonment?" suggested Anne, and he said seriously, "Something like that. I have always used, and find I still continually use, many of the techniques of the mystics, without requiring their faith."

They spoke then of loyalty. "Always a bad thing," he said incisively, "always suggests an ethical ambivalence."

Anne was shaken. "I'm trying to write a book about why people are loyal and to whom and what," she said.

"Why should they ever be?" Bertie asked. "If they do what is right, loyalty isn't necessary. If they don't, then loyalty is a poor excuse."

Anne thought of the Pétainists in France, the men of the 1944 Putsch in Germany, all now branded as traitors; of the neo-fascists, and of the ex-communists. "Josiah Royce and Gabriel Marcel would not agree with you," she said.

"Oh, Royce," Bertie replied with a malicious twinkle. "When I first went to Harvard in 1911, I was constantly being told, 'William James is dead, Santayana has retired, but, alas, Professor Royce is still with us.' He had had a stroke and was pretty gaga."

Bertie then turned to Adam and asked him how he liked Balliol. "I once had a German friend at Balliol," Bertie told him without waiting for his reply. "I once asked him why his parents had sent him there. He answered, 'I was overworking badly at Göttingen, and they feared a breakdown, so, as I needed a complete rest, they sent me to Balliol.'"

When they left, Anne, thinking of the thirty-five years she and Bertie had known each other, said, "What an hors d'oeuvre of a friendship ours has been."

"Yes," agreed Bertie, "and now we have got, you might say, into the soup."

The best-loved of all the children's friends was Marmaduke Pickthall, the Norfolk parson's son who had gone to Syria at eighteen and had, like so many Englishmen before him, fallen in love with the Arabs. At twenty-eight he published his first novel, *Saïd the Fisherman*, which was required reading for all candidates

for the Egyptian Civil Service and remains a classic. He became a superb Arabic scholar. A convert to Islam, he had a holy
horror of what he called "bogey-bogey"—of every god man has
made. The basic problem, Did God make us or we Him? was
resolved for him by Islam, and no one ever said the Moslem creed,
La illaha il Allah—the Shahada, "There is no God but God"—
more fervently. He saw the children almost daily, as they would
walk or ride the two miles from Possingworth to the Pond House,
which Mama had lent him.

When Marmaduke drank wine (forbidden to Moslems) or
broke the Ramadan fast by smoking, Anne and Clare were allowed to beat him. Marmaduke, as he described himself to Mama,
was "a childless man who loves children," and the trio spent sunlit
afternoons in a punt on the pond with a jam jar known as the
Pickthall pot, collecting tadpoles, larvae, water boatmen, and
other forms of pond life. There were water lilies too, also scented
rushes and water hyacinths. And the three took long walks in the
bluebell- and bracken-filled woods, or on the heaths, among the
bell and ling heather. The girls fought to walk on his right side,
as in both Christianity and Islam the distinction between where
the sheep and goats would be found at the final judgment was
clear. And always, as they leaned over a five-barred gate, or sat
on a stile, or gathered blackberries, the talk came back to Him "to
Whom is the return," Who is imageless Light, and "for Whom
is our living and our dying."

Marmaduke had been horrified by what he regarded as the children's idolatry; he did not approve of *puja* offered to trees or to
pagan gods and goddesses, and his passionate perception of the
Unity of God as the only Existent brought Anne, with Clare
docilely following, to Islam. Marmaduke must have had personal
mystical experience of the "one true Light," for somehow in all
his novels there were oblique references to It, or Him. He was
a man of much prayer and taught Anne to pray the Moslem
prayers five times a day, first translating them for her, then teaching them to her in Arabic. He also translated the whole Qu'ran

for her, calling it an "interpretation," for the divine text must, or rather can, never be translated, since it was dictated to the Prophet Mohammed in Arabic by the Archangel Gabriel. Mohammed was illiterate, so when the archangel said, "Write," the Prophet asked "How can I?" but did. Marmaduke's translation is the only one approved by Al Azhar, the great Cairo university, the foremost Islamic theological school, and has sold well over a million copies. Anne was received at the mosque in Woking by the Imam, Kwaja Kamal-ud-din, when she was ten; she merely had to say the Shahada to him in public. Papa was not pleased; Mama did not mind at all. Being a Moslem meant, besides saying the prayers five times a day (on a small rug or mat that is a prefiguration of the six by three feet of earth that will be our grave and is all the earth we can ever claim), keeping the fast of Ramadan, a dawn-to-dusk month-long fast, which infuriated Anne's and Clare's governesses.

Devoutly observing the Moslem rules (the prohibition of wine, pork, and shellfish did not weigh heavily on her at ten), Anne found the absence of images a marvelous release. That God not only should be "without body, parts, or passions" as the Anglican Thirty-nine Articles declare, but also "begetteth not nor is begotten," and that His Spirit, which in both Hebrew and Arabic is feminine, is not a dove, nor even a rushing wind which pigs could see even if she could not, but totally formless, so that it is as true to say He is not as to say He is (both are equally inadequate and nonsense), was curiously satisfactory. So was the fact that "No" is also an answer to prayer, to petition, or to inquiry. Not this, not that—and Anne jettisoned as so much excess baggage all the crucifixes, Thorwaldsen's Christ that stood in their nursery (given by Hans Sonne, the children's guardian after Papa's death), the Madonna di San Sisto that Mama loved, all pictures, statues, beads, and even hymns, for Marmaduke said they raised the spiritual temperature artificially.

Somewhere, deep down, in Anne's ten-year-old sloughing of all forms was an atavistic puritanism, coming perhaps from Scottish covenanting ancestors who prayed on bare moors and in ugly, empty churches, or from North German quietists who, in the fifteenth century, near Bremen, produced the mysticism of the *devotio moderna*, as it was then called. With this was coupled a dislike of clutter or decoration as being bad form. Never wear lace on your underwear, Mama insisted; never have anything but very plain clothes: to decorate is to defile. The best lines in architecture are Greek; in dressmaking, Chanel. In cooking, the best foods are broiled sole, roast lamb. So Anne delighted in the bare Moslem worship and in the Moslem *dhikr*, the repetition of the name of God, which is the Moslems' private prayer *par excellence:* its object is to realize that God's is the only real existence. That is the true *tawhid*, the separation of the eternal from the contingent. Man is God's mirror, but only God may be seen in that mirror; light waved in a circle looks like a circle, but only the light is real.

As Sultan Veled, son of Rumi, one of the greatest Islamic mystics, wrote:

> Thou art the unseen and the seen
> Had no clue
> Thou art hiding in bodies and souls
> Had no clue
> I was looking for a sign of Thine in this world
> Have found that the world itself is a sign of Thine
> Now I have a clue.

Marmaduke's departure to become editor of the Bombay *Chronicle* was the first sorrow in Anne's and Clare's life. He became one of Mahatma Gandhi's inner circle during the days of the Ali brothers and the Khalifat Committee, and sent Anne and Clare *khaddar* (homespun) cloth and Gandhi caps and Khalifat badges, which they insisted on wearing day-long, looking like bedraggled Halloween ghosts.

Marmaduke became head of a big high school in Hyderabad, and tutor to some of the Nizam's sons. He arranged the marriage of the Prince of Berar with the Princess Nilufer, granddaughter

of the last Sultan of Turkey, who was also the last Khalif, hoping
that the Khalifat would then pass to India. But it did not. His last
novel, finished at his death in May 1936, but never published, was
Dust on the Peacock Throne.

Clare's "beaver," Cousin Ernie Meinertzhagen, who was Chairman of the London County Council, because he was a relation,
was in another category.

Frogs in the pond
And all cousins of cousins

goes the *haiku*, and it defined for Anne her posse of relatives. For,
though there were many varieties, they all had something in common that friends did not. Papa and Mama had each started with
seven siblings. Papa's sisters were large, handsome, public-spirited,
and unlucky in love. One was divorced, one a widow, one a
spinster.

Mama's sisters were small, beautiful, but hardly less unlucky.
Aunt Lily, with red hair she could sit on, wrote a novel, *Peri-
winkle.* When Mama stepped into Bumpus, the bookstore, to ask
how it was selling, the reply was, 'Mostly to friends." Aunt Lily
got the clap in North Africa as a girl, but kind, handsome Gerald
Collier, a painter and a peer's son, married her to save her. Their
eldest son became a doctor in the slums and rejected the peerage
he inherited. Their youngest son teaches at Edinburgh University
and recently (1968) taught in the Chinese University in Canton.
Aunt Lily shocked Anne when she and her family were staying
with Mama and Papa at Tresserve, by saying she thought the
Imitation of Christ a wicked book. Anne, aged eight, shocked
Aunt Lily by taking William, also eight, to Mass. When he whispered he must pee, she raced him through the village to a British
home more than a mile away. She had not then, or for ten years
after, any idea of the masculine anatomy.

On the same visit Anne took Uncle Gerald up the Corsuet, a
small wooded hill some thousand feet high, to show him the

splendid view of the Lac du Bourget, and ran with him the whole way down. At the bottom they both drank ice-cold water from a spring. Uncle Gerald was dead in a week from pneumonia. Shortly after, Anne persuaded her fencing master, a white-haired, white-mustached man of seventy-four, to teach her boxing, as she despised fencing, which Mama wished the girls to learn in hope that it would improve their figures. Anne landed a fatal blow on her dear teacher's head. She deeply regretted these manslaughters.

Aunt Iseult went to India as a missionary. There she lost her faith, and returned to Europe, to Berlin, where she studied psychoanalysis under Hanns Sachs. In spite of her success in this second profession she and a female companion, when both were over seventy-five, consumed between them a bottle of aspirin tablets. The companion had become bedridden with arthritis. The coroner's verdict was that each lady had taken forty tablets more than was necessary to kill herself. Aunt Iseult's death was, indeed, totally unnecessary. She had written to an old friend who had studied with her under Hanns Sachs and lived now in Mexico, to tell him of her intention of double suicide. He had cabled her to come; he would pay her fare and take care of her for as long as she lived, since he was rich and lonely. She got the cable but did not reply; leaving a bedridden friend to seek serener climes was something Grant Duffs didn't do. Their motto is "Stand fast, Craigallachie."

Aunt Dot, Mama's favorite sister, was so lovely when young that (Sir) Owen O'Malley, husband later of the novelist Ann Bridge, fell in love with her at first sight when he was seventeen. She later died from the bite of one of her own race horses in Alexandria, Egypt. Uncle Piggy (Arthur) died in his bed but previously had had all his possessions bombed in Sussex in World War II.

One cousin Anne and Clare never knew was Aloys Obrist. He had come to a mysterious end; his photograph, in a heavy black frame, hung in Mama's bedroom at Aix, but Anne could not learn more than "your poor cousin Aloys" was dead. Then, in New

York after World War II, Anne met Elizabeth Mayer (to whom W. H. Auden dedicated his *New Year's Letter*), and Elizabeth told her that when she was dining at Dresden before World War I, before attending Tosca, she saw at the next table a strikingly handsome man dining alone. She was told he was the brilliant orchestra conductor Aloys Obrist. At the opera's end that evening he shot the leading soprano, with whom he had been having an affair, and then himself. His wife, who was pregnant, hung pictures and climbed ladders until she miscarried. His brother, Hermann, Anne and Clare knew and disliked.

Hermann's daughters, too, came to bad ends. The younger, Amaranth, was killed with her mother in the bombing of Munich in World War II. Leila, the elder, was murdered by a lover after that war and incinerated in the furnace of the block of flats where she lived. As she had inherited Auchterlies, Anne had to testify she was "presumed dead" before the property could pass to Andrew Campbell, to whom she had left it.

Papa's relations included a brother, General Ernest Jackson, who built a mosque in the Sudan. He was said to keep a harem; certainly he never married. A cousin of Papa was the vegetarian Chancellor of the Exchequer, Sir Stafford Cripps. Sir Stafford's daughter married a Negro, but he, unlike Dean Rusk, did not feel it necessary to offer his resignation on that account. Papa's relations also included a monk at Ampleforth and a daughter of the Lady Carlisle who was so against alcohol that she poured the priceless vintages in the Castle Howard cellar down the lavatory. Little wonder her poor daughter Ankaret drank heavily and died from a fall from her horse during World War II.

Relations were likely to descend at any time on either Possingworth or Tresserve or even Rutland Gate, but the girls regularly went visiting only twice a year. They spent Christmas with Grandpapa Jackson at Birkenhead, and hated the dull, square house of yellowish brick, with sooty grass lawns and big black cedars. Grandpapa, who even at ninety-nine went to his office regularly, was a magnificent "beaver," with snow-white beard.

He always wore a fresh carnation in his buttonhole, and gave each grandchild a fiver on Christmas day. There were no books in his house except sets of the English classics and bound volumes of *Punch* and the *Illustrated London News;* there was nothing to do except go for cold walks in desolate country, or visit the Liverpool Art Gallery, full of Pre-Raphaelite pictures, which the girls despised. Mama had gazed so long at Rossettis before Anne's birth (together with an equally pregnant friend) that Anne looked like Rossetti's Beata Beatrix, and was always being told in front of visitors to put her head up in that dying-duck-in-a-thunder-storm attitude. The only advantage that ever accrued from Mama's deplorable taste was that the son born to Mama's friend also looked so Pre-Raphaelite that at Oxford he and Anne were taken for brother and sister (they were no kind of kin), so he was allowed to visit her in her room at Lady Margaret Hall.

The worst thing at Birkenhead was the food. There was an immense amount: two turkeys on Christmas day—one roasted, one boiled—umpteen plum puddings, mince pies, brandy butter, a daily breakfast table heavy with viands. Such a glut made the girls feel sick. Their hearty North Country cousins despised finicky southern appetites as much as the girls were revolted by their cousins' gross natures.

In summer Anne and Clare went to Delgaty. The castle had a huge round staircase, known as the Painted Room. Rachel Grant Duff had dreamed it had a medieval painted ceiling; she had it uncovered and found it exactly as she had seen it in her dream. Life at Delgaty was blissful: breakfast at ten, then all day fishing salmon in the Deveron, or watching cousin Julian shoot, or catching trout in the lake, or going out to sea after mackerel or herring. Or scrambling among the local ruins: Eden, which had belonged to the family; or Findlater on its rocky stretch of gorse-bright coast; or Tarlair, with its huge caves. Or playing tennis with the Urquhart children at Craigston, where in the attic was their family tree going back to Adam. Or playing golf on the Banff links and looking up at the "little white church on the hill" of MacDuff, that Matthew Arnold had written about when he stayed with Mama's father.

Rachel herself was fey, very beautiful and very dirty; her room stank, not only because her two little King Charles spaniels slept in her bed. Her hands were exquisite, but above the wrists her arms were gray. Delgaty was a gay place, with lots of Scots dancing and a piper who played around the table before dinner, and the girls had the run of the walled kitchen garden, which had hot pipes inside the walls to ripen the delicious peaches and apricots, and even sometimes figs, which grew along them. There was a wishing well, and a dovecote, proof that in the old days Delgaty's owners had the right to hang villains and also had the *jus primae noctis*. There was, too, a chapel filled with pious emasculated wishy-washy saints painted by Rachel, a devout Episcopalian.

Rachel's mother, lovely Aunt Fanny, had had also three sons, whom she had called romantically Douglas, Percy, and Julian. As soon as they could speak, they called themselves Dug, Pug, and Jug. Rachel was a fervent Jacobite, and Anne and Clare were taught to drink to the King "over the water": Rupprecht of Bavaria was their rightful sovereign, they were told. And they were regaled with tales of a heroic ancestress, an old lady who was at home when some English barged in after defeating Jacobite forces at Culloden and then slaughtering the wounded. She made them welcome and offered food and drink. It was death to drink to "the Pretender," and they wanted to catch her out. "The King," the English colonel toasted. The old lady, raising her glass, quoted: " 'The tongue can no man tame,' James the third and eighth." Her knowledge of the Bible saved both her life and her honor.

Rachel could be tough too, like her ancestors. In 1927 she was invited by Sir George Abercromby, whose estate of Forglen marched with Delgaty, to come to a ball he was giving and to bring Anne, then aged seventeen. Rachel took her dear fat brother Julian, who was between wives, as partner. She asked Anne whether she could provide herself with a young man. The only one within hundreds of miles that Anne could think of was Lord Cawdor's brother, Andrew Campbell, for Cawdor in Nairn was only a county and a half away. But Rachel said, "No Campbell has ever entered this house, and none ever will if I can help it," so Anne was left behind at Delgaty and missed the ball and never met the handsome bachelor Sir George.

Perhaps the highlight of Anne's Scottish experience was being taken by Rachel to Iona. It was April and icy. They both had so little money that they could afford only bed and breakfast in a small guesthouse. But in the ruins of the cathedral, in the spouting cave, on Tun I, a hill holy even before Christ, Anne felt as never before or since the glory of belonging to so ancient a race and of being in so sacred a place.

XVI

Partings

Delight in people, friends and relations; delight in places—
Anne's and Clare's life was illuminated, irradiated, by both, and
they never really knew if they were cat people, who preferred
places, or dog people, who preferred people. Possingworth, the
Maison, even Rutland Gate, with its balconies full of pink geraniums, with roof gardens planted with roses and laurel trees in
pots, and fountains and little iron staircases one could scamper
up and down—each provided joys, all different. And then there
were pets. There were the baby pigs, who lay on either side of
the smoking room, waiting for Papa to come in from shooting,
and squealed with delight when he did, and were so clean they
used the bath for their natural necessities; there was Punch, the
pony, who would let one ride him bareback and gallop about and
pretend to be Prince Rupert at the battle of Naseby, and then
throw one off when he'd had enough, or maneuver one under a
tree with low branches so one was suspended, Absalom-like, in
the boughs. And there were the guinea pigs, who arrived in
Easter eggs and bred so fast that the girls ran out of names—
especially female ones, as every guinea pig, whether named Lenin,
Trotsky, or Savonarola, always proved herself to be a mother.
All gave pleasure. But sooner or later there was always the prob-

lem of parting. The pigs' fate was horrid; Tunky, the black lamb, grown into a sheep, became remote and bad-tempered; the guinea pigs, after every child on the estate had, willy-nilly, received one or several, were donated to a pet shop, all except the housekeeper's Stumps, who lived to be six, an all-time high.

Partings occurred with people too. Governesses left, suddenly or serenely; nurserymaids vanished into shame or marriage. Places remained; but when Papa decided, in the glorious summer of 1921, to sell Possingworth Manor, Anne and Clare for the first time realized that partings came to places too. Marmaduke's house, as an appendage of the manor, was also to be sold. Anne and Clare spent the day of the auction (of farm implements, furniture, and so on, before the land sale) sliding blissfully down the sides of the haystacks and tearing around, enjoying themselves.

But they were sad too, very sad indeed. That evening, at home at Possingworth, Anne played on the piano, and they both sang, a favorite hymn:

> A few more years shall roll,
> A few more seasons come,
> And we shall be with those that rest
> Asleep within the tomb. . . .
>
> A few more suns shall set
> O'er these dark hills of time,
> And we shall be where suns are not,
> A far serener clime. . . .
>
> A few more struggles here,
> A few more partings o'er,
> A few more toils, a few more tears,
> And we shall weep no more. . . .

It was only a few months, not years, later that a major—the major—parting of their lives took place. And they wept a lot. For the weekend of November 30, Clare's ninth birthday, Papa had gone down to Possingworth to shoot. Clare had invited several grown-ups to Rutland Gate for dinner at eight, as it was a family practice for the "birthday child" to stay up and come down to late dinner. Marmaduke was in town and came, also Bertie Russell and Anne's second painter godfather, Lindsay Macarthur, and Uncle Hampden, Clare's favorite uncle. There were silver candlesticks on the table (and turtle soup, and a glass of port each at dinner's end). But Mama was not there. She had hurried to Possingworth that day, as Harold, the chauffeur, bringing up the flowers (flowers and vegetables came up twice a week from the garden in trugs), told Mama he was worried: Papa had a high fever and looked wretched. Three days later, on December 3, 1921, the girls were sent for. Neither of them ever forgot meeting Mr. Johansen, the beloved Swedish masseur, at Victoria Station: he was arriving from Possingworth and told the governess, "It's all over." Thus they knew their father was dead before they had been told he was ill.

The whole way down, Anne tried to warm peepholes in the icy windowpane to see the black pines and hoar-white fields, the mud rucked stiff like wood. When they got to the station they were driven the five miles home in silence.

Pink let them into the big hall, where they so often had played sea lions with him—you jumped from red island to red island or were caught. But he did not greet them today. He did not speak until Mama came down the wide oak staircase, all in black.

"The young ladies, madam," Pink announced then.

"Your father is dead," she said, without touching them.

Clare flung herself, sobbing, into her arms. Tiny led them upstairs. "Come and see him," she said.

They went to her bedroom, where curtains were drawn and three candles were lit. There was their father, lying in the big double bed, white and waxy, with a crucifix between his hands, and a bunch of Easter lilies in a vase. Tiny knelt and said the Lord's Prayer. "Kiss him," she commanded, and with immense distaste they kissed the folded hands. He lay there almost a week, the last two days in an open coffin, and at the end there came from him a smell that was stronger than the lilies. The girls never had to kiss him again, but each evening said their prayers beside him and loved him daily less. And resented Providence more and more.

Marmaduke Pickthall came each day to take them out for a walk. They wandered all over the desolate icy park, and sometimes Anne would fling herself on the dead bracken under a cedar and sob out her fury: why did Father have to die, who was only fifty-eight—why not Grandpapa, who was eighty-eight? Why was life's end so nasty? One should be given the choice, as with the food on one's plate, to eat the best bits first or leave them for a *bonbouche* at the end. Marmaduke only replied by quotations from the Qu'ran: "By the early hours and by the night when it sheds darkness, thy Lord has not forsaken thee nor does He hate thee," and, "Say: my living and my dying are for Allah, Lord of the worlds, and to Him is the return."

The girls learned more from their father's obituary than they had ever known about him. The London *Times* on December 5, 1921, wrote:

DEATH OF MR. HUTH JACKSON.
A FAMOUS BANKER.

We regret to announce that Mr. Frederick Huth Jackson, the prominent London banker, a partner in the City firm of Frederick Huth and Co., and a director of the Bank of England, died on Saturday morning at his country residence, Possingworth, Cross-in-Hand, Sussex.

The Rt. Hon. Frederick Huth Jackson from the first showed great force of character. He went to Harrow (of which he afterwards became a governor), and it was at the dinner table of the then Headmaster, Dr. Butler, that he met Dr. Jowett, the late Master of Balliol, who was so struck with the force of his conversation that, before the end of the evening, he had persuaded him to abandon his idea of going to Cambridge and enter his name at Balliol. The friendship thus inaugurated lasted through, and after his Oxford days. The Master was delighted to have an undergraduate who, while knowing how to listen, was not afraid to converse freely, and after his undergraduate days would ask him down to Oxford "to talk about bills of exchange." It was in the Master's drawing room that he first met Sir Mountstuart Grant Duff, whose daughter he afterwards married. At Oxford "Fritz Jackson"— as his friends always called him—formed fast friendships with Cosmo Gordon Lang, now Archbishop of York, Cecil Baring, Lionel Crawfurd, now Bishop of Stafford, and Henry Bowlby, the present Headmaster of Lancing College, as well as with the late Lord Brassey. Thanks, perhaps, to his having travelled round the world before going up to Oxford, he always seemed more mature than the ordinary undergraduate, but he entered fully into the life of the University, and passed out with a 2nd Class in the History School in 1887.

Coming to London, where he lodged with Cosmo Lang, he began to read for the Bar, and would doubtless have made his mark there, though the work was not wholly congenial to him, and he used in after life to refer to the "immorality" of a busy counsel who would take fees to plead a case to which he knew he had little or no chance of attending. But his relationship, through his mother, to the famous firm of merchant bankers, Frederick Huth and Co., led to his being offered a clerkship there, which quickly developed into a partnership, and it was as representing this great firm that he was shortly afterwards elected a director of the Bank of England, at a younger age than any previous recipient of that honour. Though handicapped by ill-health, his immense power of concentration, his sanity of judgment, and his clarity of vision, combined with real driving force, soon brought him to the front in the difficult years following the Baring crisis, and only the calls of his own firm's business prevented him from becoming the youngest Governor of the Bank of England.

Huth Jackson quickly became a director, and later chairman, of the Indemnity Mutual Marine, a director of the Eastern Telegraph Company (whose ramifications particularly interested him), the Northern Assurance Company, and the London and South-Western Railway, and was at one time also chairman of the Anglo-Chilean Nitrate and Railway Company. From 1909–11 he was also president of the Insti-

tute of Bankers. He was an ardent Free Trader and a strong
Liberal Unionist, and it seemed at one time that he might have
represented the City in Parliament. But perhaps he felt, with
Lord Randolph Churchill's biographer, that "political tri-
umphs are necessarily tarnished by vulgar methods," and that
"the cant of phrase and formula," and "the burrowings of
rival caucuses," would have filled him with weariness. His
public service, however, was not restricted by his deliberately
eschewing active politics. He tried especially to promote the
more harmonious working of capital and labour, and his
house was a meeting-place for all shades of opinion. He even
found time to be an active member of the Political Economy
Club and president of the National Association of Employers
and Employed.

He was also one of the British delegates with Sir Mackenzie
Chalmers at The Hague Conference on bills of exchange, and
when the inner history of the war sees light, the part he
played in organizing the nation's resources will be recognized.
He took an active part in the discussions which led to the
establishment of the moratorium.

One of the most remarkable facts is that he studied before
the war in the abstract the problem of victualling these islands
in time of war, which led to his being asked by the Defence
Committee of the Cabinet to appear before them for exami-
nation. We believe it to be a fact that his cross-examination
stands adjourned *sine die,* from some day in April, 1914. His
theory, which proved unassailable, was that, while it was the
duty of the Navy to insure the safe arrival of vessels, it was
the duty of the Government to indemnify their owners
against loss, and so ensure their starting. Anyhow, when the
European war was imminent, Mr. Asquith offered him the
nation's purse, and asked him to put his scheme into force.
This request he was, for business reasons, obliged to refuse,
but he acted as chairman of the Committee appointed to consider a scheme for national insurance of vessels in war time,
and his recommendations were adopted en bloc in an Act,
which was rushed through both Houses at the beginning of
August, 1914. The result fully justified Huth Jackson's the-

ory, as, from that moment, ships which had been held up by their owners in Buenos Aires and elsewhere, immediately put to sea.

Huth Jackson was also chairman of the Accepting Houses Committee and took an active part in the negotiations with regard to pre-war indebtedness of enemy aliens. He had urged on the Treasury six months before it was adopted the plan of mobilizing dollar and other securities by deposit with the Treasury so as to provide a fund for stabilizing the exchanges, and it is not too much to say that, had the plan been adopted when he suggested it, untold millions would have been saved to the State. Later on he was the moving spirit in, and acted as honorary treasurer of, the Vienna Relief Fund.

The only distinction Huth Jackson coveted was one which was conferred on him in 1911—namely, membership of the Privy Council, but it is an open secret that he declined a hereditary honour. In 1893 he married, as mentioned already, Clara Annabel, the eldest daughter of Sir Mountstuart Grant Duff, and leaves a son, who married a daughter of Sir Paul Vinogradoff, and three daughters, the eldest of whom married Arthur, second son of Henry Hobhouse.

Papa was cremated at Golders Green Crematorium. Later there was a memorial service in St. Paul's, Knightsbridge, at which the Archbishop of Canterbury officiated and to which the Prime Minister and the leader of the Opposition (Ramsay MacDonald) came, together with an immense crowd. When the little box of ashes was put into the ground at Waldron, Anne and Clare threw snowdrops and violets after it, and Anne knew then that life would never be the same—knew, as Mama had known when she left India, that the best was over. A happy childhood, she realized later, leads to a great lack of ambition: one knows quite well that in the nature of things the best is behind, and, like Thomas Traherne, one would prefer to walk with "backward steps." Contrariwise, an unhappy childhood leads to enormous ambition: obviously, for the sake of balance, the future beckons.

XVII

Tresserve

After Papa's death, Mama found herself terribly hard up. He had died at a bad time for his firm, and every penny he left went to shore up Frederick Huth and Company. Mama had only her marriage settlement, her jewelry, and the houses. Possingworth had been sold, now Rutland Gate. (Anne, showing the Turkish Ambassador, a prospective buyer, around the latter, assured him that the mews, the many roof gardens, and the several exits would be useful in a revolution. His government did not buy.) Pink left for his Anglican monastery; Marie-Louise retired, on the annuity Papa had left her, to Aix-les-Bains, where she built herself a little house. Mama did not sell the Maison; instead she decided to spend a year there to economize. She had dismissed Maria Reinshagen, deciding the girls would make do with a daily governess who would come up from Aix, and Monsieur le Curé would be persuaded to teach them Latin. The girls were dressed in unrelieved black for the year, serge in winter, cotton in summer. Mama wore black too, of course, including widow's weeds—that is, a cap and over it a black voile veil that flowed down her back. A white line at the forehead too. . . .

Madame Roulet was hired. A *rousse*, a ginger-haired Norman, she was very fat because, she said, she always swallowed her cherry stones. She had been governess to Henri de Régnier's children; Mama admired his *La Canne de Jaspe* and hoped that the girls would learn to write French as well as that. Madame Roulet was an atheist in a tidy nineteenth-century French way. This Mama approved; to balance her, there would be Monsieur le Curé, Antoine Prémilieu. Mama asked him to lunch. He came, and won everyone. A peasant, he was both hardheaded and holy, and remarkably well educated. It was agreed the girls would walk up to the presbytery next the church two days a week for one hour's Latin, and one day a week Monsieur le Curé would come down to the Maison, give them a lesson, and stay for lunch.

Humbert Michaud would have lessons with them. He was an only son and an only grandson. His grandfather, Baron Michaud, was mayor of Tresserve and lived next to the presbytery in a small house with the best view of all; it included to the west the great *massif* of the Granier, under which lay Chambéry and behind which the Grande Chartreuse was hidden. From Humbert's terrace the whole lake could be seen, bluer than Mama's eyes. Anne and Clare had first seen Humbert in church, kneeling on a prie-dieu in the lady chapel (everyone else sat on benches). He had bare legs, a gray suit, and a white open-necked shirt, and from his jacket pocket protruded a pale beige silk handkerchief with a crest woven on the corner. He was ashy blond and tall for his age (ten). His grandfather was very devout; indeed, many people thought him a saint. When the Loi Combes had decreed in 1901 that nuns must be secularized, Baron Michaud had driven up to the Tresserve convent, half a mile beyond the church, to remove the sisters himself. Sœur Marthe, Sœur Philomène, and Sœur Agathe—the only three that were left—appeared in lay clothes, climbed into the victoria beside the Baron, and were escorted by him to a small house nearer the church, which was his property. There he installed them, and there they continued nursing—their profession, now that they were *en civil.*

Humbert's father, a waxy-faced, thin, good-looking dark man with a Dali mustache, had tuberculosis. His handsome, stout Swiss wife, in spite of being tightly corseted, had a perfect complexion and curly light brown hair. She was kind, shrewd, common, and, luckily, healthy and practical. Humbert had one sister, plump, pretty Ernestine, with goggly eyes that indicated some thyroid imbalance. She was Anne's age but did not share in their lessons; instead she went daily to school in Aix. Humbert, Anne, and Clare climbed trees together; Humbert was shocked that the girls did so in whatever they were wearing, including their *broderie anglaise* Sunday-best frocks. They in turn were shocked that quite often he panicked when aloft, and one or both of them would have to help him down. "So like a silly kitten," Clare said. They had a gun, a .22, and he a carbine. But whereas they shot only at targets, he shot songbirds and sparrows. "How beastly," Anne said. But Humbert only asked, "Why?" and invited them to eat a pie made of *bec-figues*, chaffinches, larks, and robins.

Fishing was less divisive. Humbert led them to the butcher's, where they bought fat white *asticots* to be used as bait. "They live in putrefying meat," Humbert explained. "I used to keep some in my washstand basin, but Mummy said the maids gagged so when they did my room that I must give up. So now I keep snails instead."

"Snails?" Anne said. "Do you use those as bait?"

Humbert was horrified. "Bait! I sell them to Mama for the table—get a good price, too. And as I feed them on her lettuce—the cook gives me the outside leaves—it's pure profit." This started Anne on her own unrewarding snail project.

Opposite Humbert's house, on the other side of the pebbled *parterre*, was a duplicate house that was a haybarn, chickenhouse, and storehouse. On the second floor was a loft where Humbert, Anne, and Clare spent rainy hours. Anne found a trunkful of old papers, among them many letters from Mazzini to Humbert's great-grandfather, whom Victor Emmanuel had ennobled; he was a country doctor devoted to the *Risorgimento*. Savoie had been first named, it was said, for *sale voie*, dirty road, since the passes through the mountains had for centuries been manned by robber barons, who fleeced travelers and fought each other for the spoils. Then gradually it became *sauve voie*, the safe way, when the sea route to Italy became infested by Barbary pirates. Also, with the unification and pacification of France, some law and order spilled over to the kingdom of Savoie. Humbert's attic was full of old books of history, geography, and local lore, in which the girls browsed. Humbert was puzzled and bored by their enthusiasm, but pleased and flattered that they cared.

The girls were wholly and unexpectedly blissful at Tresserve. They had thought that leaving behind Possingworth, their lake and favorite haunts, the bluebell woods and primrose banks, would be going into exile. Instead, French life proved far preferable to British. They rode, on hirelings it is true, but in such infinitely lovelier country, scrambling up to high sunlit flower-crammed Alpine meadows; they swam in the crystal-clear blue lake, beside which their Sussex water seemed in retrospect a mudhole; their lessons—reading Saint Augustine in the original with Monsieur le Curé, translating Virgil, Ovid, Catullus, parsing Caesar, or learning by heart Athalie's great soliloquy or the charge to Cinna— were pure joy. As were the expeditions—to Madame de Staël's house at Coppet, with the dinner table set as in her day, and the lovely *toile de jouy* wallpaper; to the League of Nations in Geneva to hear Briand or Stresemann speak or to watch the Turkish delegation arrive to triumph over Venizelos; to Annecy, to the castle where Saint Francis de Sales was born; to Les Charmettes, where Jean-Jacques Rousseau had lived happily with Madame de Warens.

And they were gluttons for the marvelous food: *ombre chevalier* or stuffed eggplant and *blettes au gratin* from their own garden; snails (bought from Humbert) galore; and, of course, always *croissants* with Rumilly butter and honey for breakfast, sometimes their own (acacia) honey, at other times chestnut honey from Drumettaz or clover honey from Clairafond. And for special desserts there were wild strawberries soaked in white wine, or *mille-feuilles* or *babas-au-rhum*. The girls became greedy and rather fat; but they also learned to market, to cook, and to keep house in French. They learned, too, where the best *civet de renard* (fox stew) was to be had—at the station restaurant in Aix. And where was the best *galantine de foie truffé*—at the Chapon Fin in Chambéry near the *Quatre sans-queues*—the monument of four tailless elephants erected to Comte Benoît de Boigne—the general who had fought against James Grant Duff in India.

In the winter there was skiing on Mont Revard, and sometimes sledding down their own Tresserve hill. There were chestnut roasts, and, as Monsieur le Curé allowed the girls to sing in the choir, they learned all the great Gregorian tunes: the Masses, the hymns, Vespers, Compline, and the special sequences and proses for Christmas, Easter, Pentecost; and, best of all, the *"Dies Irae"* for funerals. Indeed, the girls could not think of funerals as sad, they were such fun, with the ostrich-plumed hearses drawn by black horses, and the black velvet trappings embroidered in silver thread. Humbert's father died, and then his grandfather, and the girls couldn't have enjoyed their funerals more.

But of all the delights, learning was the greatest, and for Anne, above all, learning Latin. And Latin meant liturgy—the great sentences of the Mass—and theology. When Monsieur le Curé had asked Mama, "What about religion?" she had shrugged her shoulders and said, "Make them Catholics if you can." Both girls were still Moslems, and this shocked Monsieur le Curé as much as finding them pagans had shocked Marmaduke. Monsieur le Curé had expected them to be Protestants—most English were—but Moslems he had never encountered, and they were a challenge. He began innocuously, with *De Viris Illustribus*, a textbook, and with Virgil. But some of Virgil's greatest lines are theistic statements: for example, *"O passi graviora, dabit deus his quoque finem"* (O you who have suffered greater miseries, God will give these too an end); Aeneas' adjuration to his colleagues in the fourth book of the *Aeneid;* or the fourth Eclogue. From these, the transition to Saint Augustine's passion for Virgil (shared by Anne), and thence to Saint Augustine himself, was easy.

Anne came to love the meaning because of the language; Marmaduke's translations of the Qu'ran paled before Augustine's Latin. For example, "*Dominus non dixit, vade in Orientem ut quaeris justitiam, abi usque ad occidentem ut accipies pacem. Ubi queris, ibi invenies, quia ad Eum qui ubique est, amando venitur non navigando.*" (The Lord did not say, travel to the East to find justice, go to the West to find peace. There where you seek, there you shall find, for to Him who is everywhere present, one comes by love and not by sail.) And again: "*Ego sum cibus grandium, cresce, ut manducabis me, sed non vero Ego in te, sed tu in Me mutaberis.*" (I am the food of the strong, grow, that you may eat me, but it is not I who will be changed into you, but you into Me.) Above all, Anne learned from Augustine the human dimension. In the *Confessions* he explained how, in Plotinus, he had learned that "in the beginning was the Word, but that the Word was made flesh there I did not learn." From Augustine, Anne learned too that "in the beginning was the Word: behold Him whom Mary worshiped. And the Word was made flesh: behold Him Whom Martha served." She learned that "He who made me without myself cannot save me without myself," and that man's salvation *caused* God's wondrous incarnation; that since man has denied and betrayed his Creator, only that Creator (not, repeat not, His Son, but *Himself*) could repair the primal fault. Love loving Itself *is* the Trinity: the Love that loves is the Father, the Love beloved is the Son, the Love by which Love loves is the Holy Ghost. And she came to tolerate the external paraphernalia that she had learned to despise, as one tolerates family photographs on a piano: they have nothing to do with the living reality, they are vulgar and out of place, but because they are pathetic evidences of affection, however trivial and banal, they have their value, for they, as everything else does, contain Him

> Whose secret Presence, through Creation's veins
> Running quicksilver-like, eludes your pains;
> Taking all shapes from Máh to Máhi, and
> They change and perish all—but He remains.

She was back at Omar Khayyám again; but now there were Christian statements also; for example, Victor Hugo:

> *Vous qui pleurez, venez à Lui car Il pleure,*
> *Vous qui passez, venez à Lui car Il demeure.*

Or, better, Jacopone da Todi:

> *Fac ut portem Christi mortem*
> *Passionis fac consortem.*
> (In the passion of my Maker
> Be my sinful soul partaker.)

Or Heine's verses, which Anne had long known but came to understand only now:

> *Als ich grosser würde, Kindchen,*
> *Viel gelesen, viel gereist,*
> *Schwilt mein Herz, und ganz von Herzen*
> *Glaub' ich an den heilgen Geist.*
> (When I bigger grew, my dear one,
> Studied more and wandered most,
> Stretched my heart and with heart wholly
> I affirmed the Holy Ghost.)

So Anne was no longer a Moslem, but under the Curé's aegis became a Catholic catechumen, since Mama had forbidden any further public change of religion until she came of age.

Lessons were only in the morning. On most afternoons Mama and the girls paid or received visits. The local gentry were poor and proud; they lived in charming castles, agreeably furnished, since during the tasteless nineteenth century they had had no money for so-called improvements. The walls were hung with verdure tapestries or faded family portraits, Claude-like landscapes or Salvator Rosaesque holy pictures. The furniture was late-seventeenth- to late-eighteenth-century, the garden usually a scythed field starred with cowslips or autumn crocus, according to the season, offering at all times a superb view of lake or mountains, and dotted with bushes of lilac, mock-orange, magnolia, mirabelle, and persimmon—the latter in November covered with great golden balls shining on the leafless trees against the gray landscape; these could be eaten only after the first frost. Among the locals, each of whom "received" on their *jour* (day) one afternoon a week, were the de la Rupelles, who lived on the Corsuet, an *alpille* of some thousand feet. Their family consisted of five hideous daughters and, finally, two sons. The girls never married, but at least four out of the five appeared at every other Savoyard hostess's *jour*. They kept a small fierce Pekinese. Some years later, when Anne was engaged and walked over to introduce her fiancé, Christopher Fremantle, the eldest (and fattest) Mademoiselle de la Rupelle, asked whether Anne was not afraid to walk home the five miles or so in the gloaming. "Of course not, she has her splendid escort," said Madame de la Rupelle. At the door the Pekinese, now very old, barked at Christopher's shins. He scuttled nervously around Anne and hid behind her while she made her adieux.

Nearer Chambéry were the de Lasseraz family, in a craggy castle too close to the railroad. They had two pretty daughters and lived in Turin during the winter, having opted to remain Italian in 1870. Near them lived the de la Celles; he was a lawyer, the only one of the local gentry with a job; their one child was the local beauty and also an heiress. In a valley between the Chambotte and the Revard, near the Gorges du Sierroz, among groves of poplar trees, lived the de Loches. Their castle was the oldest and biggest, also the coldest and dampest. Most of the local gentry kept one servant, if only a daily who officiated on the *jour*. But Monsieur de Loches explained to every visitor, "We keep two staff: I am the butler and gardener, my wife is the cook-housemaid." They had one child, a son, known as the Petit de Loches, who was in the army, in the Chasseurs Alpins. On his mother's *jour* he would appear in uniform, and all the local girls (including Ernestine Michaud, Anne, and Clare) would form a circle around him on small gold chairs. He would address a word to each in turn. He married none of them, however, but the

daughter of a silk-industrialist from Lyons. Unfortunately, this
financially wise move proved ultimately foolish; she produced
only daughters, too many of them.

In the charming little Château de Saint Innocent, on the very
edge of the lake, lived a sister of one of Mama's ex-fiancés, Philip
Somers Cocks. She was Anne d'Espine; in her youth she had been
the runt in a brilliant, musical, handsome, and witty family, and
she had been married off to an elderly Savoyard widower. He had
died. They had no children. His heirs, nephews, tried to persuade
his widow to go into a convent, at first gently, then not so gently.
But Anne d'Espine dug in her toes. She adored Saint Innocent
and firmly remained there until her death at a great age. Meanwhile, she too had her *jour*, and Anne and Clare loved it, as she
had a whole cabinet full of *lacustre* objects found in the lake,
where once a prehistoric people lived, on piles (like those in today's houses in Cambodia, Thailand, and San Blas), built right
over the water. Anne longed to live so and delighted in the theory
that at one time we were aquatic or semi-aquatic creatures.

Every year an American couple, Archibald McKay and his
wife, Nellie, rented one or another of the local castles. He was a
representative of a big American bank in Paris; she was a writer,
one of the few Americans ever to be *couronnée* by the Académie
Française for her writings in French. As a girl, barely seventeen, she had eloped with Archie just before World War I.
They had remained in Paris throughout the war, and she had gone
daily to the hospital at Val de Grâce. As she had no experience
and was so young, her job had been to sit with the dying. She told
Anne she had never seen anyone afraid to die, however young,
however much in pain or lonely. During the Joseph McCarthy
era (in New York, where she kept an apartment at the Savoy
Plaza), she became a Catholic. "Why did you do that?" Anne
asked her. "Because Catholics are under a cloud just now because
of that dreadful man," she said. She had been a friend of Eleonora
Duse and had gone with Duse to see the latter's daughter, who
lived in Ealing, a London suburb. The suburban daughter despised

her famous mother—"An actress, and so foreign," she told Nellie. Nellie's husband, Archie, was overly fond of little girls and pampered Clare, buying her unsuitable hats, pawing and pinching her.

The farthest-away *jour* was that of Henry Bordeaux, the writer. He lived on the far side of Chambéry, up toward the Granier, a splendid mountain that had broken in half in the sixteenth century. One half had fallen down, destroying two villages. The inhabitants of Myans, the next hamlet in the path of the errant mountain, had besought Our Lady in prayer. The dread half-mountain halted just outside Myans and stayed where it stopped. Naturally Our Lady of Myans still receives widespread regional devotion. Henry Bordeaux was a Savoyard boy, who became a member of the Académie Française. He wrote pious tales in exquisite French, suitable for all ages; also one marvelous true whodunit called *Le Lac Noir*. A black lake, high up in the fastness of the Granier, was the setting, and the story even today, though written in the nineties, has a splendidly spine-chilling quality.

Henry Bordeaux was the first French intellectual the girls had met. They did so at the de Lucernats', where a line had formed among the teacups. "What are you doing?" Mama asked Anne de Lucernat, the lovely daughter of the house, who was ahead of her. "I'm waiting to make my little phrase to the Master," she said. The Great Man had two girls: one plain, who became a good historian; and one pretty, who died young.

Among the visits Mama and the girls annually received was one from Lady Willingdon. Born B. Brassey, she had been supposed to marry Anne's papa, as their fathers were colleagues and great friends. But at sixteen B. had been wooed and won by the splendidly handsome young Freeman Freeman-Thomas, who went on—not unaided by his wife's millions—to be made Marquess of Willingdon and become Governor General of Canada, then Viceroy of India. B. was imperious and imperial and doted on purple; her nickname was *mauve-qui-peut*. Once, when she was vicereine, she was due to go in the viceregal train to visit some maharaja. But, like many of the *very* rich, she was also stingy. She decided a plane would be cheaper as well as quicker, and so arrived two days early. The maharaja, in her honor, had repainted the entire viceregal suite purple, including the toilet fixtures. Her Excellency, on arrival, took a hot bath; her bottom stuck to the purple paint and when disengaged was sore. For the two days of the state visit she could not (or would not) sit down—nor, of course, could anyone else.

To greet guests, Anne and Clare had devised a game. Clare would put on her dirtiest dress and most vacant expression. Anne, clutching her hand, would drag her alongside any victorias coming up the Tresserve hill, and beg in her best French, "Please, something for my poor little sister—afflicted, as you can see." Nearly always someone would oblige with a franc or even two. If the victoria turned in at their drive (as generally happened, for not many went on up to the village), the girls would run in by the fountain gate, wash, change into their tidy frocks, and appear at lunch or tea, courteous, charming, serene. Lady Willingdon earned their undying dislike, for she said severely to Mama, "Tiny, those girls are too old to beg." She also always left behind armfuls of old clothes—all mauve or purple—to be fitted to the girls. She was a stout lady and tall, so everything had to be altered, and Anne and Clare had to endure hours of standing up in a small stuffy room while the three Mademoiselles Massonat (all innocent of deodorants), with their mouths full of pins, hovered around adapting the viceregal garments to the girls' slight, spindly frames.

When Anne was seventeen, Lady Willingdon offered to take her as a lady-in-waiting; Lord Willingdon had become Governor General of Canada by that time. Anne longed to accept but could never bear to stand for more than a moment. Mama agreed she would probably wilt or faint on duty. Better go to Oxford, Mama admitted grudgingly, where Anne had just won a scholarship and could sit down to listen to lectures.

Later guests were the Stanley Baldwins, who did not stay—they preferred the Hotel Bernascon in Aix-les-Bains—but appeared for lunch or tea at least once every summer. The Aix shopkeepers did not consider the season to have begun until they saw Mrs. Baldwin's hat; she always appeared in one of the fantastic erections British matrons in those days often wore. Mrs. B. endeared herself to Mama one day when they were talking of how disagreeable, for the woman, the sex act was. "How did you *bear* to have four children?" Mama asked sympathetically. "I shut my eyes and thought of England," said Mrs. Baldwin. The last time the Baldwins appeared at the Maison was at the time of the 1938 crisis. Christopher and Anne had staying with them Rob Holland-Martin, then Director of the Southern Railway. The Baldwins came up to ask him if they should return at once to England, their cure left incomplete. Certainly not, Rob said. "There will be no war. Chamberlain is seeing to that." Anne and Christopher thus knew about Munich forty-eight hours before it happened. Like the Baldwins, they did not hurry back.

The village of Tresserve, straggling along the top of its hill, contained three foreign-owned establishments, all situated at the far end, that nearest Chambéry. Along the dusty white road, the first was on the left, a pretty white villa belonging to Ames van Wart, an elderly New Yorker who had married a fluffy French milliner many years his junior. They looked out onto Mont Revard and had a splendid garden. Farther along to the right, overlooking the lake, was the Earl of Berkeley's badly built, small, modern, ugly villa. Lord Berkeley was married to an American Lowell; with them lived his stepdaughter, Miss Jackson, middle-aged, a competent musician. The Earl had no children. Each of his brothers had one son, but, since both neglected to marry in time, neither boy could succeed to the earldom, which therefore ended with the Earl's death. The Tresserve Berkeley property is now the Town Hall.

At the end of the village, just before the hill tumbled down to the lake, on the right, stood the nineteenth-century villa of Mrs. Bellingham, an Irish widow, senile but amiable, who lived with a companion, Miss Colville. Their garden was glorious, full of edible fruits and blue cedars. In November the garden was golden with persimmon trees in luscious fruit. The house was a horror, plastered with gold-lettered texts painted on a bright blue background. "Peace be to this habitation, peace to all that dwell therein; peace the earnest of salvation; peace the fruit of pardoned sin," greeted one in the hall. The furniture was rattan; the art, oleos of the Lost Sheep and the Light of the World. Anne and Clare, however, loved lunching there, not only for the delicious meals but also for the quaint remarks of their hostess. "God always tethers the wind to the shorn lamb," she announced one day. And on another occasion she sang in a quavering contralto, "Thy love for me is sweeter far, than all the jams and jellies are." One day, when the van Warts were also present, a superb pie appeared, served with lashings of sugar and cream. After all present had exclaimed on the luscious dessert, Mrs. van Wart begged for the recipe. Later that afternoon, Mrs. Bellingham kindly dispatched her butler to the van Warts with a bundle of rhubarb and her own recipe for rhubarb pie written out. He was dismissed, rhubarb and recipe in hand, with the remark, "Madame van Wart does not need a purge." The two families never spoke again, though both lived on in Tresserve many years.

For her twelfth-birthday present Anne had asked for Monsieur Bel's cat. He was fattening it up to eat, and Anne had persuaded her mother to pay fifteen francs, an outrageous sum, to save its life. Anne carried it in a sack, through which it scratched her back raw, to the Maison, buttered its paws, and shut it up in her bedroom. Somehow, perhaps with the connivance of Madame Gal, it escaped and ran back to Monsieur Bel. Two days later, when the girls went up to the presbytery for their Latin lesson, Monsieur le Curé was smacking his lips. He explained he had just eaten the most delicious fricassée of cat at Monsieur Bel's. "He left it skinned in running water for twelve hours. Was it tender!" said the Curé.

For her thirteenth birthday Anne asked for a grave in the little cemetery at Tresserve donated to the village by Lady Whalley, who was buried in it. Mama paid five hundred francs, and Anne

planted a box edging around her plot. Now she *really* belonged to
Tresserve: born there, buried there, domiciled there, Anne felt
herself a Savoyarde.

The Aix household revolved around Madame Gal, who care-
took when the family were away, cooked when they came. She
lived with her drunken postman husband in a little house on the
Tillet; Mama had built it for her, with a laundry below. The Gals
had one son, Jeannot, a keen swimmer. One day when the girls
were swimming in the lake with Humbert, they saw someone in
difficulty. It was Jeannot, being attacked by one of the so-called
lake eagles, which must have thought he was a fish, for it dove
repeatedly at his eyes. They drove it off, but only just in time;
Jeannot was quite exhausted with swimming under water and
surfacing again and again to find the bird still there.

On the Fourteenth of July there was dancing in the village
street. Anne and Clare were delighted each year to be solemnly
asked to waltz by the already inebriated Monsieur Gal, who stank
of garlic and *marc*. Madame Gal was philosophical about him.
"Until one is thirty-five," she told Mama, "one has to have a man.
After that, praise be, one needs one no longer."

The girls had been at Tresserve a whole blessed year when
Mama suddenly announced that they would be going to school in
England in September—to boarding school. The girls were outraged. "*You* told us how miserable you were when you were taken
away from India and sent to school in England," they said. "You
can't be as beastly to us as your mother was to you." But nothing
they said would move Mama. In fact, Anne's son Adam told her,
there is probably a school syndrome, because of which those who
were unhappy at school wish their children to be not less so, and
vice-versa. In vain the girls threatened to refuse to speak any English (they kept their word for quite a while); to go on hunger
strikes (they did not); to drown themselves in the lake (they never
even tried). Leaving the Maison was almost the worst sorrow they

had ever known. Only Papa's death could be compared with the horror of returning to cold, dark, wet, flat England, with its badly dressed, drab people and its inedible food.

Waiting in London for the dread day when they must drive down to their incarceration, they cried themselves to sleep each night, shouting over and over again the last lines of Saint Thomas Aquinas's great Eucharistic hymn that ends *"Nobis donet in patria"*—Bring us to our country, or is it fatherland? or home? No English equivalent exists for the wholly Latin concept of *patria*.

In hateful London, staying briefly in a cheap, chilly hotel, Anne and Clare prayed nightly that they might return to Tresserve. Anne told Clare proudly that for her it did not matter if she returned alive or dead. "I belong there," she boasted, "dead or alive," since I have my grave. No good to you, though, as there's only room for one. *You'll* have to be cremated and put in with Papa at Waldron."

Ten years later Anne, three years married, returned to Tresserve with Christopher. They went to visit her grave and were horrified to find it occupied; someone else was in it, recently buried. There were faded pink gladioli on top, and a frightful purple bead concoction spelling out "To our beloved sister." Furious, Anne dragged Christopher with her to the Town Hall to expostulate. The mayor courteously explained that no grave plot in France could be held for longer than ten years; there was just not enough graveyard space. So plots were sold for a decade and then resold.

"But if I had been inside?" Anne asked indignantly.

"You would have been quicklimed and the next purchaser would have been put in on top of you," the mayor answered.

XVIII

Its Ugly Head

"Only the lower classes really enjoy sexual intercourse," Mama told the girls, not once but repeatedly. When the time came to tell Anne and Clare the facts of life, she merely asked, "You've both read *Madame Bovary*, haven't you?" Anne, twelve, had; Clare, two years her junior, had not. "It's all in there," Mama went on. It wasn't—and isn't.

Mama, enchantingly pretty, with a perfect oval face, tiny faun's ears, a cloud of wavy brown hair, and bushy eyebrows, had been painted in 1907 by John Singer Sargent. The splendid life-size portrait, she all in white with her head against a flame-colored cushion, hung in the drawing room in Rutland Gate. Helleu had drawn her as a girl; Alma-Tadema had painted her. Even at seventy-three, when she was dying of cancer, she kept her looks. Often she wished she were "of a different class" so she could flirt all day, beginning with the milkman, going on with the butcher, baker, grocer, gardeners, rising to the butler. Whenever she needed help she would look pathetic and murmur in Italian, "I need a man." And there always seemed to be one around. But of the sexual act itself Mama took a dim view, and she told Anne that she had not slept with Papa between the birth of Konradin and Anne's conception twelve years later.

Anne concluded that women had a raw deal. She so much wished that she had been a boy, and could not forgive the Almighty—after all, a fifty-per-cent chance! All the things she wanted to be—priest or diplomat or politician— were men's things. And anyway, even in women's fields men did better. Chefs were better than cooks, tailors than seamstresses, monks than nuns; and even with children, men succeeded in loving them better and in being loved by them more, and men were much better teachers.

Poor Papa, Anne said once to Konradin, if Mama wouldn't sleep with him, how did he manage? He was eight years older than Mama, Konradin pointed out, so after a few years it wasn't so urgent; tri-weekly became try weekly, then try weakly. A man is past his prime at eighteen already (as Kinsey later confirmed!). And there was always Marie-Louise, who had remained adoring until he died. "Maïe?" Anne asked, astonished. Anne had always adored "Maïe," as she and Clare called her, and Maïe's tame guinea pig Stumps, who lived so long because his teeth were filed, and therefore as he aged he did not die of starvation. . . . Was she really? Did she? But Konradin would not answer; nor did she know. She just hated Mama and wanted Anne to ask her about Maïe so as to make her jealous.

After the Blessed Year at Tresserve, Mama sent Anne and Clare to a most atypical school in Kent, run by her friend Gabrielle Rossignon, who had invented the Belgian intensive system of keeping hens always indoors, on dried leaves, to make them lay more. Miss Starbuck, Mademoiselle Rossignon's English friend, shared with her the running of the Old Palace, Bromley. Miss Starbuck was as British as a bulldog, and as unattractive. Mademoiselle Rossignon was round and jolly of face and figure and had experimental ideas about almost everything. During the war she had converted Mama to her "intensive" system of poultry-keeping; now she kept her fifty girls intensively too. They were housed in a lovely old red brick palace that had for centuries been the home of the Bishops of Rochester; Saint John Fisher had gone thence to the

Tower. French was compulsory at all times. The girls were put on their honor to speak no English. They were also continually spied upon by the staff, and if discovered chatting in English were reported and punished. Anne and Clare spoke French as well as they did English but so disliked the spy system that they—and all their companions—spoke English on principle. No uniform was worn, and, as most of the girls were "filthy rich" and were at school only to be kept out of mischief between the ages of fifteen and seventeen, their main interests were boys, then clothes.

Mama had strong views on female attire. At home the girls had been clad all their lives in straight, beltless serge frocks, green or red (black for the year of mourning), in winter, and cotton of the same cut and color in summer. All their clothes were made by Mrs. Thomas, spinster sister of one of the gardeners. She had had a byblow daughter, Lucy, a favorite nurserymaid until she married a sailor. Mama insisted that Mrs. Thomas be called "Mrs."—indeed, she called all women over forty "Mrs." whether they were married or not. She gave Mrs. Thomas a charming cottage for peppercorn rent. Before the girls were sent to school, Mrs. Thomas made special gym tunics for them, without pleats. "Pleats make teen-agers look bunchy," Mama said. Instead, the skirts were slit up the sides. Under these they wore white silk blouses and black woolen stockings. All the other girls at school wore beige silk stockings, and Anne and Clare, in their homemade eccentric outfits, looked like twin Orphan Annies.

Anne detested school from the first moment. She shared a linoleum-floored room with three other girls. She had lapsed back, at thirteen, to being a Mohammedan since leaving Tresserve, and would rise at dawn, break the ice in her washstand jug in order to perform the preliminary ablutions, and say the morning *rakaas*. Anne's companions nicknamed her "Cocky" because she showed none of the humility suitable to a "new girl," and would pour water from their jugs over her. By October it was already bitter cold, and she shivered in her unsought martyr's role and was lucky not to catch pneumonia. Clare, by two years the youngest girl in the school, and one of the prettiest, quickly became a much-petted mascot and very popular. Anne was constantly finding her on some sofa in the forbidden part of the house where lived "Ross and Starb," as the principals were nicknamed, tickling and being tickled. Once a month both girls were bidden to Sunday lunch with Ross and Starb. *Their* rooms were warm and comfortable, as well as attractively decorated and furnished. The girls were fed delicious food and given Emu (Australian) burgundy to drink. Anne and Clare would both become slightly lightheaded and red-faced and after lunch would retire to sleep it off in the garden or the gym, as their bedrooms were out of bounds by day.

The sixth form contained the most beautiful girls Anne and Clare had ever seen. There was Frankie Lonsdale, daughter of Frederick Lonsdale, one of whose plays was running in London. When he came to take his daughter out, he used to hide outside the front door in the pachysandra, in fear of martinet, whalebone-collared Miss Starbuck. Frankie married the son of Mama's friend Lady Alba Donaldson (Hobart Hampden) and with him ran the experimental Peckham Health Centre. Then there was Grace Dalrymple, luscious and rich; her clothes and scent came from Chanel. Peggy, a rich South African, was almost lovelier, as was Beatrice, the captain of lacrosse and hockey. There were some oddballs too. One girl's ambassador parents had left her as a baby with a nurse who drugged her nightly; she was halfwitted, and despised and ill-treated by all. Then there were Phat Pat, who had some kind of elephantiasis; and Veronica, who limped from polio and whose "love" was Kiki, a girl from Southport.

The teaching was excellent, and Anne and Clare, hitherto without competition except from each other, throve. The Scots teacher of English galloped them through chunks of Shakespeare, Spenser, and Sidney, and made them write interesting essays. Unfortunately, Mama had so convinced them that "maths" and science were not for women that they did not work at these. Games were a revelation. Mama had always despised them (except tennis) and had forbidden hockey "as it thickens your ankles." But lacrosse was glorious, and netball fun. And for Anne, who "made" both teams her first term, they afforded opportunities—every other week— for getting out of school, as matches were at home and away on alternate weeks. Granted, she got away only to other schools, but at least there was an outing by bus or train, and a different setting. Anne loved rushing up and down the field at right wing (at lacrosse), or shooting goals at netball, and sucking lemon or orange quarters at half-time and discussing tactics, and afterward eating horribly spot-making, complexion-wrecking, fattening sticky-buns at the team teas.

One or two of the older girls had beaux in London and went up at weekends in pairs (this was allowed if parents gave permission) and came back with fabulous tales of night clubs, Charlestons, Garbo films, and young men. Many of the girls contented them- selves with crushes within the school, and of these there was a continuous series; girls wrote each other long daily letters, whis- pered in corners, twined arms around each other in corridors, quarreled, made up, changed partners, and stayed with each other in the "hols."

Anne had become a kind of second string for Veronica (though Kiki still came first) by knowing more Byron, Swinburne, and Rupert Brooke by heart. At the end of the winter term, Mama said Veronica might come to stay at Aix for part of the Easter holidays. Anne, Clare, Mama, and Veronica (who had never been abroad before) were to travel out together. Mama was dubious and wrote Anne warning letters: "This is the first time you are having someone to stay whose parents I have not met. No doubt her mother is a good woman, but they live in Bickley and her father is a stockbroker." Mama did not know *any* stockbrokers socially.

The journey was hideous. The train from Paris to Aix was jammed: eight seats, eight people, all obliged to sit bolt upright all night. At about five a.m., as Mama was fainting from the stifling atmosphere, Anne boldly walked over all the feet and opened the window a chink. A fat man immediately shut it. "But monsieur, we must have it open, Mama is fainting." "Let her faint," said the fat man. During the interminable night a pink-faced, stubbleless French soldier, off to do his military service in enemy country—Germany—leaned his tired young head on Clare's shoulder and intermittently slept. Dawn came at last, and Anne stood in the corridor as the train came into Culoz, and rubbed the steam off the windows and saw the mountains, lolloping like nosy leopards right up to the railway line, dark, lithe, their crests white with snow against the pre-dawn dark sky. She murmured Grandpapa Grant Duff's favorite saying, engraved on a clouded ruby ring she always wore: "This also shall pass away." The stuffy carriage, the awful people, the choking black engine smoke—these would pass, but the eternal hills would always be there, as serene, as inquisitive, and as comforting.

They got out at Aix-les-Bains and took a *fiacre* up to the Maison. Marie-Louise welcomed them with *croissants* and hot coffee, and one look at the blue lake cradled in its hills made the long journey emphatically worth while. Then baths, for they were filthy with train dirt, and a sleep.

Anne found that Veronica cramped her style. As Veronica spoke English-accented bad French, Anne was embarrassed when they went visiting the locals. As she was lame, she would not walk or ride, and it was too early and cold to swim. Veronica, however, seemed not to sense her inadequacies as a guest and appeared to enjoy herself. One day she drew Anne to her room, the best guest room, on the *piano nobile* of the old tower (Anne, Clare, and Mama slept upstairs). "I must read you Kiki's latest letter," she said, pulling her in and locking the door. Anne sat down on the edge of the bed while Veronica read a sixteen-page handwritten missive.

Presently the door rattled. "Open at once," said Mama in a cold, hard voice.

Anne did so, to be confronted by an icy parent.

"What are you two girls doing?" Mama asked.

"Veronica is reading me a letter from Kiki," Anne replied.

"Why was the door locked?" Mama asked.

Anne replied, "I don't know. Veronica locked it. I suppose she didn't want anyone barging in to hear what Kiki said."

Veronica said nothing.

Mama looked at her directly. "I think you had better leave here tonight. I will get your ticket," she said.

Anne was bewildered, indignant. Veronica was not. Anne saw her off on the train, weeping more for the horror of treating a guest so badly than from affection. "You will never love any girl as much as you loved me," Veronica prophesied in farewell.

Back at Bromley after Easter, Anne found that Veronica bore her no ill will for the incident.

Clare, who was in another classroom and bedroom and rarely saw Anne except at meals, sought her out one day in the garden, where Anne was watching a miraculous fall of tiny frogs; all the grass was crawling with them, and they seemed to have come from nowhere.

"I think I'm pregnant," she announced.

Anne goggled. "How could you be?"

"You remember that boy, that soldier in the train going to Savoy last hols?" Clare said.

"Yes, and—?"

"Well, I think I'm pregnant. I haven't had my bad week since."

Anne didn't know what to say. "I don't know how—how you could start a baby by someone's *head* on your *shoulder*," she ventured. "Better write Mama."

Clare wrote Mama. Mama wrote Starb. Starb reflected that Mama had better come and they would "see" the child together. Mama arrived. Clare was sent for. "Boudoir," she told Anne, gloomily recalling the horrid moments of their childhood when they had done wrong and were sent downstairs to Mama's boudoir for a wigging. Truthfully, Clare told Mama and Starb what had occurred in the train. Both ladies, suddenly sorry for her, had difficulty in suppressing their smiles.

"But darling," Mama said, "how *could* you think you could become pregnant like that? You've read *Madame Bovary*."

"I haven't, it's Anne that has," Clare said, "and Anne said it's no use."

"What do you mean, no use?" Mama said indignantly. "It's one of the greatest novels ever written."

"Maybe," Clare said calmly, "but it doesn't explain what men do to girls to get babies."

Mama sighed. But neither she nor Starb offered any further explanation.

Next Easter, on her way through London, Anne went to tea at the Charles Morgans' and consulted Hilda Vaughan, Morgan's lovely redheaded wife. "Do help," she said, "or someday we'll one of us be in real trouble. I don't know why Mama threw Veronica out, and Clare doesn't know—any more than I do—what Papa did to Mama to produce us."

Hilda, sitting in their lovely flat in Chelsea, looking out onto the mud-brown Thames, told her, "You should read Havelock Ellis. He is quite explicit."

Anne sighed. "Reading *Madame Bovary* did no good at all. Do you think Havelock Ellis will be any better?"

"Yes, I do," Hilda said, fondling her blond two-year-old daughter Shirley, who proceeded to struggle and climb off her lap and be sick all over the feet of Osbert Sitwell, who was across the room talking to Charles.

Anne took a bus next day to the London Library. Henry Yates Thompson had made her a life member, and she spent happy hours among the stacks. She asked fat old Mr. Cox, who had known her grandfather, for "any one of Mr. Havelock Ellis's books."

Mr. Cox looked very shocked. "But miss, he doesn't write suitable books," he replied.

"But really, I need one," Anne said.

"We let members take them out only in a brown paper cover," Mr. Cox said.

"That's all right," said Anne. She took the offending volume in its innocuous but telltale jacket. Alas, it was all about boots. She returned it next day. Mr. Cox snorted as he took it from her.

Back at school for a glorious fall term, Anne felt increasingly frustrated. Love she must, for she decided, like Augustine, that she loved to love. But whom? Veronica was over; though *she* felt no rancor, Anne felt guilty. She tried having a crush on Mr. Coleman, the music teacher, but he was dreadfully plain and had badly fitting false teeth, a wife, and three children. Alas, her love must be ideal. She had rejected Rupert Brooke because Veronica and Kiki had torn the two photographs of him out of the *Collected Poems* and pinned them up in their room. So she decided to return to the god Apollo. She had burned incense all her childhood to the cast of Apollo Belvedere in Mama's boudoir in Rutland Gate. In the Old Palace School, on the front stairs, in Starb and Ross's part of the house, was a colossal head, in white marble, of the same Apollo Belvedere. Anne now tried, once a day, to sneak through the green baize door that separated the school from Starb's and Ross's privacy and run down the polished-oak front stairs, curtsying deeply to Apollo as she went. One day, greatly daring, she felt she must do more. She stood on tiptoe, put both her arms around the great head, and kissed him full on the lips. At that moment Starb came out of her bedroom and looked over the banisters. "Anne, what *are* you doing here?" she called down. "You know this part of the house is out of bounds except for special invitation."

Anne, terrified, pulled the Apollo off its pedestal. It fell, luckily not on Anne's feet, which it would have broken; but, alas, its flawless marble nose chipped. Anne, weeping, explained she had been running down the stairs as a dare and had bumped into the head. She was severely punished.

At the end of the summer term she got 99 in all subjects in her exams. Mama decided, since the girls had done so well—too well—that the work was not challenging enough, so removed them and entered them in her old school, Cheltenham Ladies' College, where there were a thousand girls who all wore uniforms, and where particular friendships were frowned upon.

Later Anne, married, admitted to Mama that she enjoyed the act of love.

"Darling, how like a housemaid," Mama said.

Anne hugged her and sighed. "I'm afraid I am."

XIX

To Europe by Gotha

"It is much, much grander," Mama informed the girls, "to be in the lowest *Gotha* than to be in Burke."

"What d'you mean, lowest?" Anne asked.

"The *Adels-Buch*," Mama replied, "only barons and counts."

"Are we in that?" asked Clare.

"Gracious no," Mama said, "we're only *just* in Burke, see Coll. [collaterals]. Of course we're in Burke's *Landed Gentry*, but that's quite different. No, of the English, only the Royals and the twenty-four dukes are in *Gotha*, and, of course, those who get in by marriage."

Mama, badly crippled with arthritis, was planning to spend a summer in Piešt'any, in Czechoslovakia, where there were radio-active waters. She was preparing the girls for meeting what she called "Central Europeans" and had suggested they had better bone up on their *Gotha*. "You will look very provincial and silly if you meet Esterházys or Radziwills and don't know who they are."

As Mama wrote Lady Gregory in Ireland, "The girls' school reports were fantastically creditable. But whether because they are more intelligent than the average—or the other little girls less, I can't say. The best way to bring up girls," Mama continued—

Lady Gregory had grandchildren the ages of Anne and Clare—"is entirely at home until puberty. After that I think they need others of their kind. But it is a huge mistake to let little children see any but their immediate relations and household; it makes for the herd mentality, which is so horrible a feature of modern life. . . . Anne is writing tons of poetry, much of it interesting. Her prose is bad, for a curious reason. She has done a lot of Latin and will try to write English like Latin. . . . Education is a terrible problem nowadays, for no parents ask for moral education—the one thing that really matters. And so any parent that desires it is considered a crank." Lady Gregory approved the letter and its sentiments, kept it, and kept Anne in mind.

Since they would have the whole summer before them, and the cure at Piešt'any would take only three weeks, Mama decided they would potter on the way. They started from Aix-les-Bains and went first to Alassio, where Douglas Ainslie, Mama's first cousin, was living. He did not please the girls, being that "devil incarnate, an English Italianate." He was Benedetto Croce's official translator, was himself no mean poet, and, above all, was a lifelong pilgrim who stayed often in Sri Ramana Maharshi's ashrama at Tiruvannamalai in India. Later, after the Maharshi's death, he continued pursuing a guru here, a sage there, until he died in southern California among others of his kind.

From Alassio, Mama and the girls crept along the Riviera in sooty trains to Lerici, where lived another relative, Percy Lubbock, wed to the formidable Lady Sybil. She had not improved his already poor eyesight by making him read aloud to her for hours a day in a darkened room. She feared the effect of bright light on her erstwhile English June-rose complexion. Percy went completely blind but remained an enchanting companion, living in splendor in a beautiful house with gardens going down to the only civilized sea. Anne and Clare pitied this old cousin but spent the least possible time talking to him, preferring to dive off the splendid rocks straight into the blue Mediterranean.

Years later Anne found Percy Lubbock's *The Art of Fiction*

an excellent primer for teaching her course in creative writing at Fordham University, and was able, on a subsequent visit to him, to tell him how much it meant to her. Another of his books, *Shades of Eton,* is probably the best ever written about that school—except perhaps for Lord Curzon's *A Day of My Life at Eton,* published anonymously and long out of print.

Lerici offered memories of Shelley, whom Mama approved of but Anne detested—less for his treatment of Harriet, which after all was a personal matter, than for his callous cruelty to the Irish, whom he brought to insurrection and left to execution. From there the trio stopped briefly in Milan, to see the wedding-cake cathedral, incongruous in the midst of the industrial city, and the fading "Last Supper." It had faded, Mama said, as a judgment on Leonardo, who was profoundly an atheist and shouldn't have pandered to princes by painting pieties in which he disbelieved. Many years later, when a London Catholic paper headlined the question "Was Jesus Christ a homosexual?" Anne, remembering Leonardo's "Last Supper," thought that at least one artist had painted Him as such.

Next they stopped in Verona and saw the Romanesque basilica of San Zeno, which Bernard Shaw had told Mama was for him the most valid of all churches. "If you sit in it," he had written, "you will need no alcohol or stimulants to bring you to a vision of peace." In the Verona market they found a small owl exposed on a perch in the blazing noonday July sun. These tiny owls are used as decoys: their perch is limed, the field birds come to tease them and thus are caught and eaten. Anne and Clare insisted that Mama buy an owl. This entailed buying also a cage. The caged owl proved a dirty, disagreeable, and unrewarding pet. It never grew tame, bit any fingers it could reach, stank to high heaven, and had to be fed live mice (when procurable) or minute portions of raw heart or liver. Carried by the girls around Europe, the *gabbia* (cage) cost a small fortune on trains, and hotels objected—not unreasonably—to the smelly object. The bird's fleas so devoured the girls that when they got back to England they looked as though they had the measles, and before they were sent off to school at Cheltenham, Dr. Holman, the family physician, had to certify them both as "suffering severely from flea bites."

After Verona, they visited Venice, where Admiral Wolkoff, one of Mama's great admirers, lived with his daughter Vera in a ramshackle *palazzo*. The admiral, a painter, had also written a book of art criticism, in which one illustration was a photo of Mama's Sargent portrait surrounded by smaller photographs of the most famous female portraits ever painted—the "Mona Lisa," Rembrandt's "Saskia," and others. Admiral Wolkoff himself had painted an admirable portrait of Eleonora Duse, who he claimed had been his mistress. The girls jibbed at trailing from church to church and insisted on visiting the Lido; Mama said that it was dirty and swimming there was a Philistine waste of time.

They enjoyed, however, visiting Philip Somers Cocks, a fat old papist who had been quite a creditable amateur cellist, to whom Mama had actually once been engaged but only for forty-eight hours, as both had then realized It Would Not Do. Philip had married a lady who early became deaf, so he had retired to a *palazzo* in Venice, where his wife need not fear being run over.

From Venice, Mama and the girls went by hired car to Pergine, a tiny village on a lake in the Dolomites, near Trent, which was full of memories of the Great Council. The girls' room at Pergine, which looked up onto the sun-covered mountains, had until recently been terribly haunted, but an Old Catholic bishop who had been the last visitor had scattered a consecrated Host reduced to crumbs around the room. This blasphemous procedure had disposed of all lesser manifestations of evil.

At Pergine, Mama had invited a young man to stay, ostensibly for the girls' benefit. He was handsome, tall, willowy, mustached, about thirty-five, and their uncle's First Secretary in Stockholm. (Uncle Piggy—Sir Arthur Grant Duff—was British Ambassador there.) He was Jimmie (now Sir James) Dodds, a bachelor who made himself very comfortable indeed. When he had stayed with Mama at Tresserve, the housekeeper had nicknamed him "the gentleman of the three hot-water bottles." Bedsocks, too. Now, in an Italian July, he boated, swam, and lazed with Mama and the girls, rather too patently preferring Mama.

But in the train from Trent to Vienna Anne received her first proposal. A short, balding man entered the carriage and, after observing the two girls, the caged owl, and Mama for a while, began to talk. He was, he said, a schoolmaster who lived near Graz. He had a nice house and, attached to it, a greenhouse. How well-brought-up were the gracious lady's girls, so unlike most of the brazen hussies one saw about. He himself was the quiet type. He was thirty-eight and had not yet married, as his mother had lived until a few months ago and he had taken care of her and she of him. Now he was looking for a wife. Would the gracious lady consider granting him the hand of her eldest daughter? He could promise he would be an exemplary husband, as he had been a son; he would take the greatest care of such a jewel. Mama, red in the face with suppressed laughter, said he should plead his cause himself. Anne, choking back her giggles, said demurely that she was far too young. "I prefer to remain with my mother for some years still."

Vienna was still gloomy because of the Allied blockade. Many people were wearing clothes made of paper. Food was expensive. Mama and the girls stayed in dark rooms and saw mostly Jewish writers and painters with little money and many woes. There were exceptions. Frau Irene Scheue-Riess, who wrote fairy tales and lived in a rich suburb, took the trio up to Cobenzl, where Anne danced her first waltz with Fritz Mendl, a rich baker's son. The Mendls became friends; Fritz fell in love with Anne and later pursued her to London, where he would sit opposite her in buses, saying loudly, fervently, and in heavily accented English, "You are so beautiful." Anne, embarrassed, took him walking in the Green Park, where he would not believe the guards outside Buckingham Palace, in their scarlet uniforms and busbies, were real. He stood stock still in front of one, saying in a loud voice, "That is not a live man. That is a toy soldier." The poor guardee blushed furiously, and Anne feared he would burst or bayonet them. Fritz was killed in a skiing accident, which no doubt saved him from Dachau.

Piešt'any proved to consist of an enormous hotel de luxe set in a tiny village on the river Waag, a tributary of the Danube. The countryside, the plain of Bratislava, was flat, dotted with villages of white thatched cottages, the muddy streets full of geese. The peasants wore musical-comedy costumes, wonderful hand-embroidered blouses, and black skirts embroidered in rainbow colors around the hem. Around the bottom of each cottage where there was a marriageable daughter was painted a band of bright color: two contrasting bands indicated two daughters. The church was filled on Sundays with crowds singing in nasal Slovak; the churchyard had old hand-carved stone crucifixes on every grave.

In the morning, while Mama took the waters, the girls played tennis or rode or swam in a pleasant, naturally warm swimming pool. But life really began in the evening. After supper came dancing or various games—bridge, chess, and so on—with fellow guests. The girls, who had never had any "night life" before, found it intoxicating. The hotel's clientele was cosmopolitan. There were an Argentine lady and her son. There was an old Jewish Prussian *Junker*, Herr Scottlander, with red hair and a redheaded, red-necked soldier son who on first dancing with Anne told her he would like to bayonet every English woman and child because Germany had lost the war, because of the monstrous Treaty of Versailles. He early became a Nazi, Anne learned after World War II, but was liquidated at Auschwitz. There was a charming Swedish Countess Rosenberg, with a young grandson. There was the German translator of Bernard Shaw, Herr Trebnitsch, who beat Anne at chess in four moves and grunted, "*Noch nicht der Anfang*" (not yet the beginning).

And there was, above all, the lovely, delicate, charming Irene Poncracz, who lived at Diviaky and had a town house in nearby Bratislava and was a few years older than Anne. Irene was accompanied by one of her brothers, a handsome young priest who had tuberculosis, of which he later died; she, Anne, and Clare became passionate friends. It was a friendship based on Catholicism. Irene gave the girls pious cards and spiritual books, which improved their German and widened their horizons. Irene, like many Hungarians (Slovakia had been a part of Hungary until the end of World War I), was an accomplished linguist. She spoke perfect English, French, German, and Italian. Hungarian and Slovak, which she also knew, she spoke only to shop people and servants. It was the girls' first glimpse of pious, well-born, and well-educated Europeans—of *Gotha* folk, in fact. They never saw Irene again but continued to write to her.

After World War II was over, and the Communists had taken over Czechoslovakia, Anne tried to persuade Irene to come to London or the United States. Her mother and her priest-brother were both dead; her sister was married. The authorities would have let her go, as an elderly spinster was of no value to them. She still lived in Bratislava. Diviaky, her family home near Povarska, had been nationalized. But Irene would not come. She wrote Anne and Clare in impeccable French, explaining that what had happened in her country was the fault of families like hers. The Communists could not have come to power, she said, had she and her kind done their duty. Look at England, she said—no Communists there, because the governing classes had a sense of responsibility. She felt now that she must stay and expiate. Sometimes there were intimations of the extent of expiation, of cold—she often asked for knitting yarn—and once, when her ration card had not been renewed, she wrote of hunger. In the late 1960s Anne's son Richard visited her by car with food, coffee, and messages and was made most welcome. Irene was then particularly delighted to learn that Richard's elder brother, Adam, had married "*la petite Sapieha*," daughter of Prince Paul Sapieha and great-niece of Archbishop Adam Sapieha, Cardinal Primate of Poland, who had defied both the Nazis and the Communists.

In 1969, for Anne's birthday, Clare agreed to join her in Vienna so that they could drive together to Bratislava to see Irene Pon-

cracz and her brother Nicky. They crossed the Czech frontier—
only thirty miles from Vienna—in lovely June weather and met
Nicky, gray-haired, middle-aged, at the state hotel where they
had booked. Irene had gone to Switzerland on a visit to a nephew
who had left in 1968 during the troubles and was working there.
Nicky, seventy, was retired on a pension of eight hundred koruny
a month. He had been a musician and for some years had been
head of the Music Conservatory in Bratislava and clarinetist in
the Municipal Orchestra. Now he paid five koruny a day for all
his meals—very good food, he said—at the cooperative, and paid
nothing on buses or trams. Once a year he went to Austria, to
stay a month at Graz with a friend, another musician. In Bratislava he lived in a single rented room in a warm house. Irene, who
had never worked, lived in a cold room with an old maid, now
blind, and had to pay for their food and heat; she found coal very
expensive. Their eldest brother still lived at Diviaky, acting as
caretaker in the school their home had become. Another lived in
the village near Bratislava, in the castle where Nicky and Irene
were born and where their priest brother and a beloved young
sister, who died at sixteen of tuberculosis, were buried.

The following day, after dining at the best restaurant in Bratislava, and sightseeing—Anne hoped she would never know any
town as well as she felt she knew Bratislava after doing it with
Nicky—Anne, Clare, and Nicky drove out to the village where
the castle, now a school, in which Irene's family had grown up
was located. It proved to be a stuccoed, square, not very large
seventeenth-century house in a wood on a lake. . . . Anne thought
how strange that communism and capitalism had produced, in
their cases, the same results. Possingworth was now an old people's home, the Maison a school; Diviaky too was a school, as was
this other Poncracz home.

When she was quite sure there was no one around who could
hear her question, Anne asked Nicky who were worse, the Germans or the Russians. "The Germans," Nicky said. "They thought
we were inferior racially. The Russian soldiers, the Russian peo-

ple, we loved them very much when they came and chased the Germans out and freed us. They really liberated us, and you saw their graves up around the war memorial. They died to make us free. But now—" He stopped.

"Now you don't love them any more?" Anne suggested, and he replied, somberly, "Now no one loves them any more. Not since last August."

Irene's friend Pauline Palffy came to the Hotel Thermal at Piešt'any in July 1925 to visit Irene, and she, too, quickly made friends with Anne and Clare. She was as pious as Irene and as fluent a linguist, but a very different type—an outdoor girl, healthy, extrovert, from a big family. She was a splendid rider and had won cups in steeplechase races in Prague and owned racehorses and hunters galore. She invited the girls to stay with her in Smolenice, where she lived with her widowed mother, a sister, and an unmarried brother. Two older married brothers lived nearby. With the Palffys, Anne and Clare found they were *en plein Gotha*. The Poncraczes were Hungarian gentry; the Palffys were cousins to all Europe.

When Mama's "cure" was completed, the trio went to Munich to visit Mama's beloved first cousin, Hermann Obrist. Hermann lived with his German (*Gotha*) wife and two daughters. There was very little to eat. The Obrists had a paying guest, Andrew Campbell, who fed the girls biscuits and chocolates which he hid in his room. The Obrist girls and Andrew took Anne and Clare bicycling. Anne had never met brakes controlled by the pedals. When they got into the park she inadvertently checked herself and went over the handlebars onto the green—and, happily, soft—grass. A policeman appeared out of nowhere and gave her a summons for walking on the grass. "But I wasn't walking," she exclaimed. "It doesn't matter whether you were walking on your head or your heels," said the officer. "It is forbidden to walk on the grass." Anne had to pay the fine.

On Mama and the girls went, northward, stopping in Berlin to

see the busts of Nefertiti and of Amenhotep IV, and Anne's godmother Marie von Bunsen, whose father had been German Ambassador to England and a friend of Queen Victoria. Marie von,
as Mama called her friend, lived near the zoo. She was a civilized,
broadminded liberal, a gifted painter and a prolific writer who
traveled around the world and illustrated her journeys with charming watercolors. She died in the first days of World War II,
brokenhearted.

Next came Sweden, where they arrived at the British Embassy
during the celebrations of the sixteen-hundredth anniversary of
the first Council of Nicaea. Poor Uncle Arthur had staying with
him an Orthodox Greek prelate and the Anglican Bishop of Bombay. Anne argued the *filioque* clause—the addition to the Nicene
Creed extrapolated by the Emperor Constantine—with the Greek
clergyman at breakfast, and the validity of the Anglican orders
with the Bishop of Bombay. Uncle Arthur was less than pleased
by so tactless a niece.

The weather in Sweden was glorious—air like champagne—
and Stockholm admirably architected, whether the old streets and
palace or the new Town Hall. Uncle Arthur and Aunt Kathleen
took Mama and the girls sailing to Drottningsholm. Mama was
seen at the start of the expedition curling herself up in a shel-
tered spot on a rug with a cushion. "What are you doing?" Jimmie Dodds asked her. "Preparing for a party of pleasure," Mama
said. It became a family saying.

They went to Uppsala and saw the grave of Bothwell, Mary
Stuart's husband, and Uncle Arthur suggested that *Hamlet*, like
all Shakespeare's plays, was really contemporary and was about
Mary Stuart (Hamlet's sinful mother), Bothwell (his wicked
uncle), and James I (Hamlet). In Stockholm, Countess Rosenberg
gave a crayfish party for them—crayfish plates, napkins, candle
shades, and, of course, masses of crayfish. Just when they thought
the feast over and couldn't eat another bite, a regular four-course
dinner followed. They met the United States Minister, Robert
Woods Bliss, and his most beautiful wife. Anne did not see her

again for forty years, when, meeting her in Washington, she was astonished to find Mrs. Bliss just as beautiful. It was as though she had been miraculously preserved, intact, through all the years that had lined so many and killed more. The Blisses gave the Bliss Collection of pre-Columbian art, as well as their house at Dumbarton Oaks, to Harvard University.

The trio returned to England by sea, and the girls were packed off in the family Buick, driven by Harold, to Cheltenham. It was grim—one thousand girls all dressed in navy blue uniforms, white blouses, and black stockings. Anne and Clare were in different "houses." Each of the sixteen houses contained around fifty girls of ages varying from twelve to seventeen; over-seventeens went to St. Hilda's, only for seniors; under-twelves were also in a separate pen; the rest were day girls.

Some girls were at Cheltenham for ten or eleven years. Anne endured it, miserably, for one. Demerits were given for turning the head to left or right while walking "in crocodile" or in college; for running; for walking on a lawn; for getting out of step; for a crooked tie or a rucked blouse. These not only reflected on the individual (depriving her of even the minimum leisure allowed) but were a mark against her house. In the house, meals were gobbled as fast as possible, for no one might rise until all did, and the minutes won from food were among the few moments of "free time." Walking past the boys' college was forbidden, even in "crocodile" with a mistress at the end of the line. Yet the girls were taken to good performances of *Romeo and Juliet* and *Tristan und Isolde*. This dichotomy encouraged the English schizophrenia about sex: write or read about it, but real live boys must not even see the girls.

Anne loathed school but passed School Certificate with six credits at the end of her one year; she also played lacrosse and tennis and swam for her house, but she did not make a single friend and was very, very glad at year's end to be done with school. Clare remained a full four years and enjoyed them.

Home again, Anne and Clare found that Mama had bought a charming small house in Brompton Square. Though she was now in her late fifties and an impoverished widow, beaux appeared. There was an unsavory Finn who dyed his beard with a dye that stained his lips and cheeks a purple mahogany. He also wore a toupee and a corset. A better beau was English and in trade: he was a widower and in the House, but sat as a Conservative. The girls, who at this stage would have enjoyed a conventional home life and did not enjoy being poor, rooted for him, but to no avail. When he proposed, Mama told him his views were too incompatible and wrote to Lady Gregory, "I want the Labour Party to win but I dislike all Politics. I was passionately anti-suffrage and I believe my instinct was right. But having got the vote, even the women who dislike it must use it."

The beau Mama preferred—and the girls snobbishly approved, for he was several times Prime Minister—was Ramsay MacDonald. He was very handsome and would appear several times a week, about six, and immediately would be served a raw egg beaten up in milk and laced with sherry. He was fond of the girls and, when Anne was sixteen, kindly took her instead of Mama, who had flu, to the Royal Literary Fund dinner, at which he was presiding. All went well until after coffee, when, just before the Prime Minister's speech, big Corona y Coronas were handed around. Anne, who since Papa's death had been quietly smoking in the lavatory the boxes and boxes of Romeo y Julietas he had left, took one and smoked it, very pleased and proud that her ash was longer than that of either of her neighbors. Ramsay, however, was not amused and told Mama he would never escort the child again. But he relented and came to her wedding and, later, to her twenty-first birthday luncheon party. At that time Anne had jaundice and wore a huge yellow velvet hat designed to match her eyes and skin.

Mama, Anne, and Clare were preparing to go to Aix for the summer when another of Mama's old beaux, a retired Foreign

Office official, Cecil Gosling, who had married Christine de Linden, an Austrian baroness, and bought a lovely castle in Styria called Schloss Walchen, wrote to ask Mama if Anne could join his only daughter, Primrose, for part of the summer. Primrose was all of twenty-three, plump and plain, with goitery blue eyes. Despite a handsome *dot* and a *geboren* mama, Primrose was not yet engaged. Anne arrived at the Goslings' picture-book castle—there was even a lake in front with swans, and a moat—to find provided for herself and Primrose a cousin of the latter, Courtenay Gosling, and his Dutch friend, Frankie. They could not have been more enchanting companions, although they had no interest in girls as such. It was an idyllic life: swimming in the lake full of water lilies, driving around visiting baroque churches in the countryside, where the puffy white clouds imitated the architecture (or vice versa) and where all the locals made Anne delightfully welcome and called her *du* (thou) at once.

Before breakfast—of coffee with *Schlag* (whipped cream) and delicious breads and fruits—Anne would study the *Almanach de Gotha*, and gradually came to identify various individuals and their families. "*Und wer war sie?*" ("And who was she?") was a favorite question asked by Christine of her husband about their friends, and soon Anne could remember who had married whom and who was cousin to whom. There were the Hungarians—Esterházys, Andrássys, Palffys—the most notorious being Count Polly, who had ten wives; and there were the Poles—Lubomirskis (fat and dark) and Radziwills, specifically three boys who had grown up in the Channel Islands, on Herm, whose mother, a Princess Blücher, was sister to Mama's friend Loulou Radziwill. There were Germans, among them Hans Christoph von Tucker, whose family had always lived in one city—Nuremberg. Hans Christoph was very Anglophile and eventually married an English girl. Above all, there were the gloriously high-spirited Eddy Czernin and his brother Manfred, who had an English mother. Later, in World War II, Anne and Eddy, with Otto Habsburg, to whom

Eddy was then lord-in-waiting, dined *à quatre* with Hilles Morris in Washington. Otto was violently anti-British (and also anti-German!) at the time.

Pauline Palffy, hearing Anne was at Walchen, wrote and asked her to come on to Smolenice. That visit was the nicest of all—to an old house, right in the village, with a big garden. Pauline's eldest brother had done up—hideously—their old castle on a big hill outside the village and was camping in it, as it wasn't finished (and never would be; war and revolution intervened). The days were an endless series of devised delights. Anne would ride with Pauline around the steeplechase course Pauline had designed, doing the formidable jumps as best she could. Or Pauline would drive her out into the pathless woods astride a long pole on wheels pulled by two horses, one in front of the other. Like a later jeep, this equipage could crash through the undergrowth, ford streams, go over stumps. Pauline, rifle in hand, would somehow sight a deer. She would stop to shoot and would leave the dead beast for hunters to retrieve and disembowel, then return later to be greeted with a twig dipped in the deer's blood, ceremoniously presented with the traditional "*Sieg Heil!*" In the evenings there would be the deer's head to admire and venison to eat, after corn on the cob, followed by big fruit tarts, with lots of fine tokay to drink, preceded by slivovitz. Going to dinner at night was quite a performance. Everyone dressed, of course, and the family went in first, followed by the guests, between rows of servants. The menservants bowed, the maids curtsied, and some of the maids picked up the long dresses of the ladies and kissed their hems.

There would be the poor in the village to visit, too, for Pauline's mother ran the only dispensary and gave medicines free to all who required them. Pauline was godmother to all the poorest children, so she could learn to take care of them, for in the Catholic Church a "God relationship" is as valid and binding as a real one. Vice versa, Pauline's own godmother was the poorest old woman in the village, so Pauline could also take care of her godmother. Anne wanted Pauline to promise to become her godmother when she was twenty-one and could become a Catholic, but Pauline refused. She hoped, she said, that Anne would marry her brother Peter, and if Pauline were her godmother she would not be able to. Peter never showed the slightest interest in Anne, but she was touched and flattered that Pauline would have liked her for a sister-in-law.

When her visit to the Palffys came to an end, Anne went on to the Ofenheims at Freudenau, near the Polish frontier. Baron Ofenheim—"Onkel Willi," as everyone called him—was a bachelor, a friend of Anne's father. He lived in a hideous modern castle full of fake Tintorettos and Halses, of which he was inordinately proud. Everything was new, from the shiny Packard car to the chintz curtains. There were about thirty people staying, meals were gargantuan, everyone went out shooting all day, and no one communicated, except Onkel Willi's brother Ernst, a bearded London doctor, to whom Anne confided her adolescent problems. He had three children with him—a handsome girl, Mady, who was a better shot than any of the men, and two boys, Willi and Ernst. Anne was shocked to see Pauline Palffy and Mady Ofenheim shooting, and vowed she never would again.

Then, the crowning glory of that marvelous summer, Salzburg. Anne stayed with another Mady, Elizabeth von Rauch-Hintze, exactly her age, who lived with four delightful brothers and their mother and their stepfather in an old house at Aigen, on the outskirts of Salzburg. The house was cozy, with a big garden, and was full of fabulous Chinese antiques, as Paul von Hintze, Mady's stepfather, had been German Ambassador to Peking. He had ridden there on horseback from Kabul, his previous post, in the summer of 1911, taking three months. Von Hintze told Anne he had been the lover of the old Empress and that she had allowed him to take what he liked from the cellars of the Imperial Palace. He liked a lot and had impeccable taste. (Sir Percival David, who had the greatest collection of Chinese monochromes in the world, except possibly for that of the King of Sweden, later told Anne the same thing.) Mady's own father had been a Balt, as was her mother, and Anne learned how Balts despise Germans, much as the Scots do the English. Mady and her brothers and Anne climbed the mountains, swam in the lovely local lakes, rode and explored the salt mine under the Salzburg mountain, sliding down the terrifying wooden slides with thick leather gloves on in the total darkness.

The festival was sheer delight: Mozart's music in the setting for which it was written, played by his own people under baroque skies. *Jedermann*, in the Cathedral Square, was not arty-crafty or ye olde teashoppe, for the people were still Catholic, still living as they had when the play was written, in their ancient places, believing, enduring, loving the same things.

Mady later visited Oxford and stayed with Anne; later still was her bridesmaid; later still married another Balt, Freiherr Freytag von Loringhofen. They had four sons. He was a colonel in the German Abwehr and was one of the officers implicated in the *Putsch* against Hitler on July 20, 1944. His second-in-command gave him five minutes to shoot himself, which he did, thus escaping the fate of Adam von Trott, whom Anne knew at Oxford. Adam was hanged slowly while a film was made of his and others' death struggles, viewing which gave Hitler great pleasure. This film is now in the archives in Washington.

Mady, her mother, mother-in-law, and one child (the youngest, then a baby, luckily at the breast) were jailed, and were released only after the Allied victory. The three older children were taken from Mady and placed in Nazi homes. After the war Anne went with her youngest son to stay with Mady at Aigen. Mady's step-father was dead, her mother blind. There was very little to eat; the garden was a wilderness. One of Mady's brothers had become a Communist, another a Catholic; one had fought and escaped; one had been killed in the war. Anne bought one of the Chinese Buddhas and had it shipped to New York, where it proved to be a modern copy. She walked daily to Mass across a lovely meadow full of wild blue chicory, to the local little rococo church. On her last morning she spoke to the young pastor, thanking him and making an offering. She told him there was a Catholic convert in Mady's house who would dearly love a visit from his priest. "I have no time for *ci-devant* aristocrats," he replied. "I'm too busy with my UNRRA camp."

"*Ci-devant* aristocrats also have souls," Anne suggested.

Anne hated leaving Europe to go back to England; that, for her, always meant the end of the holidays. In London her first day, after lunching at the Charles Morgans', she shared a cab home with Prince von und zu Löwenstein-Wertheim. He fumbled for money so long that Anne paid the taxi fare. For the moment, she decided she had *had Gotha.*

XX

Some Varieties of Adolescent Experience

Now Anne and Clare once more wanted to become Catholics, but they had become less obvious in their pieties. The Curé had told them their first duty, until they came of age, was to obey their mother. So at Cheltenham, Anne had dutifully gone to church, including early service, and had taken Communion, delighting anew in her favorite Protestant hymns. But whenever they traveled, she and Clare, pursued by a maid (who informed on them to Mama), sneaked off to Catholic churches. Mama persecuted mildly, confiscating rosaries she found, but on the whole leaving well enough alone. After they came to live in Brompton Square, Anne used often to slip out the back door, which opened onto a churchyard, which she crossed to enter Brompton Oratory, which is contiguous to a Low Anglican church. In the pulpit of this latter church, on a June morning when the girls had been taken to Matins, the Reverend Prebendary Gough sniffed and said with distaste, as a lovely smell of incense drifted in through the open windows, "I fear my congregation may be incommoded by the effluvia from the Italian mission next door."

Mama, worried by Anne's continuing Catholic bias, sent her to a psychiatrist. He was puzzled. Finally he said, "You seem normal enough."

"I should hope so," Anne replied. "I've just won a scholarship to Oxford. If Mama would stop fussing and introduce me to some Protestant boys, there'd be no problem."

The only readily available boy was, however, Catholic and lived four doors down the square. He was the son of Philip Somers Cocks, Mama's brief beau, and was called John Sebastian, for the elder Bach. John was already at Balliol but out of term-time lived with a pious widowed aunt. All that summer John and Anne swam in the Serpentine before breakfast; the dirty lake in the middle of Hyde Park had just been opened for public swimming. Anne would have to shower on return to remove the smuts. John had had his nose broken boxing and was far from handsome, but Anne thought him an Adonis, as he was the only young man she knew. His aunt had been a concert singer; John himself played the clavichord (and piano) very well. Anne loved the atmosphere at his aunt's house, where she often met such prominent Catholics as Maurice Baring—drooping, pear-shaped—and Hilaire Belloc.

After her marriage, when Anne was working on *The London Mercury* for Sir John Squire, she went downstairs one morning with a message to the pub (the Temple Bar) where Squire was always to be found at eleven, drinking. There that day also was Hilaire Belloc; they were arguing about what was the greatest poem in the English language and asked Anne what she thought.

"I don't know," she admitted, "but Mother says it's Cory's 'Heraclitus.'" And she began to recite: "They told me, Heraclitus, they told me you were dead," but before she could spout it further, Belloc interrupted:

"They told me, Heraclitus, that you were dead as mutton.
I answered in the Grecian tongue I did not care a button,
And then I shot the nightingales that keep a man awake,
For death he taketh all away, but those he did not take."

He had improvised the parody there and then.

Anne met Belloc's children too: Peter, who loved to sail; and Elizabeth, who fell in love with Gervase Elwes, son of that Lady

Winefride (Feilding) who had been a girlhood friend of Mama's. Gervase became a priest and eventually a Monsignor and chaplain to the Catholic students at Oxford. Elizabeth never married. Anne wrote their story in a novel called *By Grace of Love*.

Probably the psychiatrist had reported Anne's comment to Mama, for shortly after Anne's visit to him she was sent off to a dance at the Alan Gardiners', who lived "north of the Park," which in those days was very remote indeed. Alan Gardiner was a distinguished Egyptologist. Their daughter, Margaret, was Anne's age, beautiful, dark, and unkempt, a *Wandervogel*, eccentric in dress and habits. Her brother Rolf was a passionate member of the Kibbo Kift, a para-Fascist international youth movement. Mama approved of him very much and kept his letters to her. The dance was fun. Mrs. Gardiner, a Finn, had decorated their house with modern Finnish furniture while including Egyptian pieces thousands of years old—a marvelous combination.

Young men created an entirely new dimension for Anne. Hitherto, once a year at Possingworth, Mama had invited the two swarthy sons of a neighbor to tea and patball tennis; once a year they reciprocated with much better tea (sticky cakes in the drawing room instead of seed cake in the schoolroom) and much better tennis, on a hard court instead of a soggy lawn. Their sister Sylvia later was one of Anne's ten bridesmaids. But except for these and Humbert and the Petit de Loches in France, Anne had not met any young males, much less danced with them. She looked forward to her first season, which began with Mama's going to Tessier's, the family jeweler in Bond Street, and selling her diamond tiara for a thousand pounds. With this money in hand, she bought Anne some dance frocks, short and straight, also a Court dress of white sequins with regulation veil and three ostrich feathers, and gave dinner parties before the balls to which her friends with debutante daughters kindly asked Anne.

It was all very disappointing and tiring. As Anne had not been to the "in" finishing school, nor to any pre-deb parties, she knew no one, and though the balls were splendid they were formal.

There were programs with stubby pencils attached, in which prospective partners wrote their initials. Very rarely was Anne's program even half full, and she would spend a long time in the ladies' room and a short time trotting around the floor. As she was greedy, she found the best part of the evening was supper, when she was always sure of a partner and made straight for the food with no nonsense about not eating through the divine menus—generally vichyssoise first, then poached fresh salmon with mayonnaise and delicious salads, followed by strawberries or raspberries and cream. If one stayed up long enough, around three there would be bacon and eggs or creamed haddock.

There were all sorts of silly exotic parties that spring: for example, one, in one of the loveliest of London squares, was in fancy dress; everyone had to come as a baby and drink out of a bottle. And at another, gasoline was poured on a stretch of the Thames, which was then set on fire, and there was dancing to the light of the flames.

Going to Court was dreary. Mama and Anne dressed up in the cold light of a June afternoon and sat for hours in the Buick in line in the Mall, while the crowd pressed their faces into the windows and made disparaging comments. "That one's nothing to write 'ome about," they said of Anne, and, "Looks like 'er ma 'as passed out." Mama had closed her eyes in boredom.

The curtsies were easy. Anne and Clare had from the age of three been taught to "knix"—make a small curtsy—when introduced to any married woman. (It was fun doing it to their twenty-year-old sister Konradin after she married Arthur, and still greater fun for Anne, also aged twenty and just married, when her niece Elizabeth "knixed" to her.) The slightly more elaborate curtsies made to each and all the Royals—when Anne was presented there were King George V, Queen Mary, the Prince of Wales (now Duke of Windsor), and Princess Mary (later Countess of Harewood)—were no problem. A reception followed, but few girls look their best in daylight in dead white with feathers. Anne's sequins shed noisily on the parquet every time she moved, and

there were no men around except equerries. The tasteless food was
provided by a caterer.

That summer, at the ends of balls, Anne would go alone to
Covent Garden and buy vegetables and great armfuls of flowers
and get home around five. She slept until noon and then coped
with the household, which consisted only of a housemaid and Eliza
Honeybun, now cook, reluctant to "take orders from a chit like
you," as she told Anne. Mama had insisted that Anne learn household management this practical way. Eliza demanded for the
"staff" English lamb and butter and bacon, while Mama, Anne,
Clare, and their guests ate Canterbury (New Zealand) lamb and
Danish butter and bacon—far cheaper and better!

Anne did not like it when Bernard Shaw came to lunch, as he
was an absolute vegetarian and had to have lots of special complicated dishes. He ate a great deal, but not like anyone else. Once
he came with his wife and the J. B. Fagans, and Uncle Arthur and
Aunt Kathleen came too. G.B.S. started to tease Anne (who was
seventeen, fat, spotty, and plain) by saying it was difficult to
decide which of the ladies he was sitting between was the more
beautiful—Aunt Kathleen (who was ravishingly lovely), a mature
beauty, or Anne with her April looks. Anne wanted to die then
and there, but to kill him first. Another time he invited Mama
(and Anne and Clare) to lunch, adding on the postcard, "My wife
will provide a corpse."

"Educated during the holidays from Eton," Sir Osbert Sitwell
wrote in *Who's Who*. Anne sometimes wondered if her real education too had not taken place in the holidays, which were many
and various: from all summer in a day, whenever her and Clare's
guardian, Hans Sonne, Papa's New York partner, appeared from
the United States, unannounced, golden-haired and gay—in the
big gateway at Aix, or walking in through a French window
from the Brigdene lawn (Brigdene was the dull dower house on
the Possingworth estate to which they moved after Possingworth
was sold), or ringing the doorbell in London, complete with

theater or ballet tickets—to long, complicated summers in Europe or brief excursions into unknown worlds in England.

There was, for example, Anne's first hunt ball, the New Forest Spinsters. She was sent by Mama in the dark blue Buick, with Harold (who Mama said did everything but bath her), from Sussex to Hampshire on a cold December 30 to stay with Sir Beethom Whitehead, a torpedo-manufacturer, and his wife, Marian (*née* Brodrick), a girlhood friend of Mama's. Their daughter Frances (who later worked in Scotland Yard) was already "out" and had assembled a party for New Year's Eve. As Harold drove up outside the Whiteheads' rambling modern house, Anne saw unfolding from a baby Austin a tall, thin, black-haired young man and a short, neat girl with good legs and smooth, tight, dark cropped hair like a seal's—obviously his sister; the family resemblance was that strong. Anne was terrified by the large gathering of completely unknown people, all young except Frances's parents, who appeared only at mealtimes. She had been asked for the long New Year weekend. At dinner the first night she found herself next to the handsome six-foot-one Austin-sevenite, and learned he was called Christopher Fremantle, was at Balliol, and was a cousin of Marian Whitehead's. "She is one of Papa's eighty-six living first cousins," Christopher vouchsafed. "We've never met her or her husband or any of the children before."

There were several sons of the house present, as well as an elder daughter married to a schoolmaster. Margaret, Christopher's sister, was at Oxford too, at Lady Margaret Hall, reading medicine, and Anne, who at that point was secretly about to take the Oxford entrance exam, was full of admiration. Christopher had inch-long black eyelashes, wide dark gray eyes, and a nice sense of humor. He looked, Anne thought, very like the Elizabethan ivory by Nicholas Hilliard of the young man—supposedly Philip Sidney—caught in briars. He wanted to be a painter; his mother wanted him to become a schoolmaster.

"Why not both?" Anne asked, but Christopher said, "Did you ever hear of a great painter who was also a schoolmaster?"

"How old are you?" ventured Anne.

"How old do you think?"

"Twenty-four," she said promptly.

"I'm nineteen. And you?"

"Guess," Anne said.

He replied, "The same as me—nineteen."

"I'll be seventeen in June," Anne said.

"This, then, is your first dance?"

"Yes, except for one evening at Hadspen—that's where my sister lives in Somerset—when she asked six couples in and got Clare and me each a partner. With Konradin and Arthur that made eighteen. We danced to a gramophone. That was last Christmas, just over a year ago."

The hunt ball was terrifying—lots of red-faced men, some young, many old, in pink coats who pranced about and every now and then yelled; also lots of bouncy hops such as polkas and Sir Rogers and dances where the music suddenly stopped and strangers grabbed one, then let go as soon as possible and one never saw them again, as one danced so badly. Christopher danced very badly too, but waltzed competently, reversing faster than going forward, so he and Anne danced together a lot.

Each day in the daylight there was golf in a drizzle, or walking, and on New Year's Day the meet, cheerful and colorful in spite of mackintoshes and dripping bushes. Harold drove expertly down narrow lanes so that Anne, Margaret, Christopher, and several others, all piled into the Buick, were able to keep up with the hounds most of the day: Frances was hunting, as were her brothers.

Next day Anne was driven back to Sussex, delighted with Margaret and Christopher, as was Mama when she told her of them. "I knew Tom Cottesloe, Christopher's father," she said. "He was sweet but small and danced very badly. He was Maurice Fremantle's first cousin."

During the Christmas holidays after Anne's first Oxford term, she, Mama, and Clare went to Aix, and Mama invited Christopher and his sister Margaret. Leaving Mama each morning, the quartet chugged up Mont Revard in the funicular and enjoyed the snow—the first time any of them had skied. On the third day—January 14, 1928—Christopher proposed, and in the evening Anne told Clare, who was not at all surprised. The three of them decided not to tell Mama, as there was no chance of getting married for ages. It was indeed a modest proposal, as neither Christopher nor Anne had any money of their own, and both had still to get their degrees.

The following summer Lady Margaret Hall offered a prize for an essay on J. M. Synge. Anne wrote Mama to ask if she had known him, and Mama said no, but she would write and ask Aunt Augusta (Lady Gregory). By return post came an invitation to stay at Coole, and Anne set off at once. The journey was uneventful but long—a day to Liverpool, a night on the boat to Dublin, then overnight to Gort.

Anne woke to see the sunny, Spanish-looking little town set in gray, stony country; she had imagined it would be green, but the low walls were made of stones taken from the fields—so few taken, so many remained. Aunt Augusta had sent to meet Anne an old black Ford that smelled deliciously of horse; the chauffeur wore knee breeches, like a groom. Anne remembered that Sir William, Aunt Augusta's husband, had been Master of the Galway Blaziers in his day and that Lady Gregory's daughter-in-law, after her son Robert's death in World War I, had married Captain Gough, who owned Lough Cutra, the estate that marched with Coole, and was the present MFH (Master of Fox Hounds).

The lake was not visible from the drive, and Lady Gregory's house, made over when Sir William returned from his civil-service duties in the mid-nineteenth century, was more comfortable than beautiful. It was, indeed, an astonishingly livable house, agreeable, civilized; a house where one could not imagine violence, anguish, passion, or, indeed, to quote the "dear Queen" (Victoria), any "conduct unbecoming a gentlewoman." Yet, as Anne came in and stood at the foot of the gentle, pleasantly carpeted stairs, she recalled that it was here Lady Gregory had stood alone one night while the men who shot her nephew were hammering on the door, shouting at her to open, and she shivering inside, the full moonlight finding her out, though she stood quite still and hidden.

She was waiting with breakfast when Anne arrived, and what a memorable meal that was! Barmbrack, the delicious homemade currant-stuffed yeast bread, porridge with lashings of thick cream, and the best ham and eggs ever. Lady Gregory looked unchanged, though it was years since Anne had seen her. She was less alarming: still exquisitely prim, with her Quaker-gray hair flat on either side of a parting. She wore only black relieved with white lace.

"Mr. Yeats," she said, "will not be down until luncheon."

After breakfast she took Anne around the "policies," pointing out the great catalpa that George Moore had erroneously called a weeping ash, and the lawn where she had once seen AE's son, Brian, face to face with a hedgehog. They walked through the kitchen garden to the hothouses full of ripening nectarine and peach, and she told Anne to eat her fill; a dark-leaved magnolia was in blossom, trained against the brick wall, its cream-colored lemon-verbena-scented blossoms the texture of kid gloves.

Aunt Augusta questioned Anne closely, intimately. How was Anne's mother? Was it not true that Anne was her mother's favorite child? Had she not been her father's? And had he not left the two girls very well off? She seemed hardly to hearken to the replies; that there had been very little money left when Papa had died, that Mama had had only her jointure, and so on. She went on to say, "I'm so deeply touched that you want to write about me. You must ask me anything you want, and I will try to tell you and help you all I can."

Gauchely, miserably, Anne blurted out that it was of Synge she wished to write. Unruffled, sweetly, Lady Gregory began at once to speak of him, saying he had stayed but seldom at Coole because of his wretched ill health, and telling how when he was dying in a Dublin nursing home he asked, "May I have my bed pulled up to the window, so that I may die with my eyes upon the blue Wicklow hills?"

She showed Anne her magnificent library. "I understand you are very interested in the East," she said. "Your grandfather was a great scholar and a friend of my husband's. He was Governor of Madras; my husband was Governor of Ceylon." She pointed out Sanskrit grammars and volumes of Singhalese poetry, splendid tooled-leather editions of Oriental history and philosophy. She told Anne of her marriage when she was twenty-eight (she was born March 5, 1852, and died in 1932).

She was the youngest of three Miss Persses, who lived with their mother at Roxborough, only seven miles from Coole. She had been very happy in her marriage and until her husband's death had written nothing but a pamphlet in defense of Arabi Pasha, the Egyptian rebel. When Sir William died, she did a superb job editing his journals. She had adored her son, and, "You shall see my grandchildren," she promised Anne. "They are coming over for luncheon with their mother. Ann is about your age; she has golden hair. Richard has a new car his mother and I gave him for his twenty-firster; he will be bringing them over in that."

She said that it was for Richard's sake she clung to Coole, though she felt herself rattling around in the big house like a dried old pea. Then she spoke of her great-nephew, Michael Shawe-Taylor, who had a fine place, Castle Taylor, but a few miles away. "He'll be coming also for luncheon. It would be so nice, dear girl, if you would marry him; that is, of course, if you like each other. Your sweet mother would, I am sure, not object; he is a good boy, and did well at Eton and the 'Varsity."

Anne objected that she was already engaged. "That doesn't mean anything at your age," said Aunt Augusta firmly. Anne quailed. How dare she withstand the sibyl of the Irish Renaissance, the Grand Old Woman of Irish letters?

They walked back into the house, and while Aunt Augusta went to see how Yeats had slept, Anne browsed amongst her books, marveling at so rich a life. She had, indeed, been "wise all her life long." Forty plays she had written, and all had been produced in Dublin, and some in London and elsewhere. And this was not counting her translations, from Goldoni, Sudermann, and Molière. For forty years her house, buried in the deepest, remotest country, had been the heart and focus of the whole Irish literary revival. The Abbey Theatre was hers or it was no one else's, not even Yeats's; and what, indeed, would Yeats himself have done without her? A slow worker, content to write from five to nine lines a day, and forever rewriting these, he needed the serene surrounding care she gave him, protecting him from social and intellectual distractions, attending to his digestion as well as to his meter. His passionate devotion to the fiery artist Maud Gonne did not fulfill his need for a governess as well, and this, self-effacing yet peremptory, Aunt Augusta was. Nor did his late marriage make the faintest break in their friendship, for "Georgie," Yeats's wife, and later their two children, came as freely and constantly to Coole as Yeats himself; yet when he needed peace he knew he still could come alone. Aunt Augusta read to him every evening, or he to her; Tolstoi's *War and Peace*, Spenser's *Faerie Queen*, Johnson's *Rasselas*. And, as he wrote to Anne after her death, "Wherever I went, I always gathered up news and stories for her."

Lunch came, the table bright with zinnias, and with it Mrs. Gough. Ann and Richard Gregory came too, Ann freckled, with the yellow hair immortalized by Yeats. Came also Michael Shawe-Taylor, mustachioed, handsome, dashing, a trifle stout; already, his sister told Anne later, he was well known as the youngest club bore in London. Yeats ate well, told funny stories, teased the young Gregorys.

The meal was barely over when Michael dragged Anne up to Aunt Augusta. "May I take the two Anns and Richard over to Castle Taylor? And will you and the rest follow us for tea? I think Bridget still can raise eight cups." Aunt Augusta, pleased, nodded graciously, and off they dashed.

Castle Taylor was most romantic. The windows had been broken "in the troubles," when Michael's father was killed by the

Sinn Fein, so it was a trifle drafty, and the furniture had all been burned, so there was none, except for some garden chairs in the drawing room. But the eighteenth-century porticoed veranda had escaped damage, and while Ann and Richard went in to find Bridget, the cook, and to look at Epaminondas, the cat, who had suddenly and unsuitably produced kittens, Michael and Anne leaned over the gray lichen-covered balustrade and sunned themselves.

"You know I'm supposed to marry you," Michael groaned in a sepulchral voice.

Anne shuddered. "But I'm already engaged to Christopher Fremantle."

"Thank heaven," Michael said fervently, brightening visibly. He added politely, "It's not that I don't like you or anything, but I hate the idea of being bullied into matrimony with you, just because you're an heiress and it suits Aunt Augusta's book."

"But I'm not an heiress," Anne said.

Michael whistled, "Aunt Augusta's out on two counts. Oh, my!"

Secure from each other's honorable attentions, Michael and Anne quickly became good friends. But Aunt Augusta had no intention of having her plans thwarted. She asked Michael over to Coole to stay, and—as he was living quite alone except for Bridget, Epaminondas, and the various chickens that ran around his kitchen —he seemed glad to come.

Aunt Augusta put herself out to entertain them. Each afternoon she drove them out calling upon the neighboring gentry. One day they went to the Dunsanys', and Anne was terrified because they discovered the famous playwright, Lord Dunsany, shooting at his wife with a revolver from a duckblind, as she sat alone in a boat on the lake. "Forty-eight pair of woodcock a day we used to get at Coole, and not many less teal," Aunt Augusta said placidly. Anne withdrew as quickly as possible from the scene of action. Soon their host came in and served tea. Her ladyship did not appear.

Wherever they went, people accepted Michael and Anne as

a couple. Many congratulated them, dewy-eyed, and Bridget more than once embraced Anne, crying out was it not wonderful that God had sent her to Ireland and Castle Taylor? Michael and she had competitions as to how many nectarines they could eat (which Anne always won) and how far they could spit the stones (which he won). They walked in the Wicked Wood—quite small, but ice-cold even in summer—where one always got lost. And they spent the evenings, after Yeats had left for Dublin to attend rehearsals, listening to Aunt Augusta's stories.

She would stand in Anne's room, telling a final anecdote, a lit candle in her hand, relating the marriages she had made. "This man turned out a bit drinky; this girl grew melancholy mad; this other ran away; this one killed herself." Only occasionally had they worked out for the best. With her black mantilla over her white hair, and the candle shaking in her hen-claw-yellow hands, she looked a real witch. She had an extraordinary fascination. How was it, Anne wondered, that this old woman, ugly, not rich, not powerful, was core and center of Ireland's spirit? Her power was so wonderfully indirect; to Anne, as a girl, she seemed the essence of womanliness, feeding, counseling, inspiring men, and women too, yet without self-assertion, without trumpets before her, or publicity or praise. She took all sting from homeliness and old age; if life could ripen into something like this, how good it must be! All passion spent, and so much purchased with it.

"Loneliness has made me richfull, as Bacon calls it," she said. "I sometimes think my life has been a series of enthusiasms." Her store of legends was inexhaustible. Anne now remembers little, only that Aunt Augusta bade Michael and herself, if they met a weasel, be sure to say to it, "I wouldn't be grudging you a pair of boots or shoes if I had them"—an insincere but, she assured them, essential offer. And she said, too, that on May Eve they must scatter primrose blossoms before every window and chimney and door lest the Good People carry off from the house every child of seven or less and each newly married bride.

One night, after Anne had gone up to bed, Mrs. Gough said

something that annoyed Aunt Augusta, and next morning, without any explanation or "by your leave," Aunt Augusta carried Anne off to Dublin, where they drove to the swankiest hotel, right on Merrion Square. Aunt Augusta was busy all day with Mr. Yeats, who was rehearsing at the Abbey Theatre—*The Only Jealousy of Emer*, to be played in masks—and could not be bothered with Anne. Mama, assuming Anne was to be Aunt Augusta's guest, had given her only pocket money. When Anne found she was expected to pay her hotel bills she was flabbergasted and found she could just afford "bed and breakfast." So, with Aunt Augusta watching intently, she would eat her way each morning steadily through cereal, herrings, bacon and eggs, sausages, cold ham, toast, butter, and marmalade, muffins, and coffee, and for the rest of the twenty-four hours would fast, mooching lonelily around the city. Aunt Augusta, after watching Anne eat her huge breakfast for two mornings, wrote off to Michael (who subsequently sent Anne the letter), "She would not do for you at all; she is not as well-off as I thought, and she would eat you out of house and home in a week."

Late in the evenings, their rehearsals over, Yeats and Aunt Augusta allowed Anne to join them at the Kildare Street club. Then Yeats would talk. Anne had never before or since heard any talk that was half such fun; it was like the River Liffey in spate, or the earliest Homeric legends; it was better than any imaginable sagas. And all were such droll tales, told better than anyone ever told stories.

He told how, once in the United States, a rich woman had taken him, after he had been lecturing, in her Cadillac to give him dinner. Her small, meek husband was put in front with the chauffeur. "I so loved your reading," the lady said, "and especially 'Innisfree,' but why did you not read my favorite of all your poems, 'The Everlasting Mercy'?" "I like that poem very much too," Mr. Yeats agreed, "but I didn't write it. It's by my friend John Masefield." Whereupon the silent tiny husband turned his head and spat out, "Stung again."

Of reading "Innisfree" Yeats said, too, that one young American woman asked him, "Were they *runner* beans?"

He told endless ghost stories, of which Anne forgot all but one, in which an old woman told him she had seen a ghost crossing Merrion Square on a windy night, "and it had the loikness of the *Oirish Times.*"

Mr. Yeats was a glorious gossip and told how he and Robert Graves had been staying together in some place and Laura Riding had jumped out of the first-floor window to prove how much she loved Robert Graves, whereupon Graves's wife, to prove she loved him more, had jumped out of the second-floor bedroom window and broken her leg.

Anne stayed for the first night of *The Only Jealousy of Emer,* then bade Aunt Augusta good-by and never saw her again. Michael came with his sister to Anne's wedding and Lady Gregory sent as wedding present an autographed copy of her two-volume *Visions and Beliefs of the West of Ireland.* Only Yeats could truly describe her—not only her "laurelled head" but the stories she had "to keep the soul of man alive."

Anne spent her second Oxford Christmas vacation in Anjou, staying with Courtenay Gosling, Cecil Gosling's nephew, whom Anne had met at Walchen. It was cold but bright, and his little house was enchanting, near the Loire, the landscape all pearly gray, with many willows about. Only a field path led to the house, past a castle that had belonged to Gilles de Retz, the original Bluebeard, about whom Courtenay was writing. There was a gay house party, including Rita Gulbenkian (Mr. Five Per Cent's daughter) and several White Russians, and lots of visits were paid to neighbors. The food was wonderful, and the wine, white or pink, in great barrels, outstanding. As was *thé caramelé,* drunk last thing at night (dried tea and sugar browned in a saucepan, with milk added). Years later, in World War II, though he was over forty, Courtenay was parachuted back into then occupied France, into Anjou near his house. He broke his arm and was hidden for weeks by friends, who thereby endangered their lives; many of the local gentry in Touraine were in the Resistance and behaved beautifully, in contrast to those in Savoy, where courage was left mostly to the Communists.

On her return from France by channel steamer, Anne did not fail to remember that she and Clare had been carefully raised by Mama always to smuggle. Mama declared she really believed only in three things: birth control, free trade, and the Trinity. She was a founding member of the British Birth Control Society. Anne, after she married, was asked to be treasurer, and accepted on condition the society change its name to Planned Parenthood Association—a name she coined in honor of the USSR Five Year Plan, feeling she couldn't raise money for so negative a concept as "Birth Control." The executive agreed, and Anne proved a successful fund-raiser, selling Gandhi's letters to benefit the cause. Mama thought it was truly disgusting to have more than four children, and distributed to the poor pamphlets expounding her views.

As for free trade, since Grandpapa Grant Duff had been in Gladstone's cabinet, and Papa's grandfather had been liberal M.P. for Cheshire, it was an article of family faith on both sides. Even as tinies, Anne and Clare had been given some contraband trifle to hide in muff or cap or glove or pocket, on principle. Later, Clare would pretend pregnancy, swathed in forbidden goods. And once Fritzl was stripped and sat parleying with customs officials on the French-Swiss border with many, many watches in the pockets of the greatcoat he had nonchalantly hung on the chair on which he was sitting naked. (Anne once, on Channel 13 television in New York, mentioned her family faith in smuggling, and the next time she re-entered the United States she was well frisked.) On this occasion, on her arrival in England, Anne ostentatiously carried a big bottle of nondutiable rosewater. The young customs officer would not believe that the sinister-looking bottle did not hold alcohol. He solemnly lighted a match, poured some rosewater on paper, and tried to light it. It sputtered out, and Anne rejoiced, publicly snickering as he grew scarlet.

XXI

Oxford

"Lady Margaret Hall offers scholarship without emoluments," the telegram read.

Mama looked nonplused. "What on earth does that mean?" she asked.

"Haven't a clue," Anne replied rudely, "unless it means what it says."

"I'll call Ursula," Mama said. Anne's Aunt Ursula was the widow of Mama's brother Adrian.

"Congratulations," Ursula said over the phone. "It means that Anne is bright, but you are rich."

"Rich!" Mama exclaimed in horror. "I haven't been able to pay Anne's and Clare's school fees at Cheltenham since their father died. Their guardian has been paying them out of his own pocket."

"You're too rich anyway to get out of paying a hundred and fifty pounds for Anne's board and tuition," Ursula said cheerfully.

"Was Lady Margaret Hall founded by the wife of that dull Jim Hall I used to dance with?" Mama asked.

"It was named for, not founded by, the wife of John de Balliol, who founded Balliol in the—was it thirteenth century?"

"Oh," Mama replied. "Nice to think of a Balliol connection."

Mama had not approved of Anne's desire to "go up" to Oxford, but the scholarship convinced her she must consent. A woman's education should above all be surreptitious, Mama declared. After all, both girls had been thoroughly grounded in French and German, also Latin, European literature and history, enough arithmetic to cope with the weekly books, and enough botany to get through "matric," the exam which was a necessary prerequisite for getting into any university. But enough was enough, and for Mama the four C's—church, children, cooking, clothes: her translation of the German K's—were sufficient field for woman's energy. To charm, to cosset, to console—men first, of course, but also women ("Never be rude to a girl, you never know whom she'll marry" was one of her axioms)—should be the whole of female endeavor. However, she was secretly delighted with Anne's success, especially as, unlike Ursula's daughters Jean and Sheila, and all who were not scholars at Oxford, Anne would not there be dubbed a "commoner."

Mama gave Anne furniture for her room at Oxford. A big screen to hide the washstand, with its jug and basin of white china. A small upright Bechstein that had been in the girls' schoolroom. The desk and chair Papa had at Balliol. A good long mirror. Lady Margaret Hall (generally known to its inmates as London, Midland, and Hottish) provided an armchair, a table, a wooden chair, and a coalscuttle, which was filled once daily in the Michaelmas and Lent terms. Anne brought with her a big map of Asia, which she had had pinned onto her wall at Aix ever since Papa had given her a subscription to the *National Geographic* for her seventh birthday. Also a signed photo of Cardinal Newman and a small oil of Oxpasture, a bluebell-filled wood near Possingworth. And a firescreen. During her three-year residence she completely papered this screen with rejection slips from newspapers and magazines and for the rest of her life she could face with equanimity the horrid phrase "The editor regrets"—even on a Monday morning.

Anne took the train from Paddington to Oxford one drafty October day. The approach to the city of spires through the cemetery and gasworks did not depress her, nor did the long taxi ride up the Cowley Road, then up Norham Gardens, which were planted on each side with Victorian villas of quite peculiar ugliness. LMH, moreover, proved to be a pleasant amalgam of one Victorian Gothic gray house, "Old Hall," and several Georgian redbrick buildings of impeccable taste. The garden was a swirl of autumn leaves flying; lots of roses were still blooming, and the Cherwell flowed around two sides of the grounds. Anne was unpacking in her room in Lodge, the Sir Giles Scott–designed building in which she had been assigned a room on the ground floor—it had steel shutters that were locked at night—when a phenomenally plain girl, with sallow skin, spots, and black greasy hair, came in.

"My name is Frances Smith," she said. "How many men do you know here? I know five."

Anne reflected. "I know Christopher Fremantle," she said. "I met him last New Year's at a hop."

"Is he a brother of Margaret, third year?"

"Yes," Anne said. "And I know my cousin, Neill Grant Duff."

"Jean's brother? At Balliol, isn't he? Then I expect you know Jean's young man, Bob Newman?"

"No," Anne replied, "but I know Andrew Campbell at the House, and, oh yes, John Sebastian Somers Cocks at Balliol—he lives next door to us in Brompton Square, and he and I swam across the Serpentine every morning last June. That's all."

"That's only four," said Frances as she left triumphant.

Anne was Modern Languages Scholar, but as soon as she had got through Pass Moderations at the end of her first term (which exempted her from Divvers, the Divinity exam, failing to pass which caused many otherwise bright people to be sent down), she switched to History. Her tutor was the Vice-Principal, Miss Evelyn Jamison, a beautiful woman with prematurely white hair, lovely skin and figure, and exquisite clothes. Miss Jamison's many-windowed room, full of flowers, looked out on Charles I's artillery parks. Her special subject was the drainage system of medieval

Milan. She was very unlike the Principal, Miss Lynda Grier, huge, hideous (nicknamed Mrs. Hippo, after a comic-strip character), who was also the Economics don. Miss Grier once confided to Anne, "My body has never given me a moment's pleasure." Her parson father had been in charge of a home for incurable inebriates, which had given the "Princ," as she was generally called, a phobia about drink. None was allowed in Hall, and the girls consequently imported sherry and even gin, in medicine bottles labeled "One tablespoon to be taken at bedtime."

Life at LMH began with breakfast in Hall. All meals were self-service, and the food was so good that young men could be lured to come to meals in LMH from colleges like Balliol and Univ, where the food was traditionally inedible. Few ever came from the House (Christ Church, Aedes Christi), Magdalen, Trinity, or New College, which boasted of their cuisines. After breakfast Anne bicycled the two miles down Norham Gardens and Parks Road to whichever college her nine-o'clock lecture would be given at—a different one each day. For some reason bicycling was "not done"; it was more chic to walk.

Most of the colleges were ancient and beautiful. Sitting in the great halls, looking up at fan-vaulting, as at the House, or at splendid portraits, as in most every one, was so agreeable that it was hard to concentrate on the lecture—the more so as there were no microphones and most of the lecturers mumbled. Their listeners sat at the hall tables, huge solid-oak affairs, and, as all lectures were mixed, brash young men could kick pretty girls under the table, and friends could spend a pleasant hour writing each other silly notes. Attendance at lectures was not obligatory and no one signed in for them; indeed, some people never went to any. But those who so abstained found they were at a disadvantage when it came to exams, for the examiners—who were also the lecturers—took malicious delight in asking questions only about subjects they had previously discussed.

Lectures were given from nine through one, but no one went to as many as four in a morning. Free time was spent having coffee with female friends, or sherry with such males as lived out of college; girls were not allowed in college men's rooms until after lunch, and then only in pairs. But if one had friends who roomed in digs, a scout would appear with a decanter and biscuits as one arrived. "Makes yer liver as 'ard as a nut," one scout warned Anne regularly as he poured the Bristol Cream.

Anne generally returned to Hall for lunch, stopping by the porter's lodge to see if there were any telephone messages. Sometimes she found she was bidden to a lunch party in some man's rooms or digs, or at the George, the preferred pub. The food provided in men's rooms in college was superb—whitebait, or fresh salmon with mayonnaise, or local trout, or grouse, pheasant, or partridge in season, watered by such vintage wines as Pommard or a light Anjou. After lunch, especially on weekends, the men would drink a '96 or '06 port. No girl ever drank port, or, in public, whisky (one of Anne's aunts was considered dreadfully fast, because on returning from hunting one very cold day she had poured herself, *coram publico*, a whisky and soda). Young men in digs fared more simply: fried plaice or roast chicken with bread sauce were sample menus. Once, when Anne was lunching with a famous Oxford aesthete at the House, the blue Wedgwood plates were covered. When the covers were raised, a single lemon was revealed in each plate. "Let us gaze," said Harold Acton, who was next to Anne. Lewis Clive, a Rugger Blue sitting on Anne's other side, grumbled rather loudly, "I'm hungry." Lewis, descended directly from Clive of India, was killed later fighting with the International Brigade in Spain. At the end of his tame Anglican memorial services in St. Margaret's, Westminster, Anne heard, for the first and only time in her life, the "Internationale" sung.

After lunch Anne played games. Games were despised at LMH, but Anne had played lacrosse for her house at Cheltenham, and she played for LMH all her three years there and won her colors. In summer the men had a lovely stretch of river, called Parson's Pleasure, screened off for them with canvas, where they swam nude. The women swam in the loathly icy public baths, reserved for them at certain time on certain days. Anne swam for Oxford against Cambridge, which rated her a half-Blue. Only the major sports—rowing, rugger, and cricket for men; lacrosse, hockey, and tennis for women—rated a whole Blue. Anne played tennis also and gave mixed tennis parties on the excellent LMH courts.

After games, tea in Lodge common room, pleasantly full of good modern pictures loaned by Sir Michael Sadler, head of University College. Tea, as always in England, was the nicest meal and moment of the day—quantities of brown or white thickly spread bread and butter, lots of jam and plain cake, and huge dark brown pots of strong station-type tea, to be drunk with milk and sugar. Then work, either in one's own room or in the LMH Library or, better, in the glorious circular baroque Radcliffe Camera, open until ten p.m. Anne found doing an essay a week for each tutor—most terms she had as many as four tutors—hard work. Except for Miss Jamison, all her tutors were men, and at various colleges. There was her tutor for economics, Lindley Fraser, who had a huge gramophone with a loudspeaker that filled his small room. He would play classics loudly, which both he and Anne enjoyed more than studying price curves. He married another of his students, became a big wheel on the BBC, and died young.

Many Oxford dons married "undergraduettes," one who did so being Oliver Franks, a handsome Fellow of Queens, whose wife, Barbara Tanner, was at LMH with Anne. Barbara and Oliver both got Firsts. Oliver became British Ambassador to Washington and a peer.

The most attractive girl at LMH with Anne was Elizabeth Harman, a granddaughter of Joseph Chamberlain. She was known as "Balliol's Betty" from the number of her admirers there. The man she eventually married, however, Frank Pakenham (now Earl of Longford), was briefly a don at the House. He had been a pacifist at Eton, refusing to belong to the Officers' Training Corps (OTC), and began life as an Anglican. Elizabeth was a Unitarian. Frank started as a Young Conservative but at one of Sir Oswald Mosley's Fascist meetings got hit on the head by a brick and was badly concussed. When he recovered he became—and he has remained—a Socialist and a Catholic. Elizabeth and he had four boys and four girls. Both he and Elizabeth and three of their eight children are very successful writers. Elizabeth has written best-selling lives of Queen Victoria and the Duke of Wellington; Frank, among other books, the best account of the founding of the Irish Republic, *Peace by Treaty*. Their daughters Antonia (married to Hugh Fraser) wrote the life of Mary Stuart. Frank was a cabinet minister in every Labour Government until 1968, when he resigned over the Education Bill on a matter of principle, refusing to concur in Labour's diminished plans and budget for education. Thomas, the eldest son, writes history and the third daughter, Rachel, novels. Another distinguished contemporary at LMH was the historian C. V. (Veronica) Wedgwood, who has received the Order of Merit (OM).

Anne's only don conquest was "old Crutters"—C. R. Crutwell, the principal of Hertford. He was her tutor for the Concert of Europe, with documents. (Modern history ended at Oxford with Waterloo, so that years later, when Anne visited the United States, she had no knowledge of the Mexican-American War or of the American Civil War.) Crutters was so anti-feminist that—since he could not forbid females to attend—he began each of his lectures by describing an island where, praise be, men only were allowed. It was somewhere, he said vaguely, in the Indian Ocean. When his outraged women listeners rose to leave, he would say suavely, "Just a minute, ladies, I'm sure you can't wait to get there, but there is no boat for a month." He was most courteous to Anne, and used to ask her to preside at his dinner parties, which she did with great delight. She refused him because she was already engaged, and also because he was singularly unkempt, unwashed and uncouth, with false teeth that fell out at inconvenient moments. He came once to stay with Mama in France and took her and the girls over to Geneva, some fifty miles away, for lunch. He drove very dangerously indeed. When Mama asked him, as they rushed around Alpine curves, "Do you find it difficult to drive on the right?" he replied, "No, not at all. Plenty of practice in England." He died early of a tumor of the brain, leaving an admirable account of World War I.

Anne's favorite tutor was the Dean of Balliol, "Sligger" (Francis Fortescue) Urquhart. He was the antithesis of Crutters, immaculately clean, cherubically pink, a white-haired bachelor whose father had brought the Turkish bath to England. A "cradle Catholic," he had reading parties of young men during vacations, in the spring in Devonshire (they knew, by the smell of incense, when they were nearing the boarding house he had chosen) and in the summer in a chalet he owned near Mont Blanc. He had exquisite taste, and his room was hung with Edward Lear watercolors. Ordinarily he took no women pupils, but Mama was a friend of his sister, Lady Tyrrell, so he accepted Anne. Anne doted on him, though he slept throughout their tutorials, with a college cat sleeping no less soundly on his knee. Anne never knew whether it was more correct to tiptoe away without disturbing him or to ask in a loud voice for next week's assignment. While Lord Curzon was Chancellor of Oxford, the Queen was scheduled to lunch in Balliol for some centenary or other, and Sligger was in charge of the menu. "I suppose we start with soup," he ventured. "Certainly not," Lord Curzon replied. "Only the middle classes have soup for lunch." Sligger wrote Anne a kindly letter when she got only Second Class Honors in her finals. "It was a very good second," he told her. And he gave her a dozen silver fish knives and forks with ivory handles as a wedding present. When he was dying of tuberculosis in an Oxford nursing home, he wrote Mama saying he had had far too pleasant a life and it was only fair he should have a modicum of discomfort before the end.

LMH being on the Cherwell River, punts and canoes were part of life. One could work in them; one did flirt in them. But foursomes it had to be, as no girl was allowed out in a punt alone with a boy (unless they were engaged), in spite of Miss Grier's having pleaded that it must be harmless in view of the public nature of such activity. "You forget there are creeks," croaked a crusty male don when the problem was being threshed out in committee. Even being alone in a punt with another girl could on occasion get one into trouble: two young LMH lovelies were sent down for having slipped into a punt to sleep one glorious June night when they found their rooms stuffy.

The authorities' views on sex were strange indeed. Anne learned no girl could have a man alone in her room unless he was a brother, a clergyman, or a fiancé. Naturally many girls changed fiancés as often as was permitted, which was once a term. Anne, when announcing her own engagement to the Princ, ventured to suggest it was odd to allow into a girl's room only a man with whom a girl was likely to misbehave. "Your morals do not interest us," the Princ replied firmly. "Your work does. A girl who has various men in her rooms, for whatever purpose, is less likely to concentrate on her studies than she who has one only." Indeed, girls were sent down mainly for failing in exams, rarely for misconduct. Sometimes, when their behavior was too flagrant, they were "rusticated"—i.e., sent down for a term, then readmitted.

By and large, the women at Oxford knew they were there to work, and did so. There were about a hundred and fifty of them at LMH and about the same number in the other colleges, compared with five thousand men. Many women were going to teach when they went down. In any profession the quality of the degree obtained matters tremendously. Anyone who gets a First is sure of an interesting job and a good income for life. Most of Anne's LMH contemporaries knew they would be obliged to earn their own livings from the age of twenty-one on, unless they managed to snare themselves rich husbands. And even were they to get married, a good degree was always an insurance (financial) against divorce or widowhood. Almost all the girls at college—a good eighty per cent—were there also because they didn't get on with their mothers. As Mama said to Anne, "The only person an English girl hates more than her mother is her elder sister." Anne, who was devoted to her Mama, was for that reason considered odd.

Within LMH, life was completely communal. Anne and her friends soon made up a group of about twelve, among whom everything was held in common. If one girl had a date, the others would contribute everything that could embellish the wearer. Fur coat or evening wrap, jewels, kid gloves, evening bags—whatever was needed, even including lipstick, could be, and was, borrowed. Everyone knew who had what, and if one were giving a "mixed party" in LMH, either in one of the common rooms or in her own room (allowed if a female don was present, or a parent, or a priest), food, cutlery, china, kitchen equipment all were loaned. This communism applied also to cars. Only three girls in Anne's year were rich enough to afford cars, and as undergraduates they could keep cars in Oxford only after their first year. But these three cars were at the disposal of anyone wishing to go places with her best—or second-best—young man.

Most evenings there were "cocoa parties" in someone's rooms, to which all came in dressing gowns, though cocoa itself was never drunk. The "in" beverages were China tea (with lemon, of course) or Turkish coffee, or—considered very dashing—smuggled beer. At the end of each corridor was a pantry with several washbasins with hot and cold running water, and a gas ring, where simple suppers—eggs and bacon, kippers, omelets—could be prepared. The bathrooms were beyond.

One evening soon after her arrival, Anne was working when someone knocked on her door.

"Come in," she said.

A large round-faced lame girl walked in. "I'm Dorothy Miller," she said in an American accent. "May I borrow a frying pan?"

"Why, certainly," Anne said, producing hers.

Some hours later, wishing to use it herself, she knocked on her neighbor's door.

"Come in," a voice said. Anne turned the doorknob, found it locked. This was most unusual; no doors in LMH were ever locked. Dorothy unlocked it, peered out. "Oh, it's you, come in."

She stooped, called under the bed, "You can come out." A man appeared, stood up. "Meet my husband; he's at Cambridge, came over on his motorbike."

All that term he climbed into LMH every Friday night and spent the weekend with Dorothy. Anne used to watch in the corridor to warn while he took a bath. But at term's end she told Dorothy, "If you don't tell the Princ, I will. Someday he will get caught, and I'm not willing to get involved."

Dorothy went to Miss Grier. "I'm married," she announced.

"I thought as much," said the Princ.

The next term, and until she took her Schools, Dorothy lived out. She and her husband later had one handsome son, then divorced. Dorothy never remarried and lived most of her life in Rome; her father, the producer Gilbert Miller, whose only child she was, gave her enough to live on.

On evenings when Anne didn't have to work, Oxford offered a variety of delights. She joined the Poetry Society, and among her fellow members were Wystan Auden, Stephen Spender, Louis MacNeice, Robert Speaight and his brother Hugh, Arthur Calder-Marshall, and Brian Howard. The society met quite often, and members read each other their own poems and also invited distinguished guests from London and even from the Continent. There was a flurry of excitement when Alistair Crowley, the authority on Black Magic, was announced. Bobby and Hugh Speaight, because they had invited him, were rumored to have been refused Communion at the altar by Monsignor Ronald Knox. Another rumor had it that Crowley had been to Communion himself at Saint Aloysius, where, unrecognized, he had been able to carry away a consecrated Host, having slipped it out of his mouth into his prayer book, for later use in a Black Mass. Yet another, subsequent rumor had it that Crowley killed his wife by pushing her into the crater of Vesuvius. Less dramatic guests who spoke at the Poetry Society were Walter de la Mare and Edith Sitwell. When Eric Gill came the undergraduates poked fun at him, laughed openly at his fat belly billowing over the hempen cord of his beige cassock or smock.

Although the Town Hall had splendid concerts, and Balliol too every Sunday night, musical life for Anne revolved around the Denekes, a German family who lived next door to LMH. Their father had worked for Frederick Huth and Company. Mrs. Deneke, a widow, lived with two daughters—Lena, Professor of German at LMH, and Marga, who had been a pupil of Clara Schumann and was a concert pianist. Marga toured the United States every year to raise money for LMH, and persuaded Mrs. Harkness to give enough for a whole new building, which she insisted be called Deneke.

Mrs. Thomas Lamont contributed very generously too. She also endowed a Chair at LMH, whose first incumbent was Albert Einstein. He spoke in Hall, very simply, without notes, and, while he spoke Anne had the impression that everyone, including herself, understood every word. But afterward, reading his lecture, she knew she had not understood anything at all. Years later she was for five years his very near neighbor at Princeton. He had never read Saint Augustine, and she gave him a copy of her own *The Age of Belief*, which contained Saint Augustine's theory of time, and he made little marginal notes in German, such as "Here the wish is father to the thought" and "Would it were so." He was sought out at Princeton by the great and the near-great. The Indian Undersecretary General at the United Nations, a Moslem, came once a month just to sit at his feet and get his *upadesha*. Dr. Einstein also suffered much from the attentions of cranks. One day Anne met him just as he had triumphantly routed one. "He talked and talked," Einstein told Anne. "Suddenly I said, 'Look, do you see that crayfish there?'" "No," said the astonished chronophage. "There, just by your foot." "I don't see it." "Neither do I see your argument," Einstein replied, pushing him out through the screen door. Shortly before he died, he told Anne that the tapping of the earth's water table was a greater threat to humanity than the development of atomic power, because it completely upset ecology. "If the roots can't reach down to water, they cannot give it off and make clouds. If no clouds, no rain. If no rain . . ." He shrugged. He died in the Princeton Hospital. Anne asked the nurse who had been attending him whether she had been able to preserve the last words of the greatest thinker of this century, and she replied, "Oh, no, when I looked in he was just mumbling away in German." There was no one in the room with him when he expired.

For theater at Oxford there was the OUDS, among whose members were Michael Redgrave, Val Dyall, John Fernald, and Peter Glenn. J. B. Fagan was producing repertory, which included Shaw, Elmer Rice, Ibsen, and O'Neill. Among his actors were Giles Ischam and John Gielgud. There was also a plethora of clubs: language clubs, cinema clubs, a fencing club, and, of course, the Oxford Debating Society, the Union, where all of England's Prime Ministers until Lloyd George had cut their milk teeth. Anne never attended it once, so unpolitical was she, but knew well two of the great lights, Quintin Hogg and Duncan Sandys. The latter was enchanting, with dead-bracken-colored hair and eyes, and much wit. He had digs—he was at Magdalen—with a passionate Buchmanite (as an adherent of Moral Rearmament was called then), and one day, playing golf with him at Frilford, Duncan could bear it no longer. "Edward," he said firmly, "drop Jesus Christ and take a niblick."

Duncan was the author of a massive joke played on the authorities. He managed to steal the Proctors' Seal. The Proctors (two) are responsible for the good conduct of the undergraduates. The keep "bulldogs"—agile men who case the young who are out at night without their gowns or are seen climbing in. When/if these are caught, the "bulldogs" present a summons. This is called being "progged." Such *billets doux* can also be sent by mail. Duncan sent summonses, duly sealed, to all the most unlikely characters—meek curates from Keble, timorous Welshmen from Jesus, Indians from Balliol—all of whom he bade appear at ten a.m. one Monday at the proctors' building. At the appointed hour the street was crowded, not only by the bewildered victims, all terrified and unable to imagine how they could have fallen foul of the university authorities, but also by Duncan's friends, including Anne, gathered to see the fun. At the height of the commotion Duncan summoned the City Fire Brigade and two ambulances. It was a glorious scene of complicated distress: the proctors turning away dozens of trembling young men, fiercely yelling at them that they had *not* been progged, the amused crowd in the Broad, finally dispersed only by the water hoses of the Fire Department. Traveling home in the same train at the end of term, Colin Ritchie, an inoffensive Scot, albeit with red hair, told Anne the authorities had got as far as discovering that the hoax had been perpetrated by a redhead. They had even grilled him. "Sandys is said to be rubbing brown boot polish daily on his hair," Colin added. Duncan was never apprehended. He rose to be a Conservative cabinet minister, for some years was Churchill's son-in-law, and is a passionate advocate of flogging, capital punishment, and white Rhodesian racism.

All the scholars at LMH were obliged to eat supper at High Table (with the dons) twice a week. Their billowing black gowns were quite becoming, but it was local etiquette that a scholar's gown should always look messy, remain unpressed, and preferably be torn. Anne used hers instead of the *Times* to make her fire draw and soon had it looking smutty and smoky. When some bits burned off she felt she had arrived. She found, in spite of going to all the same lectures as the men, having mostly the same tutors, passing (or failing) exactly the same exams, that women at Oxford were still very much second-class citizens. Dancing one vac with John Hope (Lord Linlithgow's twin brother), she asked him—as he had told her he was up at the House—whether he knew any girls at Oxford? "Girls?" he said, and looked so shocked that Anne blushed and said, "I only meant girls who are up at Oxford." "There *are* no girls at Oxford," he replied. "Oxford is still, thank God, for men only. Of course, one's sisters and their friends come up for Eights Week, for Commem, or to watch one play cricket, and very welcome they are. It's not too bad, d'you know, for if one pines for female company one can always get up to dances in London; it's very easy to climb back into college, we all do it."

Only one young man known to Anne frequented prostitutes, paid for by his father, who thought thus to keep his son healthy. Alas, it had the reverse effect, and the young man, suffering from some unmentionable disease, was obliged to visit a doctor daily, to the general amusement.

No girl of Anne's generation had an illegitimate child while at college, though three of her friends later did so, deliberately. Elizabeth Barker, the Senior Scholar of Anne's year, daughter of Sir Ernest Barker, the great Cambridge Greek classicist, had an illegitimate son. She never married. Margaret, Alan Gardiner's daughter, who went to Cambridge, also had an illegitimate son. Kitty Trevelyan, daughter of Sir Charles Trevelyan, briefly Minister of Education in the Labour Government, had a college career that included spells at both Oxford and Cambridge. She then married a German and had children by him. He became a Nazi, but when he turned his old nurse over to the SS, Kitty could bear it no longer. She went home to her father's place in Northumberland, where, eventually, she had an additional illegitimate brat, as she describes in her autobiography, *Through Mine Own Eyes*.

Religion meant little to Anne at Oxford. From snobbishness, she often asked Father Ronald Knox to tea, and Evensong at New College was "in," but that was the extent of her devotions. She loved singing in the Bach choir. Indeed, participating in the *"Sanctus"* provided as near a religious emotion as she felt for some years, though she and Christopher saw a lot of the Buchmanites, especially of Marian and Ken Twitchell. And they once went to a Buchmanite "house party" for a weekend near Oxford, as they could go together there unchaperoned. Coming into the bedroom she was to share with another girl, Anne found her roommate hanging up a silk dress. Anne politely exclaimed how pretty it was, and the girl said with enthusiasm, "You can't *imagine* what a difference Jesus Christ makes when you are wondering whether or not to send a dress to the dry-cleaners." One of the few actions in her life of which Anne was proud was refusing an offer from the Buchmanite (now Moral Rearmament) high command to join a team that was going round the world, all expenses paid. She longed to go for the ride but knew she would never forgive herself. Later, when MRA's founder, Frank Buchman, "thanked God for Hitler," she felt justified that she had made her decision against them. Her first article for *The English Review* was on the political implications of MRA.

One could go away for weekends, provided one spent the requisite number of nights in Oxford to complete one's terms. Anne's sister Konradin lived in Somerset, not too far, and Christopher and Anne would sometimes go to Hadspen and be made to work hard on the farm and also be taken to visit the neighbors. In the summers Konradin rented a house on Lord Leicester's place in Norfolk, at Holkham. The great avenues of ilex trees were all grown from ilex branches used to pack Greek antiquities bought in Greece and Italy in the eighteenth century by the then Earl. He had bought further afield too. One day a huge crate of porcelain arrived from China. The current Earl called the Chinese Embassy before unpacking it to say he had placed no order and there must be some mistake. "You didn't, but your grandfather did," the Chinese Ambassador replied. "The hundred different hand-painted plates for each course have only now been completed." Lord Leicester's grandfather had paid in advance; the porcelain was already priceless.

Holkham was breezy, energetic fun. Konradin drove a fast motorboat, behind which Christopher and Anne "planked," dragged precariously on a coffin lid, often swimming perforce in the cold sea. Often they were invited by Dr. Pember—the Warden of All Souls, who had been at Balliol with Papa and with Lord Cottesloe—and his wife to his small red sandstone castle in Shropshire, on the Welsh marshes. Anne loved to go there, and sometimes Christopher came too. Mama and the Cottesloes approved, for they were well chaperoned and there was nothing to do but work and walk. Mrs. Pember was weatherbeaten and small, and very bright and fierce; at Oxford many people were afraid of her, as she always said exactly what she thought. For example, after a dinner party she telephoned her hostess and said, "My dear, last night your party was most delightful—can't think why." Once, when she realized no one called her by her first name, she telephoned five acquaintances to advise them, "From now on call me Maggie." She and her sister, the wife of Henry Gladstone, the last surviving son of W. E. G., had "come out" with Mama. Mama and Anne went to stay at Hawarden one April; Anne remembers only the Great Man's desk, the cold, and the fields of tiny wild daffodils.

One of Anne's weekend excursions from Oxford was to stay for the Grand National with Eleanor Hyde Watts—who was at LMH with her and was to be another of her bridesmaids—at Eleanor's parents' country house somewhere near Chester. It was country that Anne despised as being dotted with Jackson aunts, rich, dull, and divorced; how different it appeared during a gay house party! Evelyn Waugh was there, slim and chic; he was to be met again years later in America, sent to Anne there by Father Martin D'Arcy, S.J. (rumored to be the Father Rothschild of *Vile Bodies*), who had received Evelyn into the Church. Anne had completely forgotten their Grand National encounter when, in 1950, the telephone rang one day in Christopher's and Anne's cockroach-crawling New York railroad walk-up.

An English voice, totally unfamiliar. "You know me, or should," the voice chided. "We both stayed with Ellie Hyde Watts twenty-five years ago."

"So we did," Anne replied, manners brighter than memory "How is she?"

"She married a baronet," the voice said, "and has three very satisfactory children."

"Is she still beautiful?" Anne asked.

"Very, I'm glad to say. Will you lunch with me tomorrow?" Lunch was to be in his room at the Plaza—number 1651, the date of the Battle of Worcester. Most suitable for a royalist.

Waugh's arrival had been heralded by preliminary flutterings in New York papist literary circles, and there had been the usual speculations—would he address this Communion breakfast, would he say a few words to that Newman Club convention?

Room 1651 was no royal suite—no view. Evelyn carried the twenty-five years since their last meeting lightly. The same cherubic face, the same complexion. "What will you have to drink?" he asked, greetings over. "It will have to be here. Can you drink sherry?"

Anne assured him that she could, and they consumed comfortable amounts of Bristol Cream. Over caviar, Evelyn explained that Laura (Mrs. Waugh) was lunching with Mrs. Kermit Roosevelt. He told of his early life, his publisher father, his old school, Lancing, on the South Downs, where he was perpetually chilblained and always hungry. In World War II, he said, he fought in the Royal Marines and then the Horse Guards.

"Your first wife was my *bête noire* when I was a girl," Anne told him, "though I never met her."

"Evelyn Gardiner? Why?"

"Her mother, Lady Burghclere, was a friend of my mother's," Anne said, "and Mama was always coming back from lunching with her to sing Evelyn's praises and tell me how much she wished I would be and behave 'like that charming Gardiner girl.' When you got divorced I *was* pleased! '*Now* do you still wish me to imitate Evelyn Gardiner?' I asked Mama triumphantly."

"Laura Herbert, my wife, is thirteen years younger than me," Evelyn said inconsequently.

When the waiter brought the bill, Evelyn asked him, "Do you really want me to sign, or is it just that you want my autograph?"

Later, when he came to dine, Christopher's and Anne's tenement flat was illuminated by the splendor of his dinner jacket. He gallantly endured the discomfort of a buffet supper but seemed saddened by the lack of napkins. "Use the back of your hand," Anne suggested.

Next time he came they sat down to eat. Anne had remembered—too late to iron them—that she possessed some immense linen napkins left her by Mama, dated 1906. They gave an air to her table, she thought. "I hope," she said, turning to Evelyn over the soup, "that you noticed that this time I have provided napkins."

"Yes indeed," he replied. "Very scrumpled, aren't they?"

"I've asked Dorothy Day," he said later, "to lunch tomorrow, at Chambord. Do you think she will come?"

"Probably," Anne replied, "if she's not in jail. I don't expect she knows about Chambord. But she will be softened by its being on Third Avenue, her beloved bums' own avenue."

Dorothy accepted lunch but insisted Evelyn be her guest at the *Catholic Worker*. About to drive down to the Bowery in Mrs. Henry Luce's Cadillac and company, Evelyn phoned Anne. "Perhaps we had better not drive to the door? Maybe we should leave the car around the corner?" Anne said perhaps that would be more tactful.

Anne suggested to Evelyn that he should meet Jacques Maritain at Princeton, and he was delighted. On our way to the Plaza to pick him up, she had a flat tire and arrived breathless and lunchless; later Evelyn kindly refunded her the price of the repair. "After all, you're saving me a train ticket to Princeton," he pointed out.

It was a cold clear winter's day as they set off through the Lincoln Tunnel, and Anne felt a sense of mission, driving a great English Catholic novelist to meet a great French Catholic philosopher. The frozen landscape was lovely, the bare trees like good bones in an old face, the rimed fields like a pretty woman set in a facial. Anne commented on the still, waiting beauty, but Evelyn, his eyes averted from the countryside, took her up with asperity.

"I am so horrified at the dreadful thing you've done, I can't possibly pay attention to *scenery*," he said with a shudder.

"What have I done?" Anne asked, and added, "You *must* look at those rust-colored barns—aren't they sheer Grandma Moses?"

Silence.

"What have I done?" she asked again.

Evelyn had learned that Anne had become an American citizen. "Every human being," he said pontifically, "is born in sin. Original Sin. But every American is born in actual sin—the sin of treason to the British Crown. Of course, many are unaware of their dreadful condition: this is the reason for the well-known, oft-commented, but never sufficiently explained American inferiority complex.

"Sin," Evelyn went on, "just the simple result of sin. And you, with full consent, have deliberately committed this horrid act." (A year later, when Anne arrived to stay with him in Gloucestershire, Evelyn opened the front door, and there were his six children lined up. "This," he told them, presenting them to her, "is an American. Look well, you may never see another.")

Tea with the Maritains was not a success. Anne steered the two great men off the Spanish Civil War, the Social Encyclicals, and several other obviously tangential points. But it was quite obvious they had no possible agreement other than participation in the same faith: they hated each other in Christ. The delicious baba-au-rhum and tea with a dash of rum was French to the last drop and crumb. Evelyn, as it was the Eve of the Feast of the Immaculate Conception (fast and abstinence), refused to eat.

On the way from Princeton to visit the Henry Cliffords in Radnor, Pennsylvania, Anne lost her way and took two cold hours to reach their destination. Evelyn gallantly wetted his feet several times getting out to ring obscure doorbells in remote houses perched in muddy lots. He warned that his toes might fall off from frostbite, but they finally arrived at the Cliffords' in time for supper.

The Italian garden tumbling down between the cypresses to the flagged pool was a perfect ski run next morning. Nineteen point eight inches of snow had fallen in the night. As the host, the children, Evelyn, and Anne were piling into the car for Mass, she borrowed a pair of her hostess's galoshes.

"Here are some for you," their host said, passing Evelyn a pair.

"You don't expect me to put those things *on*," came the horrified reply.

"If you don't, your feet will be even wetter than they were when you arrived last night," his host warned.

"Why?" Evelyn asked, shocked. "Is there no one to sweep?"

He went off across country on a lecture tour and on his return asked Anne again to lunch at the Plaza. "Laura will join us after lunch," he said. "She is shopping."

"May a friend of mine, Virgilia Peterson, also join us after lunch?" Anne asked. "She wants you so much to go on her television program, 'Author Meets the Critics.'"

"She can come for coffee," announced Evelyn.

They had caviar (Evelyn confessed he ate it at every meal, including breakfast), followed by braised beef and California Cabernet. ("French wines should not be drunk here," Evelyn declared. "They are frozen en route, and shaken, and arrive undrinkable. The local brew is perfectly acceptable.") Evelyn said that the Trappist Abbey of Gethsemane, where he had visited Thomas Merton, impressed him most of anything he had seen in the United States. "I edited the English edition of Merton's *Seven Storey Mountain*," he said. "I was a bit taken aback when the Abbot, bidding me farewell, said, 'Wish you'd given us more notice of your coming, my dear fellow. Would have gotten you to talk to the boys.' What," he asked with a comic gesture of despair, "would a successful English novelist have to say to a covey of American contemplative novices? Perhaps this country's true vocatio is silence. It has such a need of it."

At this point Virgilia joined them.

"Go away," Evelyn told her. "I'm still eating. Come back at three."

On the dot, she obediently returned.

"Why did you come back?" Evelyn asked as he poured coffee.

"I suppose because I'm a masochist," replied Virgilia, "but also because I wish to ask you if you would do us the honor of speaking on 'Author Meets the Critics.' "

"How much do I get?" asked Evelyn. "Would you give me five hundred dollars to give to Dorothy Day?"

"I'm afraid you get nothing," Virgilia said firmly. "Our authors are *guests*."

"Do *you* get paid?"

"Yes, I do," she said. "It's the way I make my living."

"Could you not do something else? Domestic service, for example? There's a great shortage of domestic servants here, I believe."

"I do that at home," Virgilia said, "but no one pays me."

A moment or so after Virgilia had left, Laura joined them. "I have just been insulting an adulteress," Evelyn told her. Virgilia, a Catholic, had recently divorced her husband, Prince Paul Sapieha, also a Catholic, and married (civilly) C. G. Paulding, another Catholic.

Next day Anne opened her pressure cooker too soon, and the chicken and rice blew up in her face, reaching (and spoiling) the ceiling also. Evelyn had asked her to dine a week later with Mrs. Henry Luce before a talk he was giving on Belloc and Chesterton. Anne arrived, still skinless and tomato-faced, and shook hands with Mrs. Luce for the first time. Mrs. Luce suggested Anne would feel better in a veil, and left off greeting her guests to take Anne to her room and lend her a pretty sequin-spangled affair.

When Anne, on a subsequent visit to England, brought her youngest son to stay with the Waughs, Laura cried out, "We must hide him instantly. Evelyn doesn't like children." (He and Laura had had seven; one died; one, Auberon, became an author like his father.) So Hugh Dominic Fremantle was delivered to the servants in the kitchen and was put to sleep early in his mother's bed. Although they spent three days at Piers Court, Evelyn never to his dying day knew that Hugh Dominic had been his guest. But on another occasion Anne brought her Balliol son, Adam, and Evelyn could not have been more civil, providing champagne for the *partie carrée* and putting himself out in every way. The last member of Anne's family to see him was her son Richard, at the wedding of Anne's great-niece (Mama's great-granddaughter) Victoria Eden to Asquith's great-grandson, John Jolliffe. It was a nice family occasion and Hadspen was suitably *en fête*, but Evelyn huddled in a corner, sad, chilly, and dotty. Happily he died soon after, on Easter Sunday, just after hearing a Latin Mass said by his friend Father Philip Caraman, S.J., who was staying with him.

Weekends at Oxford could be spent in a variety of ways. In the fall there were the grinds—steeplechases in which undergraduates rode their own, or hired, horses. Girls and the less horsy men followed on foot, running from jump to jump, watching their friends roll into ditches or soar over fences. The best of the grinds was the Bullingdon, one of the racing clubs, with wonderful colors worn by members (and ties, too, when on foot). There was hunting too, with the somewhat poor packs nearby, the Bicester and Whaddon Chase—lots of wire and many tarred roads. Anne didn't hunt and was glad to learn from friends who did how rarely they ever saw a fox, let alone caught one. There were, too, the Berkshire Downs to walk over, with all sorts of unexpected pleasures, such as a prehistoric White Horse near East Hendred, and an Armenian parson who wore fifteen (some said sixteen) colored embroidered waistcoats against the English cold. There was sometimes skating; one winter even the Thames froze, and all the canals, so the most energetic (Anne not among them) skated over to Cambridge. That year there was the traditional ox roasted whole on the Isis, and a lovely moonlight binge.

There were excellent pubs around Oxford, for those in funds: at Watereaton, at Binsted, and at Thame (the Golden Cockerel). Every spring, there were "toggers," bumping races, when Anne trotted along the muddy towpath and looked for pussy willow while pretending to be rooting for Balliol. Later, at the end of

May, there was Eights Week, when everyone watched the racing
boats (with eight oars) from barges anchored at the bank and the
college coaches ran madly up and down the banks shouting advice
and encouragement to the crews through megaphones. When
bumps were made, everyone shouted and cheered, and when a college became head of the river, its coach, crew, and friends traditionally threw themselves into the cold, muddy water.

After Eights Week came Commem, when each year several colleges gave balls. These were tremendous affairs, with huge
marquees and marvelous suppers. They were most romantic—the
perfect lawns ("Roll and mow for five hundred years" their
recipe), the crowded herbaceous borders, the best bands down
from London, and the loveliest debs descending in droves. After
dancing that went on all night, there was a splendid breakfast
about seven; then one's whole party was photographed, and everyone went on the river. Anne enjoyed Commem balls as she never
had enjoyed the dances during her one London season. Then, each
night she had been obliged to go, with a partner, to some unknown
house or other. She had tried to spout the necessary inane plati-
tudes to each young man who asked for a dance. Her partner
would often leave to go to some other, and better, dancer, after
which there would be long sojourns in the powder room so as not
to be seen sitting out. (Anne had only once really enjoyed a London ball, at the Runcimans', where Steven—now Sir Steven—had
spent most of the evening on the balcony with her, looking out
over Westminster and talking of Byzantine art.) At last a kind
friend, Kenneth Rae, had told Anne, "Don't try so hard. Just say,
'Isn't Jack Buchanan great?' and you won't have to utter again."
Anne did so and found it worked, although she never did discover
who Jack Buchanan was, or why he was great. But at Oxford
Commems she danced delightedly all night.

But most of all the joys of Oxford, Anne enjoyed the quiet dinner parties. She loved being set down for at least two hours in
some such room as the oval dining room of the Pembers, friezed
with Bartolozzi prints, where she was penned between two—

usually intelligent and amusing—men. At Oxford, too, there were international houses to dine in, such as the Willerts': Sir Arthur had been the *Times* man in Washington. Or literary, such as the John Masefields' or the John Buchans', where his daughter Alice and her handsome Scots husband entertained for her father. A favorite expedition for Sunday lunch was Wytham Wood, where the ffennells (who had changed their name when they bought Wytham Abbey with money made in their native South Africa) entertained in a tent, being unable to get their tenants out; aided by his guests, Mr. ffennell would drive his own pigs (alas, in vain) into his tenants' pheasants. There were also to be dined with such brilliant conversationalists as (Sir) Maurice Bowra, of whom Anne persuaded Angus Malcolm to do a cartoon for the undergraduate paper, *The Cherwell*, as the Buddha, with Lord David Cecil as the lotus; and (Sir) Isaiah Berlin, who later was a paying guest of Anne's in her wartime Georgetown house in Washintgon. (He left only when he got a house for himself by arriving at the same time as the police after a secretary in the British Embassy had been murdered by her lover. He used to put fresh red ink where the blood had been on the floor when he gave dinner parties.)

Many of the men and women with whom Anne was at Oxford remained friends for her whole life. Alan Pryce-Jones, whom she met with John Goldman (her Pre-Raphaelite "twin"), is today as kind, brilliant, amusing, and delightful as he was when an undergraduate. He has had a distinguished career, being for many years editor of the *Times Literary Supplement*, later coming to the United States for the Ford Foundation and writing for many daily and weekly journals here. Nancy Balfour, a good friend at LMH, became an editor of *The Economist* and received the CBE. And Anne considers that she had been above all blessed to have known Wystan Auden for more than forty years. He is, to her, one of the best and greatest human beings—quite apart from being the greatest living poet—and to have stayed with him at Kirchstetten is a crowning delight of her sixth decade, as staying with Yeats and Lady Gregory at Coole was of her second.

XXII

Nightingales Awake

Since Anne and Christopher had now been engaged for over a year, they decided to tell Mama and his parents. Mama kept their letters, which Anne found after her death. On May 14, Christopher wrote:

> I am writing to ask you (the most difficult of all letters) if I may marry Anne. We were engaged at Aix, but said nothing there because it seemed uncertain and because we knew each other so very little. Now we have waited and it seems a little less improbable. I hope you don't feel it was very unfair to say nothing. It is very difficult because I cannot possibly have enough money to marry (having only what my father allows me and what I earn) until we are *quite* tired of each other—and it seems impertinent and ridiculous in such circumstances to ask if I may marry such a delightful person. . . . But I hope that if she is to be wasted on somebody you will forgive me for wishing it to be myself.

Anne wrote:

> My darling—in the same post—indeed in the same pillar-box—Christopher is writing to tell you that we are engaged and asking you to let us get married. We got engaged at Aix on January 14 on Mont Revard. We did not tell anyone be-

cause we were not—and are not still—at all sure it will last. But we told anyone who asked—Clare and Margaret did—and are now telling the Cottesloes by the same post, and I suppose you and they will talk it over. I like Christopher so much that I am (at present) quite willing to marry him in spite of all you have said against marriage. I like Christopher even before breakfast, and can even contemplate using the same toothbrush—if washed.

That summer Christopher went to Sligger Urquhart's chalet in Savoy, and Anne journeyed to Central Europe to stay with an old friend of her father's, Julius Meinl, a millionaire grocer. Mama had been given to understand that Meinl's daughter-in-law and son would be staying (he was a widower). Anne's host met her in a big Lincoln in Vienna, and they drove incredibly fast across dirt roads for a hundred or so miles south—past Graz, and into Yugoslavia. Meinl's house was grand, in dull country, and the food—above all the coffee, for he was the coffee king of Europe—was good. The only other guest was the Reverend A. S. Duncan-Jones, the Dean of Chichester—no sign of any female at all. Old Meinl rode daily with Anne, and within forty-eight hours the need for a chaperon became painfully obvious. Anne confided in the dean, who was neither worried nor shocked. "Wire your fiancé to telegraph he has been hurt and you must instantly return," he suggested.

Anne bribed the chauffeur to send off a telegram, and after two harrowing days, mostly spent locked in her room, a reply arrived: "Christopher injured flying. Return immediately. Cottesloe."

Anne found no one in London at all. Christopher was still abroad with Sligger. Mama and Clare were at Aix. Anne spent a weekend at Konradin's in Somerset—too much like hard work, haying. And then she set off at Mama's suggestion to stay with Mama's friend Madame de la Panouse at Le Mortier in Touraine—a huge modern castle, waiters behind every chair at meals, whispering the vintage and year before filling one's glass, "Nuits St. Georges '17, mademoiselle," or whatever it might be. And at night seven different tisanes: lime blossom, verbena, ash leaves, cherry stalks, camomile, orange flowers, or mint.

The Crowes, the four children of Sir Eyre, the permanent head of the Foreign Office, were staying, a boy and three girls—one, Sibyl, Anne's age, was at Girton—as well as their mother. Also Doreen Jessel, at London University, and her parents. Daily the guests were chauffeur-driven to one after another of the Loire châteaux. Anne wrote to Mama:

> Blois is wonderful, a lovely staircase. François I built it for his son's mistress—French *mœurs* are odd. The nice young French diplomat, M. Dumaine, has gone, and now there are only the Jessels, the Crowes, Lady Arthur, and myself. We played seven sets of tennis yesterday and bridge at night. . . . Today we went to Loches. It was horrible. In the darkest part of the dungeon two bishops were shut up. They carved a tiny ledge and a cross above it with their hands. With some of the bread and wine they were given through the grating, they said Mass daily for five years. There was so little air that they had to climb up to the ledge every so often on their hands and knees or they would have been asphyxiated.

Madame de la Panouse had five daughters (one died at eighteen) and several who died in infancy, and a son by Roger Cambon, her husband's colleague in the French Embassy in London. This boy, Artus, was about Anne's age, an unattractive creature before whom, and for whom, Doreen, Sibyl, and Anne were trotted out. Madame de la Panouse had a home for ninety illegitimate children in her park, and a pretty chapel, complete with a chaplain, the Abbé Engelbert, who was rich and erudite. Anne and Christopher were to meet him years later in America, to which he escaped after the fall of France. He was quite a good writer, *couronné* by the Académie Française, and Christopher and Anne translated into English his one-volume *Lives of the Saints*.

Anne was writing prose now as well as poetry. Her first published piece was a letter to the *Daily Mail*, entered in a competition for the best reply from a female under twenty-one to the query: "Do you want marriage or a career?" Both, said Anne, and was paid five guineas. She was reviewing for *The Times Literary Supplement* before she went to Oxford. At twenty, she tied with herself to win the *New Statesman's* under-twenty-one short-story competition. Her second entry was under the pseudonym Petronella Elphinstone, which she snobbishly much preferred to her own bourgeois name.

In the Christmas holiday of 1929 Mama paid a state visit to Christopher's parents, Lord and Lady Cottesloe, at Swanbourne. She would rather have been asked to Wistow, their Leicestershire place, as that had belonged to the Vaughans, cousins of Mama's, for centuries, and she had hoped Christopher and Anne would inherit it (they did not). It was an unsuccessful visit. On Sunday at the second service (Holy Communion) Mama genuflected in the Creed, which horrified the low-church Cottesloes; and the Old House shocked Mama. It was a most beautiful small manor house, seventeenth-century in part, but was drafty, cold, and uncomfortable, no room being really a sitting room. There was only one bathroom to some eleven bedrooms. Nor was there any meeting of minds. The Cottesloes were stanch Conservatives. Christopher's father was Chairman of the local Conservative Party—though Lady Cottesloe surreptitiously gave Anne five pounds when, after her marriage, she stood as Labour candidate for the St. George's division of Westminster. (Anne had been offered Ealing, Acton, or St. George's and said she'd prefer "Charles James Fox's old constituency." "Charles James Fox, 'oo's 'e?" asked Herbert Morrison, her—and London's—boss.)

The Fremantle children had been raised to give their weekly allowance of twopence to the Missions, and Lady Cottesloe had many missionary friends and a missionary daughter. Mama and Papa had both thought missions insufferably insulting to other people's beliefs. On Mission Sunday, Papa would stand in Waldron Church with his customary offering of a pound note in his

hand, Mama with ten bob, and Anne and Clare each with half
a crown, and they would ostentatiously not put anything at all
in the collection when the plate was passed. None of the young
Fremantles had ever been to the theater—except one of them
once, to *Chu Chin Chow*—whereas Anne and Clare were taken
to Shakespeare, Chekhov, Ibsen, and so on, from the age of seven.
Food, Lady Cottesloe considered, was of no interest, and clothes
were to make everyone look as inconspicuously like each other
as possible. Mama doted on her dressmaker and thought a lot, perhaps too much—at least Christopher thought so—about food.

However, since the Cottesloes and Mama were all genuinely
fond of their children and wished them well, everyone behaved
properly, though icily. The visit was never repeated. Mama and
and the Cottesloes met only twice again—at Christopher's and
Anne's wedding and at the christenings of their two oldest sons.

During the spring following the official announcement of their
engagement, Christopher and Anne were allowed to go to Tus-
cany for Easter, chaperoned by his sisters Margaret and Bride.
They had an uneventful trip out, the only excitement being that
in their carriage on the train were two men Christopher said were
Communists. "The most etiolated is the chief Communist of the
London University Students Union," Christopher whispered to
Anne in the corridor. "He has made a cell there, and has got one
going at Balliol too." "And the other?" she asked. "Just a hench-
man," Christopher said. Anne sat as close as she dared, hoping to
overhear seditious talk, but only one suggestive word fell from
their lips. The chief, looking out at sodden osier-fringed fields,
pointed to them, unsmiling, and said, "Steppes." A young French
officer talked of "going over to the enemy," as he was stationed
in the Saar; and somewhere between Turin and Florence an Italian man chided the three girls roundly for letting Christopher
darn his own socks. They did feel it was blush-making, but Christopher wisely would not yield the socks to any one of them.

They stayed in a *pensione* with a view, over San Miniato and
the David, down to the Arno and the Ponte Vecchio. Anne wrote

Mama: "Margaret and Bride have one room, Christopher and I each our own (very large rooms), the beds are clean, there are gardenias growing in the lounge . . . baths are dear—5 lire each—so we aren't having any. We go on tomorrow to Arezzo, Gubbio, and Assisi."

Next day, complete with rucksacks, they took a five-a.m. train to Terontola, bought bread, cheese, tuna fish, and wine, ate breakfast out. Later they took another train to Lake Trasimeno and stayed the night at Magione; then on to Perugia, where the streets are all nobly named—Street of the Angels, of the Trinity, of the Holy Ghost—and the pictures are unique in their douceness. They spent Easter in Assisi, where Anne wrote the first of many articles for the London *Times*—about the little town noisy with lambs bleating on Good Friday, and on Saturday the shops filled with dead lambs in their skins, mouths open, electric-light bulbs inside, or flayed, posed on green-paper lawns. On Easter Sunday they went to the Carceri, Saint Francis's hermitage, where he preached to the birds in a big ilex and slept in a stone coffin. The grounds were carpeted with scillas, hepaticas, mauve croci, violets, and purple anemones growing wild, with great snowdrifts around them.

Going anywhere was fun, and by the time they married, Anne and Christopher had acquired such a taste for travel that they rushed off to the Continent whenever they had a few days and had ten pounds each to spare—then the fare "abroad." They walked in Sicily, Anne writing for the *Times* about the Syracuse dramatic festival, seeing Aeschylus in the open-air theater for which he had written his great plays, seeing the most perfect of temples at Segesta, built of honey-colored stone, and Enna, where on Easter morning a huge image of Mary and a no less huge image of Christ entered the great square from opposite ends, and their bearers when they caught sight of each other ran to meet in front of the Cathedral with a great clamor of bells. Enna was largely destroyed in World War II, but outside Palermo the great basilica of Monreale has its mosaics intact; and in the cathedral at Palermo is the huge porphyry tomb of one of the greatest men who ever lived, the Puer Apuliae, Emperor Frederick II, which the Germans removed in World War II.

Later, Anne went to the USSR, and was the first *Times* correspondent ever to go officially into that country. Before that, all dispatches to the *Times* had been "from our Riga correspondent." She went to report on the Moscow theater festival. She traveled by boat, taking the *Smolny* from Tilbury to Leningrad. On the boat were some Cambridge madrigal singers and Lewis Casson. Anne persuaded him to direct a performance of *Comus*, which they gave in the calm of the Kiel canal, with the Soviet crew in their gas masks as the rabble. (Anne, of course, hogged the part of the Lady.) In Leningrad there was an exhibition of Scythian gold, and the marvelous ballet. Anne thought the anti-God museum most appropriately housed in the ugliest and most vulgar nineteenth-century cathedral she had ever seen. In the train from Leningrad to Moscow she was put into a double sleeper with Humphrey Sumner, a most beautiful (bachelor) Oxford don; she was mortified that he preferred standing all night in the corridor, drinking endless cups of tea from the samovar, to sharing her compartment. In Moscow she got almost no food or sleep. Breakfast in the National Hotel was only from nine-thirty on, by which time she was sightseeing; in the afternoon she watched children's theater or puppets; in the evening she saw always one play, often two, or ballet or opera—she saw the first performance of Shostakovich's *Lady Macbeth of Mtsensk*—and when she crawled back to her hotel about two a.m. it was too late to eat. She saw a good deal of Walter Duranty, who told her that Stalin had said to him at their first interview, "I wish I had thought of bread and wine first"; and of American Ambassador Bullitt and his wife, who took her out to their dacha; and of Irena and John Wiley, just married and most hospitable. John was later U.S. Ambassador to Colombia, Portugal, Iran, and Panama.

After Anne had been beaten in the 1935 General Election by Duff Cooper, then Secretary of State for War, she consoled her-

self by going to the United States for the English Speaking Union
—she spoke in thirty-two states and traveled forty-two thousand
miles in six weeks—then took a week's holiday in Mexico, staying
with Sir Owen O'Malley, then British Minister there, whose
daughter Jane had been at Oxford too. Owen took Anne to the
pyramids, which she hated; they were as blood-drenched and evil
as the Tower of London or the palace at Mycenae, the only two
other buildings where the very stones seemed to cry aloud in
horror at what they had witnessed.

Anne took a bus to Taxco, where she spent a night with Elizabeth Anderson, a delightful Southern lady who wrote cookbooks,
and met William Spratling and bought a splendid Toltec piece
from him. Miss Anderson took her to the bus stop at eleven p.m.,
when the bus was supposed to arrive from Acapulco on its way
back to Mexico City. Midnight came, but no bus. It was cold, late
November; Elizabeth confided Anne to the care of the night
watchman and went home. It got colder; around one a.m. the
watchman gallantly offered Anne his coat, which she refused:
she feared it would be crawling with vermin. As she shivered
more and more, he walked her to a *bodega* and bought a bottle
of tequila and bade her drink. She took a swig and almost choked.
He drank deeply and tried to make her drink. "You are no friend
to Taxco if you will not drink with me," he said. After another
hour he grew maudlin. "Come to the park," he said. Anne refused.
"Then I will shoot you," he said. "I will myself be shot for drinking on duty. I am not allowed to drink on duty. First I will shoot
you, then myself."

Anne, foolishly, started to run, pursued by the night watchman,
who was shooting, but luckily wildly. In her terror she took the
right direction, found herself at the high wall outside Elizabeth
Anderson's house, somehow scrambled up, and got to the porch.
The night watchman was too drunk to climb after her and, after
wasting a few shots on the wall, gave up. Anne managed to wake
Elizabeth; she took the bus when it came later in the morning, in
daylight. When she got back to the O'Malleys', she learned that

a young relative of Lord Maugham had also been shot at in Taxco, and his companion killed.

On her way back to England via the United States, she visited New York and stayed with her guardian, Hans Sonne, in Tuxedo Park. When she commented to her dinner partner that everyone there was Republican, he asked in surprise, "Are there any white Republicans?" He came from Tennessee. She discovered the Melchetts were in New York and asked Hans if she might ask them out to Sunday lunch. He was delighted but on learning the Melchetts were Jews said, "Oh dear, then we can't lunch at the club, as we do on Sundays; we always let the butler go out." No Jews were allowed into the club, or to live in Tuxedo, so Hans hired a butler for the day and entertained Lord Melchett, the head of Imperial Chemical Industries, and his South African wife, at home. The hired butler was Norwegian, a cousin of the present King Olaf. Lady Melchett told Anne at lunch that she hated New York; it was odiously "full of all those mongrel people in their concrete cages."

But the return home, after all their traveling—and home for Anne and Clare was the Maison—was the best of all. The gray Maison covered with scented mauve wistaria in May, with purple grapes in September—one had only to lean out of one's window to pick and eat. The Maison was the happiest house Anne ever knew, and after she and Christopher were married, Mama lent it to them every summer, and they filled it with their friends. During World War II the German High Command took it over as headquarters. Prisoners were interrogated there, and the Maison became feared and hated locally. After Mama's death and after the war was over, it was sold to an Orthodox Jewish charity, which turned it into a school to train young rabbis whose parents had been killed by the Nazis. A good example of the tidiness of the Almighty.

The three Oxford years passed like a dream, and final Schools came all too soon, when, wearing "sub-fusc"—black suit, black socks or stockings, a mortarboard on the head—men and women were shut up all day daily for a week in the Schools Building. As she went down when Schools were over, Anne was aware that her years at Oxford had been as golden as the laburnum trees flowering along Norham Gardens. For Oxford has had more than seven hundred years' experience in making young people happy and does so supremely well.

Anne was twenty, and Christopher, who had gone down at the end of Anne's first year, was at the Royal College of Art, where he was working for a diploma under Sir William Rothenstein. Anne and Christopher met rarely, and their engagement had gone on far too long. Mama, though devoted to Christopher—she declared he was engaged to Anne only because he really loved *her*—was worried because as a painter he was not likely to make any money. "You will not be good at living in poverty," Mama told Anne. "You will be messy, and Christopher, who is clean and tidy, will not like it. You will never make a good man happy."

By the time their banns were read, Christopher and Anne felt more desperate than devoted. They were quarrelsome, and poor Mama was bored by them both; also she scolded Anne for being heartless about leaving her. Actually, Anne didn't leave Mama until almost the end of Mama's life: she and Christopher lived nearby in London, and Mama saw, if anything, too much of them. She had one rule: never let grandchildren stay the night; she welcomed them by day but said that, after four children of her own, she was not going to have her nights disturbed. Anne had said at Oxford, when she was reading medieval history, that she would have three sons and call them for the Victorines, three monks of the Abbey of Saint Victor, outside Paris, who became famous: Adam of Saint Victor as a hymn-writer, Richard as a theologian, Hugh as a mystic. "What will you do if you have a girl or girls?" Ellie Hyde Watts had asked. "I won't," said Anne, and didn't. (She named her three sons as planned.)

Mama, when war seemed inevitable at last, decided to go back to India. Anne could not accompany her, having small children, nor could Clare, just married. So Mama took with her a young

pansy, whose fare she paid. The sea was rough, the food on the
P&O boat was ghastly, and in Bombay her escort abandoned her
for a local boy. She went on alone to Madras, where the Governor and his wife were kind and courteous, but Mama was sadly
disillusioned. British India, on its last legs, was bitter and brutal;
the Indians she met seemed to be either toadies or traitors. She
returned, sick in heart and body.

Anne motored to Aix to meet her, taking Mama's maid with
her through April-blossoming France. World War II cast coming shadows over everything: a young hitchhiker Anne picked
up turned out to be the hero of the film *Carnet de Bal;* "I shall
be dead soon," he said, "so I am taking a holiday now." He was
killed even before Dunkirk.

Anne found that Mama had seen the local Aix doctor, who
had diagnosed cancer of the rectum. "Luckily it's small and we
can operate," he said. But Mama said she must go home, consult
the other children. Back in London she decided, on Konradin's
advice, not to have the operation, as it would mean wearing a
bag and what she called "unmentionable horrors." She would last
only six months, the London doctor said, and he would keep her
doped. It took four years of war, bombing, of blackout and rationing, before she died. Clare and Konradin were with her; Anne,
who had got compassionate leave from the British Embassy in
Washington, was on her way. "Tell her I tried to wait," Mama
said, then asked, "Will it never end?" and died on January
12, 1944.

Anne arrived in time for the funeral service and carried her
ashes up to London from Somerset en route to Waldron. Most of
Tiny's ashes were buried next to her Fritz, but Konradin took a
few to scatter on the Hill O'Doune above Banff. As she climbed,
she was followed by a dog. Mama had always detested dogs;
"ambulating dunghills," she called them and insisted that people
kept them only in order vicariously to enjoy their sexual license.
Konradin said she thought the dog was assuredly "sent." Mama
had wished to have the words "She left the world cleaner than

she found it" added to the stone she had put over Papa, which read: "Frederick Huth Jackson 1863–1921: Sometime squire of this parish. A great Merchant, a great Friend, a great Lover. His ashes lie under this stone, and underneath are the everlasting arms." But the vicar objected to the proposed addition. "Most unsuitable," he wrote Anne's son Richard.

At her wedding Anne had ten bridesmaids, all of whom are still alive in 1970, all still good friends. In this "sad century" she has had an exceptionally lucky life; if she is allowed two last words they will be "No complaints." (Christopher asks what if only one is permitted? Neither "no" nor "complaints" sounds well alone.)

Christopher and Anne were married by the Archbishop of Canterbury, the Bishop of Buckingham, and the Dean of Chichester (the Reverend A. S. Duncan-Jones, who had saved Anne's honor in Yugoslavia) in the presence of Mama, the Cottesloes, Marmaduke Pickthall, and many other friends and relations, including Arthur Grant Duff and Sir Henry Mather-Jackson (who gave Anne away), at Holy Trinity, Sloane Street, on November 12, 1930.

———

FOR A.J.

Ashes her eyebrows, finely tapered,
And ash her pointed ear.
With what, in interstellar silence,
Will she now hear?

Dust are her eyes; and dust her eyelids,
No worms her sight assay.
With what will she, if comes the morning;
See the new day?

Index

Orwell